Strategic Studies Institute Book

CHINESE LESSONS FROM OTHER PEOPLES' WARS

Andrew Scobell
David Lai
Roy Kamphausen
Editors

November 2011

*****

*****

Comments pertaining to this report are invited and should be forwarded to: Director, Strategic Studies Institute, U.S. Army War College, 632 Wright Ave, Carlisle, PA 17013-5046.

*****

Published by Books Express Publishing
Books Express Publishing, 2011
ISBN 978-1-78039-987-4

Books Express publications are available from all good retail and online booksellers. For publishing proposals and direct ordering please contact us at: info@books-express.com

CONTENTS

FOREWORD

I am delighted to introduce this 2011 publication by the Strategic Studies Institute (SSI), the National Bureau of Asian Research (NBR), and the United States Pacific Command (USPACOM), which focuses on the lessons learned by the People's Liberation Army (PLA) from the experiences of non-Chinese armed forces during the previous 30 years. The papers contained in this volume could not be more timely or valuable to policymakers and scholars alike.

Throughout my career, and currently as the USPA-COM Commander, I have consistently sought a solid and relevant understanding of China, and the PLA in particular. The importance of China stems not only from its current international role and its influence on the Asia-Pacific region in particular, but also because China's impact on global developments will likely continue to grow. One of our enduring imperatives, therefore, is to accurately survey China's experiences as a means to grasp its existing perceptions, motivations, and ambitions. More than ever, solid, evidence-based scholarship that evaluates what the PLA has learned from the use of force and conflict elsewhere in the world is needed to shed light on the prospects for its cooperation, or rivalry, with the international community. This jointly sponsored study by SSI, NBR, and USPACOM is an important contribution toward this end.

The judgments associated with the PLA Conference in October 2010, and this volume, provide unique, valuable insights on how the PLA has applied the lessons learned from others' military actions to its own strategic planning. For example, the PLA rapidly oriented itself to the importance of airpower, command and control, and precision munitions from the U.S. experience in Operations DESERT SHIELD and DESERT STORM. Of equal significance are the lessons learned by China's armed forces that now apply to its new non-traditional military roles; such as the best practices to address all-hazard disasters and common transnational threats of piracy and terrorism.

The expertise and scholarly analysis provided by SSI and NBR inform the decisions that affect our operations and approach throughout the Asia-Pacific region. I commend both organizations for their commitment to excellence with the presentation of the annual PLA Conference and the resulting conference volumes. *Chinese Lessons from Other People's Wars* is an essential source for those seeking to understand China's strategic judgment and calculus, and will help prepare us to address the challenges and opportunities that lie ahead.

ROBERT F. WILLARD
Admiral, USN
Commander, U.S. Pacific Command

CHAPTER 1

INTRODUCTION

Andrew Scobell
David Lai
Roy Kamphausen

The annual Conference on the Chinese People's Liberation Army (PLA) took place at the U.S. Army War College (USAWC), in Carlisle, Pennsylvania, on October 22-24, 2010.[1] The topic for this year's conference was the "PLA's lessons from Other People's Wars." Participants at the conference sought to discern what lessons the PLA has been learning from the strategic and operational experiences of the armed forces of other countries during the past 3 decades.

Why did observers of the PLA want to study what Chinese military analysts might learned about non-Chinese wars? The answer is twofold. First, the PLA has not fought an actual war since 1979. Yet, during the last 3 decades, fundamental changes have taken place on the battlefield and in the conduct of war. Since the PLA has not fought since 1979, it had no experience in the changing face of war, and thus could not follow Mao Zedong's admonition to "learn by doing (在战争中学习战争)"; instead, it must look abroad for ways to discern the new pattern of warfare in the evolving information age. Studying Chinese military analysts' observations of non-Chinese wars therefore provides us a glimpse of what the PLA takes from others' experience to improve its capability and to prepare itself for dealing with China's national security issues, such as Taiwan, the South and East China Sea disputes, and

1

internal unrest in Tibet and Xinjiang, to name the most obvious ones.

Second, Chinese military analysts have noticeably more freedom in assessing and commenting on the strength and weakness as well as the success and failures of other countries' wars. Indeed, for political reasons, Chinese military analysts have to emphasize the heroics and triumphs of the PLA's war experience and downplay setbacks and failures.[2] While there is certainly recognition of the daunting challenges—in Korea, for example, accounts readily acknowledge that the Chinese People's Volunteers (CPV) were totally unprepared logistically and devastated by airpower—there are limits to the levels of candor. To date, there is no critical analysis of the PLA's claimed success or dismissed failure in the Sino-Vietnamese Border War of 1979 by Chinese military analysts (however, there are a few studies done by scholars outside of China[3]). Studying Chinese military analysts' observation of other people's wars, therefore, provide us key hints as to what Chinese military analysts consider important aspects of current and future military operational success and failure.

CHINESE MILITARY OPERATIONAL EXPERIENCES AND LESSONS

In more than 80 years since becoming a formidable political and military force in China, the Chinese Communist Party (CCP) and the PLA (first as the guerrilla Red Army during the First [Kuomintang (KMT or the Nationalist Party]-CCP Civil War [第一次国共内战] of 1927-37, then as a "semi-professional" branch of the KMT-CCP anti-Japanese coalition, the 8th Route [八路军] and New 4th Armies [新四军], the PLA during

2

the Second KMT-CCP Civil War [第二次国共内战] of 1946-49, and finally a standing military of the People's Republic of China (PRC) have survived a tremendous amount of military conflict. Their experience spans from guerrilla warfare to large-scale campaigns and fighting against foreign armed forces in the Korean War of 1950-53, the Sino-Indian border war of 1962, the Sino-Soviet border skirmishes of 1969, the Sino-Vietnamese naval battles of 1974, and the Sino-Vietnamese border war of 1979 (there were also naval skirmishes with Vietnam in 1988 and with the Philippines in 1994 over the Spratly Islands).[4]

In addition, the PLA has been employed domestically to deal with widespread civil unrest, protests, riots, and rebellions.[5] Recently, the PLA has adopted a more serious and systematic approach to noncombat missions. As a result, Chinese military doctrine has evolved to include the concept of Military Operations Other Than War (MOOTW). What this has meant is that, whereas in the past, nonwar missions were part and parcel of the military's job, these operations are now becoming formally integrated into PLA doctrine.[6] Nevertheless, PLA leaders are quick to stress that the military's "core mission" remains warfighting.[7]

The richest PLA operational legacy is in land warfare—there is an extensive record to reflect upon. Some important lessons were learned, including the importance of concentrating forces for an attack, the value of massed firepower, and seizing and maintaining the initiative.[8]

Yet, some lessons do not appear to have been learned or perhaps they were learned but then promptly forgotten. For example, one major lesson of the Korean War concerns the importance of logistics. Since the campaigns against the KMT and the Japanese were fought on Chinese soil, the supply lines were short or, more often, nonexistent. The PLA was used to producing its own food, living off the land, or capturing supplies from the enemy. None of the approaches were available on the Korean Peninsula. These initial problems were addressed as the CPV put considerable effort into building a logistics tail. But keeping roads repaired and supplies flowing were constant challenges for CPV commanders. Yet, the logistical lessons of Korea seem to have been forgotten a quarter of a century later when the PLA went on the offensive against Vietnam.[9]

Moreover, another lesson of Korea was the importance of air defense. The U.S. Air Force wrought tremendous devastation on North Korea and seriously impaired CPV ground operations, especially ravaging supply lines. The Chinese adapted to this by operating at night, fortifying positions and hardening facilities.[10] The CPV also focused efforts on anti-aircraft batteries. Indeed, because of Korea, the Chinese gave concerted attention to improving air defenses for military installations and cities throughout China. Chinese military "volunteers" gained invaluable experience while serving in Vietnam in the 1960s as anti-aircraft units countering U.S. Air Force bombers.[11] As a result of these lessons and the reality of deficiencies in aircraft and pilots, the PLA Air Force (PLAAF) has funneled extensive resources and attention into air defense efforts.

As far as the lessons from air wars, the PLA had very limited wartime operational experience upon which to draw. Indeed, the only significant air combat operations conducted were in Korea and over the Taiwan Strait in 1958.[12] In the early 1950s, the Chinese air force was on a steep learning curve, albeit with significant Soviet assistance in terms of aircraft, training, and even actual personnel.[13] Chinese airmen and their flying machines acquitted themselves remarkably well but recognized their limitations and focused on air defenses for ground operations. While the tactical experience was extremely valuable and carefully monitored, operational lessons were few, if any, because airpower was viewed as a mere adjunct to the main event—operations on the ground. There was no air war in the 1979 Vietnam conflict,[14] and the last "significant aerial combat" was in 1958.[15] Thus, it was not until the 1991 Gulf War that the PLA leadership began to appreciate airpower not merely in a "supportive role" but as a dimension of battle space in its own right.[16] The PLA also studied the North Atlantic Treaty Organization's (NATO) air war against the rump Yugoslavia in 1999.[17] Of course, China was not merely a disinterested observer because a NATO targeting error resulted in the accidental bombing of the Chinese Embassy in Belgrade. The direct hit resulted in death and injury to Chinese citizens and severe damage to the building.

Similarly, the PLA has traditionally viewed sea power as an adjunct to land power. Other than attention to coastal defense, the focus of PLA Navy (PLAN) efforts has been on amphibious operations with the target of Taiwan foremost in their minds.[18] It was only very recently, particularly since the late 1980s and 1990s, that concentrated attention has been given to developing blue water naval capabilities and off-shore defense. PLAN operations were largely limited to the defense of seaports and coastal cities, modest amphibious operations against Hainan Island and some off-shore islands during the 1950s, and several naval skirmishes against Vietnamese forces in 1974 and 1988. Although China seems to have focused significant attention on its submarine fleet, the PLAN has no experience whatsoever in submarine warfare. As a result, the Chinese navy had to turn to other people's wars for operational lessons of sea power.[19]

Where ballistic missiles are concerned, the PLA has perhaps the least amount of experience. Missile tests are the extent of this, including, of course, those conducted in the context of the 1995-96 Taiwan Strait Crisis. Nevertheless, the PLA has invested heavily in building up a potent arsenal of short-range ballistic missiles. Therefore, China must look elsewhere in search of operational lessons for ballistic missile employment.[20]

PLA LESSONS FROM OTHER PEOPLE'S WAR

One should not simply assume that a military learns from experience. Learning a lesson requires a sequence of distinct processes—analysis of experience, identifying the key lessons, and then acting to "institutionalize" these lessons. The final phase may be the most difficult, as the armed forces or service branch must follow through to implement changes in its organization or doctrine. Change in a complex bureaucracy like the military is never easy. As one U.S. Army analyst observed:

> An army learns lessons after it incorporates the conclusions derived from experience into institutional form. Out of the commander's experience may come a lesson, and from that lesson may come new or adapted doctrine or perhaps dissemination of potentially useful information. Only after its institutionalization, can the lesson be correctly described in the past tense as a lesson learned. Until then it remains just a lesson or

usable experience, a semantic distinction that few can appreciate.[21]

Douglas Lovelace, Director of the Strategic Studies Institute (SSI) and the first discussant at the conference, added "a little more texture" to the lessons learned framework with the following essential evaluation criteria, at least from a U.S. Army lessons learned perspective:

- A valid and reliable observation;
- Understanding the observation;
- Discerning the significance of the observation;
- The applicability of the observation; and,
- Assessing the effectiveness of the lesson learned.[22]

Professor Lovelace pointed out that the U.S. approach has its own idiosyncrasies. For instance, he suggested that most American lessons learned are focused at the operational or tactical levels of war. Moreover, Professor Lovelace opined that the United States almost certainly has an expeditionary bias in its lessons learned: the U.S. military looks for lessons to enhance its own ability to project military power. He also suggested that these same idiosyncrasies are not likely to be the same for the PLA. He posited for instance, that China's military may well focus its lessons learned more at the strategic level of war and have as a bias a more defensive, homeland security approach.

These are high standards against which to judge the lessons learned by a country's armed forces. But we should not necessarily hold the PLA up to these standards. First, unlike the U.S. military, the PLA does not have a unified center for lessons learned (key U.S. examples are the Joint Center for Operational Analysis, the Center for Army Lessons Learned, the Air Force Center for Knowledge Sharing Lessons Learned, the Marine Corps Center for Lessons Learned, and the Navy Lessons Learned System). The PLA Academy of Military Science (AMS) is perhaps the closest equivalent to an institution making concerted efforts to learn from foreign military experiences. Yet learning from other people's war is ostensibly only one part of the AMS's many missions; and there is no indication that the AMS has developed any systematic way to handle this complicated business.

Second, we do not know precisely what lessons the PLA learns from the other people's wars, what it dismisses, or whether it has learned wrong lessons. For instance, Chinese analysts may be led to believe that Slobodan Milosevic was defeated by air power alone in the "Kosovo Air War." They could have missed an important factor that Milosevic surrendered in time to avoid a contemplated invasion by NATO ground forces. Another possible wrong lesson can be the much talked-about American aversion to taking casualties. As the American sacrifice in Iraq and Afghanistan shows, the nation's acceptance of casualties depends very much on the situation. It would be a mistake to take aversion to casualties as an inherent problem of the U.S. military and the American people.

Moreover, we do not know how the PLA learns lessons, and how the PLA makes changes and implements lessons learned. To the best of our knowledge, the PLA does not officially report on the lessons learned from a conflict. Observers of the PLA have to piece together widely scattered information in order to speculate on the lessons the PLA presumably has learned from foreign militaries and other people's wars. Thanks to China's substantial output of publications on military topics in recent decades, there has been a growing amount of writings by the PLA and other Chinese security and military analysts on other people's wars and recommendations for PLA improvements. In addition, in recent years there has been extensive coverage by Chinese mass and military media of the PLA's frequent military exercises. Many of those news reports like to highlight the PLA's new developments in both weaponry and the conduct of war, both of which could be results of learning and implementation of lessons from foreign militaries and other peoples' wars.

In this volume, we present a number of case studies based on publicly available Chinese sources. The authors are mindful of the methodological problems that a less-than-complete publicly available documentary and analytical record in Chinese on the wars might present. Readers are advised to bear these challenges in mind when reading the accounts of each war. Hopefully, over time the PLA will see that it is in its interest to increase transparency and become more professional in conducting the lessons learned business.

The first case concerns the PLA's observation of the Kosovo Campaign. China pays heavy attention to this case for at least two compelling reasons. First, the Kosovo Campaign is a controversial foreign military intervention on the basis of the rights of individuals trumping the sovereign rights of states. China has three "sore spots," namely, Taiwan, Tibet, and Xinjiang, sharing similar features with the Kosovo issue. They have the potential to trigger foreign intervention, and China takes this potential very seriously. Second, the Kosovo Campaign was an awesome display of air power. The PLA cannot afford to ignore this war and must draw lessons from it.

A survey of the Chinese literature on the Kosovo War (the United States calls it a campaign, but not a war) reveals several important things. We see an expected Chinese criticism of the U.S.-led military intervention in the former Yugoslavia. China warns the world not to take the Kosovo case as the beginning of human rights over sovereign rights interventions and the U.S.-led West not to contemplate similar actions against China's handling of the Taiwan, Tibet, and Xinjiang problems.[23]

Another interesting finding is that the PLA has observed many aspects of the U.S.-led military operation in the Kosovo campaign, in addition to its signature features, the air campaign, application of precision-guided munitions, and the informatization of warfare.[24] These include, but are not limited to, logistics support and military equipment resupply, military transportation, mobilization of the reserve forces, psychological warfare and public relations warfare, anti-air raids, use of unmanned aerial vehicles, high-tech approaches, naval superiority, mobilization of the people, and so on.[25] The PLA even pays attention to issues such as how to survive as a prisoner of war,[26] to prevent suicide in the military,[27] to deal with troop reductions due to casualties,[28] and many more.

In 2000, June Teufel Dreyer published an SSI monograph on the PLA's study of the Kosovo War.[29] She found that different groups in the PLA learned different lessons from their analyses of this case. Dreyer identified three prominent schools of opinion inside the PLA, each claiming to have learned the right lessons and advocating must-follow solutions. The first school was impressed with U.S. air power and overall advanced military machine and support systems. The advocates of this school suggested that China

10

undertake measures to catch up with the U.S. forces and prepare for an evenly-matched contest with the United States in future conflicts. The second school, however, drew a different lesson: Milosevic lost the war because he did not know how to employ asymmetric tactics to deal with a much more powerful opponent; China therefore should modernize its national defense at its own pace, and the PLA should follow its own tradition, that is, winning from the position of the weak, to deal with the United States. The third school dismissed the claim of U.S. triumph in weapon technology and continued to advocate the primacy of people over weapons, a teaching from Chairman Mao and a tradition of the CCP and PLA.

Dreyer was invited to revisit this case at the conference. She finds that a decade afterwards, the debate is still ongoing in China. However, it also appears that the PLA has taken the views of all three schools into account: China has made impressive improvement in the PLA's capabilities; the CCP and PLA continue to follow their traditions; and the lessons appear to have been learned with "Chinese characteristics."

The second case is the Falkland-Malvinas War of 1982.[30] This war remains to this date the most classic case between two determined warring nations involving the use of sea, air, and ground forces, with long-range expeditions and close engagements. The war also had heavy casualties including the loss of major warships and fighter jets. It is a case all major powers study. But China is clearly more interested than any other nation in studying this war, presumably for this case's remarkable resemblance to the Taiwan issue, which could take China into a fight against Taiwan resistance and a U.S. military intervention.

In 2008, Lyle Goldstein of the U.S. Naval War College China Maritime Studies Center published an article on the PLA lessons learned from the Malvinas War.[31] Goldstein found that although China sided with Argentina politically, Chinese military analysts had nevertheless no problem pointing out the fundamental mistakes Argentina made in this war. PLA analysts saw that Argentina leaders had missed Sun Zi's basic teaching — they did not know the enemy or themselves well. Specifically, Argentina made a wrong calculation about the British will to fight for the Malvinas. Moreover, Argentina overestimated its own fighting capability. After all, Argentina's "war machine" was not well-maintained, without assured resupply, and there were major mistakes in Argentina's strategy and operations. The PLA appears to have taken these lessons to heart — it has been working hard to upgrade its fighting capabilities over the last 2 decades and holds no illusion as to possible U.S. intervention.

While Goldstein's work focuses on the PLA's analyses of the Malvinas War as a traditional China-Taiwan-U.S. case, Christopher D. Yung in this current volume finds the PLA's interest goes beyond Taiwan — it is learning the lessons from Britain to prepare the PLAN for carrying out missions far from its home base. Much of the British experience, such as anti-access and area denial; effective command and control; national mobilization, a sound defense economy, and a self-reliant resupply system; expedition force protection; foreign base and access facility; long-range air power; the use of merchant vessels; well-protected logistics supply lines; and so on, has provided valuable lessons. There is ample evidence that the PLA is acquiring these capabilities and preparing for these operations. Of note is that the PLA is also implementing these lessons in its naval operation in the Gulf of Aden.

12

The third case examines PLA analyses of the use of missiles in other people's wars. The relevant case that comes to mind is the Iran-Iraq War of the 1980s. The relevance of this case for China is clearly about its need to use missiles as a main deterrence force against Taiwan's push for independence and possible U.S. military intervention in a cross-Taiwan Strait confrontation.

Christopher Twomey has presented some intriguing findings in this study. Although PLA analysts paid noticeable attention to the Iran-Iraq "war of the cities" — that is, the indiscriminate bombing of civilian centers with missiles and the political and coercive impact of those missile attacks on the two nations, China did not appear to be interested in the lessons of those brute terror attacks. Instead, the PLA clearly prefers the use of precision-guided missiles. In *The Science of Second Artillery Campaign*, an official publication of China's missile and nuclear force, the PLA openly prescribes that its conventional missiles will be used exclusively against the enemy's key military targets that the weapons of other services cannot reach. These targets include the communications hubs, weapons delivery platforms, and, most practically, the aircraft carrier battle groups.

Twomey offers three possible reasons for this PLA preference. One may be that China does not want to terrify the 23 million people in Taiwan with "raids against the cities" there. As Sun Zi puts it, the worst strategy in a war is to slaughter the opponent's people. If China wants to take Taiwan intact, it is not in its interest to indiscriminately fire missiles that cause massive destruction there. The other reason appears to be that the PLA is more interested in the U.S. use of precision-guided missiles (PGM). Indeed, there are many PLA studies about the PGM and its employment in the U.S. joint and integrated operations in the last 20 years, reflecting an ostensible PLA learning from the U.S. military. Improvements in PLA ballistic missile accuracy may well be linked to an effort to create Chinese-style PGM's using ballistic missiles. Finally, it is also highly likely that the PLA has made its own efforts to promote internal innovations in the use of missiles as deterrence in the Taiwan issue. This doctrinal development is also consistent with the PLA's ongoing revolution in military affairs with Chinese characteristics. Whatever the case, the PLA clearly believes that PGMs are powerful weapons of the weak against the strong (read the United States). It is determined to make them a central component in China's missile strategy today.

The fourth case is about China's lessons from the Gulf Wars (Gulf War I of 1991 and Gulf War II of 2003). Almost certainly the greatest overall impact of a non-Chinese war was the Gulf War of 1991, which by most accounts stunned the PLA.[32] The high tech dimensions and swift victory by the U.S. and coalition forces against the Iraqi military left a lasting impression on Chinese military leaders. Chinese leaders characterized this U.S. show of force as the new revolution in military affairs (RMA). They saw that this U.S.-led RMA came as a result of the U.S.-led West taking advantage of the revolution in science and technology, namely the breakthroughs in computation, electronics, and information processing and transmission. Chinese leaders took the stunning U.S. show of force as a wakeup call and made all-out efforts to learn from the United States and improve the PLA. In many ways, the PLA has made improvements. As Dean Cheng presents in his chapter, much of the PLA's learning has been translated into its strategic guidelines and operational handbooks and is guiding the PLA to develop its capabilities.

China, however, is very critical of the second Gulf War. Chinese hold that the U.S. invasion of Iraq was a blatant violation of "international rules and norms;" it is another bad example of sidestepping the United Nations (UN) to pursue U.S. self interests (the first being the Kosovo campaign). As a result, Chinese see that Gulf War II has had a negative impact on U.S. prestige; it substantially hurts U.S. soft power; the United States has paid a heavy price for it (heavy casualties, economic expenses, and many other factors); and to a great extent, this war contributes further to the steady decline of American power, which was celebrated as having created a "unipolar moment" after the first Gulf War and expected to "rule a lasting unipolar era" for many years to come.[33]

However, the above criticism at the political and strategic level aside, China still pays close attention to the operational aspects of the U.S. military actions in the second Gulf War. Chinese characterize the U.S. "shock and awe" campaign as the United States pushing its military superiority to a new height. They also find impressive the execution of electronic and information warfare. Indeed, the PLA takes the informationization of warfare as the defining factor of the ongoing RMA. In the last three *National Defense White Papers* (2004, 2006, and 2008), China has placed the informationization of its armed forces as the goal of China's national defense modernization.

At the same time, the PLA and Chinese analysts continue to pay attention to those U.S. military operations they have been studying since Gulf War I and the Kosovo campaign (see the listing in the discussion of Case 1). In addition, as Dean Cheng presents in his chapter, Chinese analysts have paid special attention to the so-called "three warfares," namely, psychological warfare, public opinion warfare, and legal warfare. They see that the United States made unprecedented efforts to wage these "soft battles" of the war; these efforts helped the United States set the stage for the war and create the winning conditions even before the war started. In addition, the United States also made these efforts to justify the war, exercise damage control (following the Abu Ghraib scandal, for example), and maintain Americans' support for the war. Although Chinese dismiss some aspects of these approaches, they nevertheless believe that these are good lessons to learn and that they should integrate these soft-war approaches in their warfighting capability.

The fifth case is about the PLA's observation of the operations of the U.S. Pacific Command. The Western Pacific has not had a war since World War II, although there have been several land wars on its edges, the Korean War of 1950-53, the Vietnam War of 1965-73, and the Sino-Vietnamese border war of 1979; and several naval confrontations between China and Vietnam and the Philippines. However, this vast area has never been truly "pacific." There has always been an undercurrent of tension. Since the mid-1990s, the U.S.-China power transition has become the defining characteristic of this region. More recently, U.S.-China tension has come to the surface as a result of the two nations confronting each other over the U.S. military activities in China's claimed Exclusive Economic Zone (EEZ) and tensions in the Korean peninsula and in the South and East China Seas.

Much of China's direct military interaction, and at times confrontation, is with the U.S. Pacific Forces. As

Frank Miller puts it in this case study, the U.S. Pacific Command (PACOM) is the face of the U.S. military to the PLA, and so it is not surprising that China pays close attention to PACOM's strategic design and operations in the Western Pacific. The Chinese understand that the United States is concerned with a rising and increasingly more powerful China and has maintained a two-pronged policy of engagement and hedging toward China. They clearly see that while the engagement part of this policy involves all the instruments of U.S. foreign policy, including the military, PACOM is the pillar of the U.S. military preparation for a worst-case scenario against the possibility that "a rising China turns bad."

China's study of PACOM is extensive. As Miller shows, the PLA looks closely into the organization of PACOM, its force structure and equipment, training activities, regional engagement plans, outreach, humanitarian operations, and joint military exercises. Perhaps the most-studied subject is U.S. aircraft carrier battle group operations. China may be on the verge of acquiring an aircraft carrier capability, but a debate about this capability has been going on in China for decades. Proponents argue that China is the only major power in the world without an aircraft carrier and the world should not be surprised to see China acquire one; more importantly, as China seeks to secure and protect its expanding maritime interests, it must develop a strong blue-water naval power with aircraft carriers at its core. Skeptics in China, however, believe that the aircraft carrier is a war machine of yesterday; China should use its resources to develop weapons of tomorrow. The interesting convergence of this divide in China is that both schools study extensively the PACOM aircraft carrier battle group operations, with the proponents paying more attention to the useful part while the opponents, as Miller observes, "study ways to defeat the U.S. systems."[34]

In the sixth case study, Martin Andrew examines PLA observations about U.S. counterinsurgency (COIN) operations in Afghanistan. PLA analysts note that U.S. COIN operations took place on extremely difficult battlefields at high altitude and in complex terrains; they are therefore much-needed lessons for the Chinese military. In addition, U.S. employment of network centric methods and equipment in a wide range of operations informs the PLA on its transformation. In a careful analysis, Andrew highlights the PLA's interests in aviation operations such as helicopter assault, unmanned aerial systems (UAS) maneuver, close air support in combat, precision strike, and utilizing space assets to support ground operations. These are valuable lessons for the PLA in its modernization efforts.

The final case study is about the PLA's observation of counterinsurgency operations by the Russians against the Chechens. Russia's Chechen problem has much relevance to China's Xinjiang problem (and China's Taiwan and Tibet problems). Russian experience in dealing with this problem is thus very valuable to the Chinese. There is a general consensus among Chinese analysts that Russia's initial handling of the Chechen problem under the Boris Yeltsin administration was a total disaster. PLA General Yang Hui (杨晖) has rightly highlighted the key problems such as the lack of agreement among the senior Russian leaders on what to do with the Chechen independence movement, the Russian government and military's complete incompetence and lack of preparation in waging the first Chechen War of 1994-96, the miscalculation of the Chechens' fighting capability, the near absence of intelligence on the enemy, and so on.[35]

Chinese analysts, however, give high marks to Russia's tactics in the second Chechen War of 1999. They commend Putin's decisive acts taken against the Chechens, such as steadfast resistance to the Chechen independence quest, decisive military action against the armed Chechen rebels, a unified and better coordinated government and military, standing up against U.S.-led Western double standards and criticism, cutting off the Chechens' external support, and taking measures to improve Chechen economic conditions and rebuilding war-torn Chechnya.[36]

Yu Bin observes China's key takeaways as: 1) tolerance and compromise to rebellions and insurgence should not be entertained; 2) decisive action, or even preemption, is essential to stop an insurgency "at its infancy;" 3) keep the People's Armed Police (PAP) and the PLA at full capacity; and 4) stand firm to oppose outside interference.

LESSONS (IMPLICATIONS) FOR THE UNITED STATES

As we have seen, Mao Zedong's dictum to "learn by doing" provides little help to a military that last fought in earnest more than 3 decades ago. Studying Chinese military analysts' observations of non-Chinese wars therefore provides us a glimpse of what the PLA takes from others' experience both to improve its peacetime deterrent capabilities and to prepare for potential military operations in a Taiwan contingency, in the South and East China Seas disputes, against internal unrest in Tibet and Xinjiang, or to fulfill its "new historic missions." This process of "learning from

19

other's lessons learned" is what a seasoned member of the U.S. intelligence community referred to at the conference as the "extrapolation factor" and can be thought of as a military application of what the field of international political economy refers to as the "advantages of late developing countries."

However, at best this approach provides just a glimpse into PLA thinking and observers must be wary of an overly deterministic linkage between the lessons the PLA has or has not learned, and what it may or may not be doing about them. The causal evidence chain linking observations by PLA commentators about a foreign crisis to a debate in China and to subsequent concrete changes in doctrine, techniques, equipment, or strategy poses big methodological challenges for such an endeavor as ours. In many cases, the evidence is just not fully there to make these links, especially without the sorts of inputs that firsthand participants in the Chinese process might provide. What occurs more frequently are the half-associations, the emergence of lessons learned that piggy back and reinforce ongoing developments in the PLA, and lessons that perhaps support a party line in an internal political debate.

Nonetheless, the process can provide valuable insights. At one level, Chinese military analysts have noticeably more freedom in objectively assessing the successes and failures of other nation's conflicts than they do in looking at their own. While important observers of China's military such as Dennis Blasko point out that the PLA does undertake "after action reviews" (AAR) in which it frankly assesses performance and identifies shortcomings, it is likely the case that for political reasons Chinese military analysts still tend to emphasize the heroics and triumphs of the PLA's war and exercise experience at the expense of learning fully from setbacks and failures. Studying Chinese military analysts' observations of other people's wars therefore provides us key hints as to what Chinese military analysts consider important aspects of current and future military operational success and failure for the PLA itself.

Moreover, we can also enhance our understanding of PLA priorities by understanding what observations about foreign operations the PLA is *not* making. This is what one former U.S. policymaker pointed out at Carlisle as the lessons "not learned" or not adopted, the so-called "dogs that do not bark." While it may be difficult to parse real lessons learned from academic "noise" in PLA scholarly writings, we can say with high confidence that it would be extremely rare to find a topic of high importance to PLA thinkers that did not find some expression in the open literature.

This leads us to the first policy implication, namely that the military lessons that the PLA learns are embedded within a broader Chinese domestic political reality that shapes and colors them. This seems especially the case because the PLA seems to learn its lessons more at the high operational to strategic levels of war, precisely the domain where politics most inserts itself. For instance, China strongly opposed the Kosovo air war because of the terrible precedent it set. Beijing continues to worry about the specter of foreign military intervention in China, a concern heightened because of the country's history of being bullied by foreign gunboats and boots on the ground. Taiwan, as well as Tibet and Xinjiang, are locations where Beijing focuses its concern. This distorted the military lessons China learned from NATO air operations, and what China might have gleaned on the topic of air power at an operational level was diminished by a political necessity to qualify American successes precisely because it was feared that this power might be used against China itself at some future point. This then would diminish the likelihood of learning lessons about the value of low-tech people's war approaches to such sustained bombing campaigns, largely in the face of the data gleaned from that conflict. This would thus appear to be an example of a lesson not learned or one improperly applied.

A second implication emerges from the observation made by Professor Lovelace that the lessons most readily learned by the PLA are those at the high operational and strategic levels of war. This is a fortunate merging of evidence and relevance for U.S. policymakers. As Christopher Yung's chapter indicates, Chinese strategic planners place a high priority on an accurate pre-conflict strategic assessment; indeed a singular criticism of Argentina in the Falklands/Malvinas was that Buenos Aires failed to conduct a comprehensive strategic assessment in the run-up to its own actions that precipitated the conflict.

This dynamic suggests that the issue bears close attention by Western observers of the PLA as well. If the contingency or crisis involves the United States, then the Chinese will take a very careful measure of how committed and capable the United States is for the fight. And so, demonstrating the type of commitment and capabilities that convey resolve becomes a very necessary element of deterrence precisely because the Chinese pay so much attention to it. PACOM plays an important role in this regard. Everything that PACOM does to enhance regional stability, bolster alliances, dissuade provocations, and so on ultimately serves to shape how China writes its pre-combat strategic assessment. So in a very real sense issues of peace and war hinge on PACOM's daily operations in peacetime.

This, then, leads to a final policy implication, which emerges from Frank Miller's treatment of PLA lessons learned from PACOM. Miller argues persuasively that PACOM is a singular point of focus for the PLA. PACOM's regional engagement strategy, military diplomacy, and multilateral exercises in particular have been studied by the PLA and adopted for Chinese use. But PLA adoption of PACOM approaches should not in any way be construed as acceptance of PACOM. Quite the contrary, the PLA sees PACOM as both one model for how the PLA might develop, and as an obstacle to achievement of its goals — a potential adversary who must be understood and thwarted. As the U.S. Government more broadly seeks ever more cooperative approaches to its engagement with China, it remains essential to recognize that just as the United States has elements of both "hedge and engage" in its approach, so does China. Just as there are U.S. analysts who portray the PLA as the source of destabilizing operations — think of the January 2007 anti-satellite launch, the January 2011 J-20 test flight, increasing assertiveness in China's littoral seas during 2009 and 2010, and unyielding military pressure on Taiwan over the years, to name a few — so, too, does China seek to portray the U.S. military as the singular source of destabilizing actions. China characterizes U.S. military reconnaissance operations in international air and seas off China's coast as unfriendly and an obstacle to the further development of productive bilateral relations. Military professionals and decisionmakers would be well advised to be circumspect about these developments, avoiding impulses to over-correct or resort to the default settings in U.S. policy approaches. Chinese soldiers and statesmen will inevitably draw their own lessons from these American reactions to Chinese actions.

ENDNOTES - CHAPTER 1

1. The annual PLA conference has been in existence for more than 2 decades.

2. Writings of the glorious military history of the Chinese Communist Party (CCP) and PLA abound. The following are a few examples. Xiao Yusheng, (肖裕声), 中国共产党军事史论 (*On the Military History of the Chinese Communist Party*), Beijing, China: Chinese Communist Party Central Committee Archive Chubanshe, 2007; He Xin (何訛), 中国共产党武装斗争认识史 (*History of the Chinese Communist Party Armed Struggle Experience and Learning*), Beijing, China: CCP History Chubanshe, 2007; 中国工农红军史略 (*History of the Worker-Peasant Red Army*), Beijing, China: CCP Archive Chubanshe, 1987; 八路军史, (上, 下) (*History of the Eighth Route Army*, Vols. I and II). Beijing, China: CCP Archive Chubanshe, 2005; 新四军战史 (*Battle History of the New Fourth Army*), Beijing, China: PLA Chubanshe, 2000; 中国人民解放军第一, 二, 三, 四野战军战史 (*Battle History of the PLA's 1st, 2nd, 3rd, and 4th Field Armies*), Beijing, China: PLA Chubanshe, 1998; 中国军事科学学会军事历史分会与军事科学院军事历史研究所合编 (Military History Chapter of the Chinese Military Science Association and the Military History Research Institute of the Academy of Military Science, eds.), 发扬优良传统，履行神圣使命：纪念中国人民解放军建军80周年学术研讨会论文集 (*Promoting Good Tradition, Carrying out Sacred Mission: Collected Works Commemorating the 80th Anniversary of the Founding of the PLA*), Beijing, China: The Academy of Military Science Publishing, 2008; Yao Youzhi (姚有志) and Li Qingshan (李庆山), 解放军横扫千军的四十大战役 (*40 Major Sweeping Campaigns of the PLA*), Shenyang, China: Baishan Publishing, 2009.

3. See Xiaoming Zhang, "China's 1979 War with Vietnam: A Reassessment," *China Quarterly*, 2005; and Edward C. O'Dowd and John F. Corbett, Jr., "The 1979 Chinese Campaign in Vietnam: Lessons Learned," in Laurie Burkitt, Andrew Scobell, and Larry M. Wortzel, eds., *The Lessons of History: The Chinese People's Libera-*

tion Army at 75, Carlisle, PA: Strategic Studies Institute, U.S. Army War College, 2003; Harlan W. Jencks, "China's Punitive War with Vietnam: An Assessment," *Asian Survey*, Vol. 19, No. 7, August 1979.

4. For the CCP and PLA's own accounts of their history, see Note 1 for some of the primary references. For non-Chinese analyses of the CCP and PLA's historical experience, two recent publications are good sources for reference: Mark A. Ryan, David M. Finkelstein, and Michael A. McDevitt, eds., *Chinese Warfighting: The PLA Experience Since 1949*, Armonk, NY: M. E. Sharpe, 2003; Burkitt, Scobell, and Wortzel, eds., *The Chinese People's Liberation Army at 75*.

5. On the use of the PLA to restore order in the Cultural Revolution, see Andrew Scobell, *China's Use of Military Force: Beyond the Great Wall and the Long March*, New York: Cambridge University Press, 2003, chap. 5; on the PLA's operational response to the 1989 Tiananmen protests, see *ibid.*, chap. 7. On the PLA's response to the Tibetan protests of 2008, see Murray Scot Tanner, "How China Manages Internal Security Challenges and its Impact on PLA Missions," in Roy Kamphausen, David Lai, and Andrew Scobell, eds., *Beyond the Strait: PLA Missions Other Than Taiwan*, Carlisle, PA: Strategic Studies Institute, U.S. Army War College, 2009, pp. 39-98; on the PLA's domestic operations to deal with the 2008 Sichuan earthquake and other domestic challenges, see Harold Tanner, "The People's Liberation Army and China's Internal Security Challenges," in Roy Kamphausen, David Lai, and Andrew Scobell, ed., *The PLA at Home and Abroad: Assessing the Operational Capabilities of China's Military*, Carlisle, PA: Strategic Studies Institute, U.S. Army War College, 2010, pp. 237-294.

6. These new noncombat missions include peacekeeping and anti-piracy missions. On the former, see Bates Gill and Chin-hao Huang, "China's Expanding Presence in UN Peacekeeping Operations and Implications for the United States," in Kamphausen, Lai, and Scobell, ed., *Beyond the Strait*, pp. 99-126; on the latter, see Andrew E. Erickson, "Chinese Sea Power in Action: The Counter Piracy Mission in the Gulf of Aden and Beyond," in Kamphausen, Lai, and Scobell, ed., *The PLA at Home and Abroad*, pp. 295-376.

7. See, for example, Andrew Scobell, "Discourse in 3-D: The PLA's Evolving Doctrine, Circa 2009," Kamphausen, Lai, and Scobell, ed., *The PLA at Home and Abroad,* pp. 99-134.

8. Mark A. Ryan, David M. Finkelstein, and Michael A. McDevitt, eds., "Introduction: Patterns of PLA Warfighting," in *Chinese Warfighting,* pp. 3-22. See also Dennis Blasko, "PLA Ground Forces Lessons Learned: Experience and Theory," in Burkitt, Scobell, and Wortzel, ed., *The Lessons of History,* pp. 61-88.

9. O'Dowd, *Chinese Military Strategy,* pp. 70-71; Susan M. Puska, "Taming the Hydra: Trends in China's Military Logistics Since 2000," in Kamphausen, Lai, and Scobell, eds., *The PLA at Home and Abroad,* p. 554.

10. On these lessons, see John J. Tkacik, Jr., "From Surprise to Stalemate: What the People's Liberation Army Learned from the Korean War," in Burkitt, Scobell, and Wortzel, eds., *The Lessons of History,* pp. 293-326.; Yu Bin, "What China Learned from its 'Forgotten War' in Korea," in Ryan, Finkelstein, and McDevitt, eds., *Chinese Warfighting,* pp. 123-142.

11. Chen Jian, *Mao's China and the Cold War.* Chapel Hill, NC: University of North Carolina Press, 2001, pp. 225-227; Zhai Qiang, *China and the Vietnam Wars, 1950-1975,* Chapel Hill, NC: University of North Carolina Press, 2000.

12. On the overall lessons learned by the PLAAF, see Kenneth W. Allen, "PLA Air Force, 1949-2002: Overview and Lessons Learned," in Burkitt, Scobell, and Wortzel, eds., *The Lessons of History,* pp. 89-156. See also, Xiaoming Zhang, "Air Combat for the People's Republic: The People's Liberation Army Air Force in Action, 1949-1969," in Ryan, Finkelstein, and McDevitt, eds., *Chinese Warfighting,* pp. 270-300.

13. Liu Zhen, *Liu Zhen Huiyilu* [*Memoirs of Liu Zhen*], Beijing, China: Jiefangjun Chubanshe, 1990. Liu was the first commander of the Air Force of the Chinese People's Volunteers.

14. Kenneth W. Allen, Glenn Krumel, and Jonathan D. Pollack, *China's Air Force Enters the 21st Century.* Santa Monica, CA: RAND, 1995, pp. 92-93.

15. Allen, "PLA Air Force," in Burkitt, Scobell, and Wortzel, eds., *The Lessons of History*, p. 144.

16. Tian Yueying (田越英), "人民空军战略的发展演变及规律" ("The Pattern and Evolution of PLA Air Force Strategy"), 军事历史 (*Military History*), No. 6, 2009.

17. June Teufel Dreyer, *The PLA and the Kosovo Conflict*, Carlisle, PA: Strategic Studies Institute, U.S. Army War College, 2001.

18. For an overview and analysis of amphibious operations in the Taiwan Strait, see Xiaobing Li, "PLA Attacks and Amphibious Operations During the Taiwan Strait Crises of 1954-55 and 1958," in Ryan Finkelstein, and McDevitt, eds., *Chinese Warfighting*, pp. 143-172. For an analysis of sea power lessons learned, see Bernard D. Cole, "The People's Liberation Army Navy after Half a Century: Lessons Learned in Beijing," in Burkitt, Scobell and Wortzel, eds., *The Lessons of History*, pp. 157-192. See also Alexander C. Huang, "The PLA Navy at War, 1949-1999; From Coastal Defense to Distant Operations," in *Chinese Warfighting*, pp. 241-269.

19. See, for example, Lyle Goldstein, "China's Falklands Lessons," *Survival*, Vol. 50, No. 3, June 2008, pp. 65-82.

20. For PLA lessons on missiles, see Mark A. Stokes, "The People's Liberation Army and China's Space and Missile Development: Lessons from the Past and Prospects for the Future," in Burkitt, Scobell, and Wortzel, eds., *The Lessons of History*, pp. 193-252.

21. Dennis J. Vetock, *Lessons Learned: A History of U.S. Army Lesson Learning*, Carlisle, PA: U.S. Army Military History Institute, 1988, p. 128. On the specific challenges of changing an army, see General Donn A. Starry, "To Change an Army," *Military Review*, March 1983, pp. 20-27. This discussion draws on Andrew Scobell and Larry M. Wortzel, "Introduction: The Lessons Learned by China's Soldiers," in Burkitt, Scobell, and Wortzel, eds., *The People's Liberation Army at 75*, Carlisle, PA: Strategic Studies Institute, U.S. Army War College, 2003, pp. 4-5.

22. Douglas Lovelace, "Discussion Notes," 20th Annual PLA conference, Carlisle, PA, October 25, 2010.

23. See Cao Shulan (曹淑兰), "论科索沃独立对于中国稳定的不利影响" ("On the Kosovo Independence and Its Negative Impact on China's Stability"), 湘潮 (*Xiangchao*), No. 3, 2000; Chen Zhiqiang, (陈志强) "当代科索沃问题的国际政治因素" ("The International Political Factors in the Contemporary Kosovo Issue"), 史学集刊 (*Collected Papers of History Studies*), No. 3, 2010; Ji Jingfang (纪景方) "科索沃战争引发的理论思考" ("Some Theoretical Thoughts on the Kosovo War"), 军事历史 (*Military History Studies*), No. 1, 2000; Liu Shaoming (刘绍明) and Xu Bin (许彬), "世纪末的警钟: 科索沃战争留给我们的启示" ("Alarm Bell at the End of the Century: The Lessons of Kosovo War"), 湘潭师范学院学报 (*Journal of Xiangtan Normal University*), No. 2, 2000; and Qian Wenrong (钱文荣) "人道主义干预与国家主权" ("Humanitarian Intervention and National Sovereignty"), 和平与发展季刊 (*Peace and Development Quarterly*), No. 3, 2000; and "科索沃独立开创了危险的先例" ("Kosovo Independence: A Dangerous Precedence"), 和平与发展季刊 (*Peace and Development Quarterly*), No. 2, 2008.

24. This is a main lesson from the Kosovo War. There are many studies on informationization warfare. The Chinese Defense White Papers have made it clear that China makes the informationization of its national defense and armed forces as the goal of national defense modernization.

25. Jia Wannian (贾万年), Guo Shusen (郭树森), Tian Xuejun (田学军), "伊拉克战争美军卫勤保障特点及对外军的启示" ("What the PLA Can Learn from the U.S. Military Logistics Support in the Iraq War"), (*PLA Military Medical Affairs*), No. 8, 2006; Zheng Ran (郑然) and Zhou Shiwei (周世伟), "伊拉克战争美军卫勤动员及其启示" ("Lessons from U.S. Military Medical and Logistics Support Mobilization in the Iraq War"), 西南国防医药 (*Medical Journal of National Defense Forces in Southeast China*), No. 3, 2006; Liu Hongwei (刘洪卫), "科索沃战争对我军军交运输建设的几点启示" ("Several Lessons from Kosovo War on Our Military Transportation Development"), 军事经济研究 (*Military Economics Studies*), No. 11, 1999; Na Tingbin (那廷斌), "建设强大后备力量为打赢未来战争做好准备: 科索沃战争给我们的一点启示" ("Developing a Powerful Reserve Force and Preparing to Win Future Wars: Lessons from the Kosovo War"), 学理论 (*Theoretical Studies*), No. 8, 1999; Meng Xianchen (孟宪臣), "科索沃战争对心理战的启示" ("Lessons from the Kosovo War on Psycho-Warfare"), 政工学刊

(*Journal of Political Works*), No. 3, 2000; Zhang Peigao (张培高), "战争离我们并不遥远：从科索沃战争看国土防空的紧迫性" ("War Is Not Far from Us: Lessons from the Kosovo War on the Urgency of Territorial Air Defense"), 中国国情国力 (*China National Power*), Vol. 97, No. 1, 2001; Ji Xiumin (计秀敏), "北约军队的'空中眼睛'：介绍无人机在科索沃战争中的应用" ("NATO's 'Eyes in the Air': An Introduction to the Use of UAV in the Kosovo War"); Lin Yuchen (林玉琛) and Jin Mengjiang (金孟江), "无人机将成为压制防空作战的有效武器：科索沃战争经验总结之" ("UAV Will Become An Effective Weapon in Countering Air Defense: One of the Lessons from the Kosovo War"), 现代防御技术 (*Modern Defense Technology*), Vol. 29, No. 1, 2001; Ai Chun (艾春), "科索沃战争中的海上力量" ("Naval Forces in the Kosovo War"), 海洋军情 (*Maritime Military Information*); Wang Shuli (王树理), Lai Yuan (来源) and Zhang Songquan (张松权), "科索沃战争中交战双方战争动员与准备的特点及其启示" ("The Characteristics and Lessons of War Mobilization and Preparation on Both Sides of the Kosovo War"), 军事历史 (*Military History*), No. 4, 2002; Zeng Zhongqiu (曾仲秋) and Wang Peian (王培安), "科索沃战争给我国国防动员的启示" ("Lessons from the Kosovo War on Our National Defense Mobilization"), 国防 (*National Defense*), No. 11, 2001.

26. Huang Jun (黄俊) and Tao Guodong (陶国栋), "美军教飞行员如何当战俘" ("U.S. Military Teaches Pilots How to Be a POW"), 环球军事 (*Global Military*), No. 9, 2009; Cao Tingze (曹廷泽) and Pan Dahong (潘大红), "从科索沃战争看未来后勤保障" ("Lessons from the Kosovo War on Logistic Support"), 军事经济研究 (*Military Economics Studies*), No. 5, 2000; Chen Daiyun (陈代云) and Le Hanhua (乐汉华) "科索沃战争对加强我军战场军需保障的启示" ("Lessons from the Kosovo War on Our Military Battlefield Supply"), 军事经济研究 (*Military Economics Studies*), No. 12, 1999; Dong Xiaomei (董孝梅) and Zhao Jianyuan (赵建元), "科索沃战争中美军的后勤保障及启示" ("Lessons from U.S. Military Logistic Supply during the Kosovo War"), 军事经济研究 (*Military Economics Studies*), No. 8, 2000; Liu Yaqi (刘亚奇), "美军民力后勤保障的内容及成功经验" ("The Components and Successful Experience of U.S. Civil-Military Logistic Support System"), 基层后勤研究 (*Research on Rear Service at a Basic Level*), Vol. 6, No. 2; Wang Feng (王丰), Lu Baoliang (卢保亮), and Tang Guoping (唐国坪), "科索沃战争对后方仓库建设的启示" ("Lessons from the Kosovo War on Warehouse Construction"), 军事经济研究 (*Military Economics Studies*), No. 10, 1999.

27. Zhao Hanqing (赵汉清), Shi Jianan (施建安), and Wang Weihua (汪卫华), "美军在伊拉克战争中自杀的预防及对我军的启示" ("What the PLA Can Learn from the U.S. Military Suicide Prevention in the Iraq War"), 东南国防医药 (*Military Medical Journal of Southeast China*), Vol. 12, No. 1, 2010.

28. Li Peijin (李培进), Li Shuming (李书明), and Ma Jing (马婧), "美军伊拉克战争中伤病员减员分析及启示" ("Lessons from U.S. Military Handling Troop Reduction Due to Casualty in the Iraq War"), 人民军医 (*PLA Military Medical Affairs*), No. 7, 2010.

29. June Teufel Dreyer, *The PLA and the Kosovo Conflict*, Carlisle, PA: Strategic Studies Institute, U.S. Army War College, 2000.

30. The British and Americans call it the Falklands War, but the Chinese go with Argentina to call it the Malvinas War. Since this study is about Chinese learning of this war, we use Malvinas.

31. Lyle Goldstein, "China's Falklands Lessons," *Survival*, Vol. 50, No. 3, 2008.

32. See, for example, Paul H. B. Godwin, "Change and Continuity in Chinese Military Doctrine, 1949-1999," in Ryan, Finkelstein, and McDevitt, eds., *Chinese Warfighting*, pp. 46-50.

33. See Charles Krauthammer, "The Unipolar Moment," *Foreign Affairs*, 1990/91; and "The Unipolar Moment Revisited," *National Interest*, Winter 2002/03, for the discussion of the "American hegemonic opportunities." See Chinese critics in Zhou Guiyin (周桂银), "先发制人战争的道义限度" ("On the Moral Limitation of Preemptive War"), 世界经济与政治 (*World Economics and Politics*), No. 8, 2010; Luo Feng (罗峰), "美国预防性战争的逻辑" ("On the Logic of the U.S. Preventive War"), 世界经济与政治 (*World Economics and Politics*), No. 9, 2010; Li Xia (李霞), "浅析伊拉克战争对美国软实力的影响" ("An Analysis of the Impact of the War on Iraq on the U.S. Soft Power"), 学术交流 (*Academic Exchanges*), March 2010; Li Jie (李洁), "伊拉克战争的得与失" ("The Cost and Benefit of the War on Iraq"), 瞭望周刊 (*Outlook Weekly*), March 24, 2008; and Li Xia (李霞) and Lao Yanan (劳亚男), "伊拉克战争对美国霸权的负面影响" (The Negative Impact of the War on Iraq on the U.S. Hegemony"), 赤峰学院学报 (*Journal of Chifeng University*

[Soc.Sci]), Vol. 31, No. 6, June 2010, for a few of the critical analyses.

34. There is a huge literature on China's need to develop its maritime power (海权). Daniel M. Hartnett and Frederic Vellucci, Jr., *Continental or Maritime Power? A Summary of Chinese Views on Maritime Strategy since 1999*, Alexandria, VA: The CNA Corporation, October 2007, is a good analysis of this debate. There are also numerous writings about the strength and weakness of aircraft carrier battle group capabilities. There is no need to list them here.

35. See also Zhang Qinlin (张勤林), Xue Lin (薛平), and Dai Gongxun (戴功勋), "从车臣战争看武警部队未来反分裂, 反恐怖作战" ("Lessons from the Chechen Wars on the People's Armed Police's Future Operations on Anti-Separatism and Anti-Terrorism"), 警察技术 (*Police Tactics*), No. 4, 2000; Yang Wenxin (杨文新) and Zhang Qing (张庆), "俄罗斯不再妥协：1995年以来俄罗斯与车臣恐怖分子的3次较量" ("Russia No Longer Compromises: Russia's Three Battles against Chechen Terrorists since 1995"), 环球军事 (*World Military*), No. 2, 2003.

36. See Zhou Liang (周良), "试析车臣问题久拖不决的深层根源" ("An Analysis on the Fundamental Reasons for the Prolonged Chechen Problem"), 当代世界 (*Contemporary World*), No. 5, 2010.

CHAPTER 2

PEOPLE'S LIBERATION ARMY LESSONS FROM FOREIGN CONFLICTS: THE AIR WAR IN KOSOVO

June Teufel Dreyer

THE KOSOVO CONFLICT AND ITS OUTCOME

Executive Summary.

Different groups within the People's Liberation Army (PLA) learned different lessons from their analyses of the Kosovo conflict; a decade after the confrontation, the three distinct voices that emerged at the time continue to be heard in only slightly modified form. Advocates of the first school, that the PLA must match the United States weapon for weapon, have seen large increases in the defense budget each year. Judging from multiple foreign analyses, these have enabled the PLA to reach a level that would make a regional conflict between U.S. and Chinese forces a more even contest than it would have been in the Kosovo era. The second school, which argued that the PLA should rely on using existing weaponry better and employ inexpensive asymmetric techniques lest China be lured into an arms race that would bankrupt it, still castigates those who claim that battlefield victory is impossible unless and until they are provided with state of the art weapons. Leapfrog techniques and asymmetric weapons continue to be discussed in military periodicals. With regard to the third voice, which argued for the continuing validity of people's war, the passage of the National Defense Mobilization Act in 2010 specifically cited the crucial role of the civilian population in prosecuting war. Defense periodicals frequently mention the role of the people in reinforcing military operations, often referencing Kosovo as an example. The primacy of men over weapons is regularly affirmed, as is the need for political work to bolster morale and belief in the party's policies as the proper guide for action. There has been no resolution of the debate among the three schools, which can be seen as complementary rather than mutually contradictory. Only the first is expensive, and with the country's economy continuing to grow, it does not place an undue burden on the national budget.

This analysis finds certain pitfalls in the PLA's analysis: lessons learned that are suspiciously advantageous to the particular part of the military that makes a case for them, a tendency not to challenge certain factors that might challenge cherished PLA traditions, and an apparent unwillingness to consider the implications of certain issues at all.

The Setting.

On March 24, 1999, subsequent to the failure of international efforts at a summit at Chateau Rambouillet, France, to persuade the government of the Federal Republic of Yugoslavia (FRY) to halt the ethnic cleansing of Albanians from Kosovo, the North Atlantic Treaty Organization (NATO) began a bombing campaign to force the FRY government of Slobodan Milosevic to comply with its demands. The action was taken by NATO rather than the United Nations (UN) since two permanent members of the UN's Security Council, Russia and China, were opposed. Russia's sympathies lay with the Serbs as fellow Slavs and adherents to Eastern Orthodox Christianity; Moscow also feared that a Kosovo successfully detached from the FRY would embolden its own restive minority regions such as Chechnya. The People's Republic of China (PRC) feared setting a precedent for the intervention in the domestic affairs of sovereign states that could be applied to China with regard to such areas as Taiwan, Tibet, and Xinjiang. For similar reasons, Beijing also opposed western states' demands for a referendum on independence in Kosovo that, given its majority Albanian population, would certainly succeed.

Although NATO planners had assumed that Milosevic would quickly capitulate after the bombing started, he did not, presumably assuming that NATO would give in quickly. Operation ALLIED FORCE, as it was officially named, devolved into a protracted bombing effort that was hampered by unfavorable weather conditions, enemy resilience, and disharmony both among the members of the allied coalition and within the U.S. high command. Field commanders chafed under rules of engagement that inhibited their ability to carry out their missions. For example, the Dutch government refused to allow the presidential palace to be bombed because it contained a painting by Rembrandt.[1] And, because losing allied pilots to Serbian anti-aircraft fire might undermine the unity of the coalition, NATO pilots were forced to bomb from heights that made targeting more difficult.

At the same time, citizens of the FRY had to endure daily attacks from the sky that damaged more and more vital infrastructure nodes, while Serb air defenses failed to destroy enemy aircraft in significant numbers. Initial popular support for Milosevic's government began to erode even as Milosevic himself began to contemplate both the inevitability of his defeat and the growing possibility that he might be overthrown by his own people. Russia, for reasons of its own, did not come to his support. The Kremlin's analysts began to fear a NATO ground-force invasion, which would create pressure for President Boris Yeltsin to send in the Russian military. This would have been unwise from many points of view: among others, the cost of the invasion would be high; the Russian military's power projection capabilities at that time were limited; and the troops would have to pass through areas controlled by countries supporting NATO's effort. Perhaps most important to Yeltsin was his concern that confronting NATO would jeopardize vitally needed western investment in his country's tottering economy.[2]

On June 9, after 78 days, Milosevic conceded, albeit not without extracting some concessions. Although some conditions were more stringent than those decided on at Rambouillet—for example, a requirement that FRY troops be withdrawn from Kosovo was added—others were more favorable to him. NATO access was to be limited to Kosovo rather than to the whole of the FRY, as it would have been under the original Rambouillet plan. The stipulation that Kosovo's future would be decided by referendum was dropped; and the UN Security Council would affirm Yugoslavia's territorial integrity and sovereignty over Kosovo.

The People's Liberation Army Contemplates the Kosovo Operation.

In China, newspapers and journals associated with the PLA studied the unfolding military campaign with careful interest and occasional references to the fact that the lessons of Kosovo would be relevant to the sort of campaign the PLA itself might have to mount against an enemy, unnamed but clearly the United States, with technological superiority in a local war on China's periphery. The militaries of other nations, most particularly Taiwan and to a lesser extent, India, were also interested in what lessons the PLA had learned from Kosovo, anticipating that the lessons might be used against them in a future encounter with the PRC.

Jiefang Junbao (*PLA Daily*; hereafter JFJB) rejected NATO's contention that the war was being fought for humanitarian reasons. It saw NATO's clear intent as an effort to further American hegemonic aims, to remove "the last red nail of socialism" from Europe, to reinforce its agenda of global democratization, and (puzzlingly but unexplained) to "bomb the euro with the U.S. dollar."[3] Early hopes that Belgrade would be able to forge an alliance with Moscow and Minsk, thus creating a wider European confrontation leading to a ground force invasion, escalating anti-war sentiment in Europe, and a reprise of the embarrassing defeat the United States suffered in Vietnam[4] did not materialize.[5]

As NATO intensified its campaign, targeting additional nodes and deploying high-technology weapons, military sources sounded progressively less optimistic about the outcome. Anger was tinged with respect for the weapons and skill of the enemy forces, with the mood becoming more pronounced after the bombing of the code room of the Chinese embassy in Belgrade. Three journalists were killed, of whom two may have been PRC intelligence agents who may have been channeling information to Yugoslav forces that enabled them to better resist the aerial attacks against them.

Military media were impressed with the improvements in weaponry, precision bombing, bunker-busting, and network centric warfare that had been seen in nascent form in the Gulf War 8 years before. Detailed comparisons were made with not only the Gulf War but several prior U.S. military operations. JFJB noted that, while munitions dropped from the air accounted for one-fourth of all munitions expended in World War II, the ratio was one-third in Korea, half in Vietnam, four-fifths in the Gulf, and 100 percent in Kosovo. It concluded that air strikes had evolved from a supplementary role into the main combat form for future wars and that control of space would become increasingly important.[6]

Implicit in this analysis, and to become progressively more noticeable in later analyses that added comparisons with wars not yet fought in Afghanistan and Iraq, was the conclusion that the U.S. military carefully examined its performance in every confrontation and made strenuous efforts to correct perceived deficiencies. Kosovo also represented a further step in the evolution of the Revolution in Military Affairs (RMA). Mechanized warfare was giving way to informationalized warfare, with translation of the awkward term soon to be elided into "informatized" warfare. The key to victory would no longer involve the integration of land, sea, and air forces on a three-dimensional battlefield; instead, war would be fought on a five-dimensional battlefield comprising land, sea, sky, space, and electromagnetic spheres embedded in a network centric context. Control of the time gap (时代差) would give the party that possessed it the winning edge on a battlefield in which front lines and platforms were disappearing.[7] Technological advances meant that NATO forces were able to prosecute the Kosovo conflict with relatively fewer numbers of combatants: numbers had become less important. Precision bombing meant that fewer bombs need be expended by fewer pilots, and the advent of unmanned aerial vehicles (UAVs) meant that those who directed the drones would be able to remain at a safe distance while doing so. Kosovo was also variously described as the first purely air war, the first no-contact war, and the first war in which space played a major role. America's extreme aversion to casualties was noted, as was the success of its efforts to rescue the pilots of downed planes.

Ideologically, military media characterized the invasion as a setback for Chinese hopes that the unipolar world that followed the disintegration of the Soviet Union would segue smoothly into a multipolar balance of power. The United States had bypassed the UN and, while claiming to fight for democracy and humanitarian causes, had trampled on the sovereignty, independence, and territorial integrity of other countries. In the words of Academy of Military Science strategist Yao Youzhi, Washington in reality practiced the maxim that might makes right, "allowing its own officials to set off fireworks while banning the common people from lighting lamps."[8] Another lesson that must have been learned but was never explicitly stated was that Russia could not be counted on as an ally.

Since Europe had been expected to form one of the poles of resistance to American hegemonism, the willingness of European nations to participate in the confrontation called for an explanation. Here again, Yao Youzhi provided an answer: although aware of American desires to control both NATO and Europe, they had their own "sinister designs." Having fought endlessly for dominance in Europe over the centuries, participation in the U.S. use of force against the FRY gave European states "a chance to sing their operas on a borrowed stage," regaining the feeling of having some power. Yao noted that Germany had been afforded an opportunity to send troops abroad for the first time since World War II ended; he felt Berlin's exceptional willingness to do so portended a desire to reestablish its image as dominant power in Europe. Although America was attempting to use Kosovo to preclude the emergence of a separate pole of power, Yao opined that perhaps Washington had not anticipated German motives.[9] Other analysts predicted that the United States would lose its power quickly. PLA media saw Kosovo as evidence that America had emerged from the shadow of the Vietnam War and was again flexing its muscles militarily.

They viewed the Kosovo conflict in the context of other events most Americans would see as discrete, such as the enhanced U.S.-Japan security relationship; America's desire to revisit the Anti-Ballistic Missile (ABM) Treaty with the Russians; the bipartisan congressional Cox Commission's conclusion that the PRC had stolen high-level U.S. weapons technology; repeated complaints from both official sources in Washington and nongovernmental organizations (NGOs) about human rights violations in the PRC; and Taiwan president Lee Teng-hui's comment that the relationship between the PRC and the Republic of China on Taiwan (ROC) should be seen as a special state-to-state relationship. Upgraded U.S.-Japanese security cooperation might serve as the basis for the creation of an "Asian NATO" that would constitute another building block in the encirclement of China.[10] Combining these events into a strategy to block the PRC's advance toward modernization, commentators predicted ominous consequences for China, with the PLA cast in a major role as defender of the ancestral land. The bombing of the Chinese embassy in Belgrade on May 8 reinforced this scenario, with JFJB and other publications regularly repeating the phrase "war is not far from us."[11]

Three Schools of Thought Contend.

PLA planners drew certain obvious conclusions from their analysis of the Kosovo conflict. If air power were to be the decisive factor, as it had been in Kosovo, troop training would have to make defense against air strikes its focus. *Kongjun Bao*, the air force newspaper, opined that air wars would be decisive in future battles; an air force logistics specialist contrasted the efficiency of NATO operations in transporting men and materiel to the FRY area with the deficiencies of the PLA Air Force's (PLAAF) work in this regard. He suggested consulting the FRY's experience. Of particular interest was the value of secreting assets in the FRY's rear areas: the writer felt that China had been too hasty in dismantling the logistics depots in so-called "third line" areas and too eager to construct "appearance projects" in more vulnerable areas.[12] Training should stress "three offensives and three defenses": attacking stealthy warplanes, cruise missiles, and helicopters; and defending against precision air raids, electronic measures, and reconnaissance.[13] Fighting a war against a technologically superior enemy would require better educated officers and men; therefore, it was imperative that training programs stress scientific and technological knowledge. Noting the effectiveness of the U.S. Air Force in rescuing downed pilots, JFJB urged that anti-air raid preparations include counter-rescue training. The PLA must focus on defeating rescue operations from both land and air, creating both a "land net and a sky net," so that enemy pilots could be prevented from ever flying again.[14]

A succession of essays in military journals dealt with the issue of informatized war and how to counter it. One fairly typical essay suggested a three step process:

1. Use digital, computer, and global communications technology to integrate early warning in the operational space, automated command and control, and precision strikes;

2. Use the command, control, communications, computers, and intelligence surveillance and reconnaissance (C4ISR) system to combine the arms and services in an organic way to establish an integrated military force; and,

3. Use the battlefield information superhighway to achieve battlefield integration.[15]

That NATO had achieved its successes with a relatively small fighting force lent weight to plans to downsize the PLA.

While there was a consensus that the nature of war had fundamentally changed, that a threat to China existed, and that the PLA needed to reinforce its ability to defend the PRC, different voices expressed different opinions on how this should be done. One school held that it was imperative for the PLA to increase its ability to confront the unnamed high-technology hegemonist on its own terms: "the nation that manages to stay in the forefront of the big tide of science and technology will be able to gain the initiative in future war."[16] China would need UAVs, cruise missiles, and better electronic surveillance equipment, as well as

42

the ability to take countermeasures against American assets.

In June, a Hong Kong newspaper announced that a military high-tech research institute had been established under the party's Central Military Commission in response to the events of Kosovo. It characterized the institute as the descendant of an earlier group headed by Marshal Nie Rongzhen that Mao Zedong had tasked to develop the PRC's nuclear bomb. The head of the modern-day version was to be General Xiong Guangkai, deputy chief of the general staff in charge of PLA intelligence and military research units, and would include members of the cabinet-level Commission for Science, Technology, and Industry for National Defense; the ministries of information, industry, and education; the Chinese Academy of Sciences; the Chinese Academy of Engineering; as well as leading scientists, engineers, technicians, and intelligence officers from civilian and military units. High-ranking PLA officers were described as urging the central government to set aside funds as a matter of urgency in order to develop and acquire more sophisticated weaponry.[17] In a lengthy article in the August 1999 issue of the party Central Committee's semimonthly official journal, Qiushi (求是, Seeking Truth), Chief of the General Staff General Fu Chuanyou made a strong case for the high-technology option, stating flatly that military training in science and technology was the only way to win.[18]

A second school questioned the wisdom of trying to counter the United States weapon for weapon. Luo Laisheng, a participant in a forum sponsored by the Guangzhou Military Region on the theme "Implications of NATO's Air Strike on the FRY for Military Training With Science and Technology," opined that

Kosovo had broken the myth that high-technology weapons are invincible and corroborated the lessons of history in which those in a weaker position managed to defeat stronger enemies. New weapons will always have some fatal weaknesses, said Luo, while old ones, as long as they are well-placed and well-used, can prevail. He chided comrades who felt that the PLA's armaments and training were too backward. Other participants echoed his plea to eschew defeatism and enable existing weaponry to be more effectively utilized.[19]

Another vocal backer of opposition to an all-out effort to match the United States in weapons technology was Qiao Liang (乔良), one of the two senior colonels whose book, *Unrestricted Warfare* (超限战), had been published just prior to the Kosovo confrontation. In an interview with *China Youth Daily* (中国青年报), Qiao argued that for China to strive for a high technology military to deal with the United States was to fall into the same trap that had bankrupted the Union of Soviet Socialist Republics (USSR) and caused it to disintegrate. Stating that the PRC could never catch up, Qiao compared the effort to "trying to break a stone with an egg." Other measures would be far more effective. For example, he stated, never in history had a great power ever really eliminated a guerrilla force. Declaring, albeit erroneously, that Western powers had devised the rules of war in order to advantage themselves, Qiao advocated that China ignore them.[20]

In Qiao and his co-author Wang Xiangsui (王湘穗)'s analysis, as more weapons are developed and deployed, the value of each individual weapon in combat is diminished. As a corollary, no single type of weapon can be decisive, save in the highly unlikely event of nuclear weapons in a total war. Qiao and

Wang characterized Americans as being excessively fearful of casualties as well as very rich. As a consequence, they tended to see warfare as a "marathon in military technology" rather than a test of morale, bravery, intelligence, and strategy. Such a mindset, they posited, creates a different kind of vulnerability. The proliferation in types and costs of weapons that are necessary to support this marathon could even cause the American economy to collapse. Note that Qiao and Wang's characterization of the United States as a-strategic contrasts with the more prevalent descriptions of Kosovo mentioned above, as part of a larger American strategy to encircle the PRC to prevent its modernization and rise on the international scene.

The lesson Qiao and Wang drew for China, as a much poorer country, was that the PRC must use whatever means are at its disposal, refusing to be fettered by rules and codes devised without its participation and which would work against it. Biological and chemical warfare, terrorism, and the manipulation of environmental conditions — for example, producing harmful climate changes in the enemy's territory — must all be employed.[21]

Aware that if a strong country used no-limit warfare against a weaker opponent, the weaker country was unlikely to survive, Qiao noted that history proved this was unlikely to happen. "Barbarians always historically rise by breaking the rules of civilized and developed countries, which is what human history is all about. The United States has been on the rise for a century, having drawn up its own rules."[22] While the image of America as a Gulliverian giant constrained by rules of its own making must have been satisfying to patriotic readers, the implicit equation of Chinese with barbarians could not have been.

JFJB echoed Qiao's sentiments, minus the reference to barbarians, quoting Mao Zedong as having said "We are not gentlemen, and do not have to practice any 'idiotic' humanity, justice, and virtue."[23]

Proponents of this school argued for seeking out the vulnerabilities inherent in the enemy's superior strength and employing countermeasures that they generally referred to as *shashoujian* (杀手锏) and occasionally as *sashoujian* (撒手锏) — assassin's mace weapons — or, less poetically, low-cost quick-fix substitutes to enhance the PRC's military capabilities. PLA publications show awareness that the technologically superior side is also capable of using this type of asymmetric warfare, and that "U.S.-led NATO" did in fact use it in Kosovo. The tacit assumption seems to be that the Chinese side will use it more cleverly and effectively. Laser beams could blind satellites, and computer networks could be disrupted. The PLA could use decoys, such as those employed by FRY troops, to deceive NATO forces into wasting valuable munitions to kill nonexistent tanks, and deceptive tactics to lure strikes to areas where enemy troops were not located.

For the third school, Kosovo proved that people's war retained its validity in the modern age. Instances of civilians joining hands across bridges and surrounding power plants to prevent them from being bombed and of noncombatants hacking into NATO communications were much praised. PLA media described computer-literate Serbs as bombarding the NATO web site with viruses and large amounts of email; they were said to have paralyzed the computer system on the USS *Nimitz* and to have brought down the White House server for an entire day.[24] The PLA's General Political Department also pointed to the role of political work and the importance of keeping high morale among both civilian and military personnel. According to Chinese media accounts, the army and the people had functioned as one, conforming precisely to the script of people's war.

Not surprisingly, the bombing of the embassy in Belgrade elicited calls for military retaliation. Calls for militant counteraction were vociferous; according to the Hong Kong press, there had been anti-American demonstrations at military academies around the country even before the attack.[25] These became more prominent thereafter.[26] Although the U.S. embassy in Beijing was quickly besieged by rock-throwing mobs that some believed had been officially encouraged, there were nonetheless evident efforts to restrain the more militant from taking concrete action. Chinese president and simultaneously head of the Central Military Commission Jiang Zemin appears to have been in the forefront of these. Obviously choosing his words carefully so as not to invite criticisms of cowardice from his domestic enemies, Jiang assured an enlarged meeting of the Politburo's Standing Committee that party and government would never barter away its principles. Although he made no explicit linkage between the consequences of a militantly anti-U.S. policy and China's bid to enter the World Trade Organization (WTO), Jiang stressed that it was important to continue negotiations on that issue.

> Our current struggle against the U.S.-led NATO is unlikely to come to a successful end within a short period time, for the United States will continue to resort to sophistry concerning its bombing of the Chinese Embassy in the FRY and . . . we must further retain our rights for taking corresponding actions. . . . We must carry out our struggle against hegemonism and power politics, yet we cannot close our door and refuse to

deal with certain western countries, like the United States. Although we know perfectly well that the wolf is going to attack man, we still need to deal with the wolf. That is, we must "dance with the wolf." This is the reality we must face and the diplomatic strategy we must adopt. We should develop ourselves and enhance the comprehensive national strength of our country under the condition of simultaneously fighting against and having dealings with hegemonism and power politics.[27]

Jiang vowed to discuss the matter with U.S. President Bill Clinton at an appropriate time.

A provincial party chief strongly supported Jiang's contention vis-à-vis the hardline military faction. Sichuan party head Xie Shijie took direct issue with those who said that large increases in the military budget were necessary to safeguard the PRC's sovereignty and dignity, saying that:

We must unify the safeguarding of state sovereignty and national dignity with the continuation of the policy of opening to the outside world. The overall masses must differentiate between the authorities of the U.S.-led NATO bloc and improvements in the investment environment. One hand must court business and attract investments, while the other hand must increase exports.[28]

A few days later, a *JFJB* commentator who was perhaps not entirely pleased with Jiang Zemin's ruling on the need to dance with the wolf, used the same metaphor to convey a more ominous message: although the predator had yet to come, the sounds of its claws sharpening could be heard from time to time. Since war was not far away, continuing efforts at preparedness were what were needed.[29]

Jiang Zemin's view prevailed. China was admitted into the WTO, albeit not immediately; its economic and military strength continued to grow impressively; tensions in Sino-American relations abated; and Kosovo, though scarcely forgotten, ceased to command the passionate response it had aroused in 1999.

Kosovo in a Decade's Perspective.

Ten years later, the PRC was at least able to dance as an equal with the wolf, and perhaps even to assume the role of leading partner. No obvious choices had been made among the three schools, and they can certainly be seen as complementing rather than competing with each other. Indeed, General Xiong Guangkai (熊光楷), who had been chosen to head the high-technology institute research unit mentioned above, attempted a synthesis of the three. In his 2003 book, *International Strategy and the Revolution in Military Affairs*, (国际战略与新军事变革), Xiong argued that these, combined with the "important thinking of Comrade Jiang Zemin's Three Represents," were the essence of the RMA with Chinese characteristics. The PLA should study and draw lessons from all previous local wars that were conducted under high technology conditions, while not fully or indiscriminately copying them. The reality, said Xiong, is that the PLA was still in the stage of partial mechanization. The state of mechanization should be completed, using informatization to guide mechanization and mechanization to promote informatization: these should be considered dual tasks. Finally, the army and the people should be combined, attaching importance to enhancing the traditional superiority of people's war under high-technology conditions. This combination would be the basis for military superiority (优势).[30]

Only the first, high-tech focused, school is expensive, and with its economy thriving and the PLA downsized, China has been able to fund more and better military hardware. Yet the same three schools of thought continue to voice their opinions. Something close to dissent from Xiong Guangkai's synthesis can be found in *Missile Force Daily* (火箭兵報), the newspaper of the Second Artillery Corps. After a brief nod to the importance of talented personnel and forward thinking, the author states that, although "some people say" (有人說) that one can defeat a better armed adversary if one masters better ways of fighting,

> . . . this may be true of previous forms of war. In informatized war, if one's weapons are inferior, one's fighting skills may also be restricted . . . only by striving to master the scientific and technological development can we more rapidly change the model of shaping combat capabilities.[31]

With regard to the first school, as detailed by the annual reports of the U.S. Department of Defense (DoD) and a number of China's increasingly apprehensive neighbors, the PRC has made significant acquisitions in technologically sophisticated weaponry. It has the most active land-based ballistic missile program in the world, is developing and testing offensive missiles, forming additional missile units, qualitatively upgrading some missile systems, and developing methods to counter ballistic missile defenses. The air force has acquired UAVs and Su-30 fighter planes; a new bomber will be equipped with a new long-range cruise missiles. Aerial surveillance capabilities have also been improved. There is an active aircraft carrier research and development program. The navy is improving its over-the-horizon targeting capability with more capable radars that can be used in conjunction with overhead imagery from satellites to assist its next-generation anti-ship missiles to locate targets longer distances from China. The missiles themselves have longer ranges and better accuracy. A new ballistic missile nuclear submarine (SSBN) and two new nuclear-powered attack submarines have entered service, and a new base has been constructed on Hainan Island in the South China Sea that provides the PLA Navy (PLAN) with direct access to important international sea lanes as well as a port from which submarines can enter the deep waters of the South China Sea.[32]

An Indian defense journal said that China had learned the value of space as the fourth dimension, and took note of the PRC's major efforts in that area.[33] Taiwan military sources said that Kosovo had changed the PLA's strategy away from trying to take Taiwan through either a blockade or amphibious landing scenario to one of "immediate response and decisive action." A sudden, paralyzing assault comprising electromagnetic pulse technology, missile strikes, and air attacks would compel the now-defenseless Taiwan to surrender before other countries had a chance to intervene, and without incurring significant manpower resources.[34]

As the PRC's economy has continued to make impressive progress while the western world was beset by its worst financial downturn in recent years, the argument that the United States is trying to lure China into an arms race in order to bankrupt it has faded from the media. Even so, the PLA's *China National Defense News* (中国国防报) opined as late of 2006 that the U.S. edge in weapons technology had led other countries to imitate every move it made, thereby luring them into failing to learn anything valuable. Imitators would hence lose their own capital, even to making blind investments, only to be left further and further behind.[35]

Those who favor making better use of existing armaments rather than lust after the latest high technology and using innovative low technology that may or may not employ unlimited warfare techniques continue to argue their case. The example of the F-117 comes up again and again, sometimes used in support of clever tactics, sometimes in support of low technology being able to defeat state of the art technology, and sometimes in support of the value of people's war. In 2006, the deputy commander of a unit in the Shenyang Military Region quoted Chairman of the Central Military Commission Hu Jintao as saying that the military should fight on the basis of existing armaments. However, he noted, there was a tendency to deviate from this thinking: some officers and soldiers believed it was impossible to prevail unless they had advanced technology. The commander argued that several recent wars, including Kosovo, had shown that the role of traditional weapons should not be underestimated and that, conversely, high-tech weapons are not flawless and perfect. Specifically referencing the F-117, the commander advised "if one's sword is inferior, then one should try to have a better technique of using the sword (剑不如人剑法高于人)."[36]

Similar sentiments emanated from the newspaper of the Beijing Military Region, where a commentator opined that when, in the Fifth Encirclement Campaign of the 1930s, the Red Army abandoned the strategy and tactics that had previously served it well, the result was defeat. He advocated combining reliance on actual weapons on hand with careful use of strategy and tactics, concluding that good tactics, not just weapons, were an important trump card.[37]

The roles of climate control and camouflage, again referencing Kosovo, were also regularly mentioned. A 2009 report described the PLA as carefully studying the uses to which climate change might be employed on the battlefield. One of its examples was that of FRY defenders burning tires that created smoke so dense as to conceal troop withdrawals. Properly used, weather weapons could defeat opponents through surprise moves.[38] The orbits of satellites could be tracked and items of interest to an enemy moved out of their path or otherwise concealed.[39]

An engineer identified by *Air Force News* (空军报) as a camouflage expert praised the FRY's well-concealed single aircraft shelters and aircraft cave depots that he described as having protected a large quantity of operational aircraft, surface missiles, radar, and other weapons and equipment. Having learned from the FRY's experience, the PLA's camouflaging equipment and materials had now achieved serialization and possessed various camouflaging capabilities. However, he conceded, camouflage netting, paints, and other standard equipment now in service were still far from being able to satisfy the needs of air force units; high resolution satellites could still detect military targets.[40]

Another expert, Wang Jiaying, attached to the Second Artillery Corps and described by its newspaper as a battlefield magician, noticed that the vegetation camouflage used by FRY troops in the Kosovo conflict lasted up to 7 days—i.e., far longer than that in use by the PLA. Research revealed that the FRY troops had used a certain type of preservative liquid on the cut stems of the vegetation; the Chinese military then adopted the same preservative. Wang's research also led to the development of protective coatings for missiles, which depended on collecting samples in the specific areas where the missile emplacements were located. Becoming ill at a sentry post more than 4,000 meters above sea level—the location was unnamed but was almost certainly in Tibet, and the symptoms the article describes are those of altitude sickness—Wang refused to leave until his work was completed.[41]

According to Taiwan sources, the protection measures taken by the Second Artillery Corps since Kosovo were very effective: optical sensors of satellites were unable to penetrate either the thick bunkers or the mountain caves used to protect troops. Hence, while Taiwan's imagery satellites could detect the deployment locations of the missiles, it had no way to know exactly how many missiles were inside them. PLA propaganda films had shown many ballistic missiles being launched from forested areas at night, indicating the Second Artillery's ability to launch from the field. The Second Artillery had also conducted operational training in warehouses or on factory shop floors in recent years. These measures had significantly minimized the probability of detection while Second Artillery Corps troops were in training or on operations. A special militia unit had been tasked with the preparation of fake missiles that were visually indistinguishable from real ones, even to a spy satellite equipped with infrared or synthetic aperture radars.[42]

According to a July 2010 report, the PLA has set up a centralized cyberspace unit with a dedicated base,[43] and multiple reports indicate that the PLA has been at least partially responsible for cyber espionage against foreign governments and corporations.[44]

As for people's war, China's National Defense Mobilization Law, approved by the National People's Congress in February 2010, gave the state the legal right to requisition "civilian facilities, locations, and other materials owned or used by organizations and individuals," thereby broadening its powers in this regard and deepening the level of military-civilian integration.[45] As noted by former RAND analyst James Mulvenon, the concept of national defense mobilization has a clear lineage from Maoist people's war, when civilians were expected to carry out guerrilla activities against invaders and support the military according to the classic water and fish metaphor. In the post-Mao era, however, local governments have tended to resent the burden of supporting military units through supplying food, fuel, and financial contributions, thus necessitating a law that more clearly defined their responsibilities.[46]

Dennis Blasko points out that from 1998 forward, every one of China's White Papers on defense has explicitly stated that the PLA adheres to the concept of people's war as part of China's military strategy. Spokespersons explain that the notion of people's war as based on rifles, millet, and human wave tactics that emphasize guerrilla warfare and protracted conflict is a misperception: in its present day incarnation, people's war has been redefined as a form of organization of war that has nothing to do with the level of military technology.[47] Civilians are responsible for contributing their skills to the war effort, either enthusiastically or by having them requisitioned, at whatever level of time and technology the state deems appropriate. In the cyberwar that is anticipated to be crucial to success in future conflict, civilian hackers are expected to play an important part, with frequent references made to the role that they played in Kosovo.[48] A possible portent of the role nonmilitary personnel might play is the example of a graduate student in engineering in Liaoning who produced a paper on how to attack a small U.S. power grid sub-network so as to cause a cascading power failure throughout the country.[49]

As for the noncombat aspects of a winning strategy, the PLA's political work stresses the "three warfares"—media, psychological, and legal—as major weapons intended to weaken the will and spirit of the enemy with the fewest casualties. To be most effective, this should ideally begin in peacetime before the onset of hostilities in order to turn public opinion in the enemy country and among its soldiers against the war effort. Morale-undermining activities are, of course, nothing new: the example of Tokyo Rose comes immediately to mind. What is new, according to Taiwan sources, is that the relationship between the PLA's political warfare and its military operations has changed in such a way that the former has risen from subordinate status to being independent.[50]

Lessons Learned From Past Wars.

To a significant extent, the lessons learned by the PLA are lessons its leaders already knew or that served as justification for positions that advantaged their own niches within the defense establishment. For example, the PLAAF learned that air wars would be the wave of the future and that control of the air had been the decisive factor in victory[51]; its air transport division learned that air transport was a crucial element in NATO's ability to prosecute the war and pointed out that in Kosovo the scale at which support and transport planes was used approached that of main combat aircraft, enabling large quantities of weapons and equipment to reach the battlefield quickly.[52] The chief of staff of a logistics unit highlighted the importance of logistical support for the air force's operations,[53] the Second Artillery to the successes achieved by missiles, and the General Political Department to the need to maintain high morale among troops and population, and to the importance of properly carrying out propaganda work. The key to victory in informational war would be to conquer the psychology and willpower of the opponent.[54] As a retired Taiwan general pointed out, no one needed to teach the PLA the value of propaganda.[55] To be sure, there is a difference between simply knowing the value of something and learning how to use it better, as the PLA seems to have done from observing the FRY's practice thereof. Meanwhile, Western strategists expressed doubts that the domination of air conflict and absence of ground support would be replicated in any future war, which so far they have not.

Although it is obvious that the PLA studied the Kosovo confrontation carefully, some factors confronting NATO appear to have been ignored in assessing its operations. These include the difficulties of prosecuting a war by committee that presented field commanders with rules of engagement that severely impinged on their ability to carry out military operations, and an extreme aversion to casualties, two factors that would presumably not affect PLA operations to the same extent. Although these are unlikely to apply to a war undertaken by China, PLA strategists might want to contemplate whether the United States, in fighting a war that did not involve getting the consent of numerous and sometimes fractious allies, would use the same restrictive rules of engagement.

As well as whether western scruples about civilian casualties would continue to prevail when vitally important national interests or the lives of their own soldiers hung in the balance.[56]

An additional factor is that, although the experiences of Kosovo are repeated mantra-like in publications from following years, later voices appear to be repeating earlier ones with little effort at reexamination. This runs the risk of myth-creation, which, if based on falsehoods, could be dangerous. For example, there is no attention to the issue of whether the destruction of an F-117 stealth fighter was genuinely a triumph of the civilian population that can be replicated on a larger scale, a lucky shot, a consequence of pilot error, or the result of prior information on the plane's flight plan from a less than enthusiastic member of NATO.[57] Similarly, the enthusiastic support of the Serbian people for their government is presented as immutable. U.S. studies, however, indicate that initial citizen support became so frayed in the course of bombing that Milosevic's fear of an uprising against him became a major factor in his decision to capitulate.[58]

With regard to the Serbian fighters, Air Commander Lieutenant General Michael Short expected to lose many planes, but to his delight he lost only two and no pilots, and commented,

> The truth of the matter is that there were not a lot of Serbs who were willing to die for Slobo [Milosevic], trying to shoot down a NATO airplane. Their effort throughout the war was to survive, to move, to hide, to get missiles in the air, but [they] made little or no attempt to guide those missiles. Almost all their shots were ballistic shots, which means they weren't guided.[59]

This tendency to bend history in order to "prove" a point the author wishes to make is also evident in such instances as the above-mentioned Beijing Military Region commentator who argued that the Red Army was defeated in the Fifth Encirclement Campaign of the mid-1930s when it abandoned tried and true strategies. There is no acknowledgement that the differences caused by a new Kuomintang (KMT) strategy, the ever-tightening ring of blockhouses suggested by Chiang Kai-shek's German advisers, might necessitate a change in the Red Army's responses. In this regard, the author is accepting party history unquestioningly: Mao used the defeat to bolster his own sagging political fortunes. There is no indication that any counterstrategy Mao might have suggested — and an exhaustive search of the Yan'an archive could not locate any evidence of any counterstrategy Mao had advanced — could have succeeded.[60]

While PLA sources express awareness of the need to maintain high morale among troops, the issue of when and under what circumstances morale might erode remains unexplored in the PLA literature on lessons learned from Kosovo. Other issues that have passed into unexamined unquestioned mythology and could mislead the PLA are: whether the bombing of the PRC embassy in Belgrade was, as PLA publications aver, planned in retaliation for Chinese help to the FRY[61]; and, whether NATO bombed the presidential palace,[62] "wantonly and indiscriminately" [63] and used cluster bombs against civilians. In truth, the presidential palace was placed off limits, and targets were carefully chosen to avoid civilian casualties. Less than 500 died as a result. Target planners were quickly ordered to cease using cluster bombs after Milosevic's press staff persuaded CNN to run a segment on what it termed a terror weapon.[64] The constant repetition of the success of Serbian forces in concealing tanks, while an accurate observation, begs the question of how much this contributed to overall military success, since Milosevic surrendered even though many of his tanks survived. In other words, to focus on the number of tank kills may be to use the wrong metric.

Finally, while the PLA sought lessons from Kosovo that would enable it to better fight an unnamed superior military power, there is no indication that, in its avowed strategy of fighting local wars under high-technology conditions, it has considered that the Chinese military might find itself in the role that NATO had in Kosovo. Hence, while applauding the ingenuity of the people in outwitting the higher-technology enemy through employing camouflage, deception, and guerrilla tactics, there is no public acknowledgement that the PLA might find the same tactics used against it by Uyghurs, Tibetans, or Taiwanese.

Concerning the cases cited above, the PLA might wish to consider what the Kosovo war actually accomplished. More than a decade after Milosevic's capitulation, the status of Kosovo remains in limbo. The efforts of UN Forces in Kosovo (UNMIK) to get the two sides together to reach resolution of their differences have been unsuccessful. Neither Belgrade, the capital of Serbia, nor the Kosovo Serbs will agree to recognize Kosovo as an independent state, while Pristina, the capital of Kosovo, sees the independence of Kosovo as a *fait accompli*. Its leaders insist that they will agree to negotiations only as two independent states. After Kosovo issued a unilateral declaration of independence in 2008 and gained diplomatic recognition from 69 countries, including the United States, Serbia took its case to the International Court of Justice (ICJ). In

July 2010, the court issued an advisory opinion declaring that the unilateral declaration of independence did not violate international law. The Chinese foreign ministry, seeing an ominous precedent, immediately denounced the ruling. The victory for Kosovo was, however, tempered in that the ICJ, in its 10 to 4 ruling, did not go so far as to affirm Kosovo's independence.

Lessons from the Lessons?

It is instructive to compare what the PLA learned from the U.S. experience in Kosovo conflict with what the United States learned from its own performance in Kosovo. There are few similarities in the analyses. Whereas PLA publications emphasized the impressive levels of technology and training, American analysts tended to focus on significant shortcomings and errors, to the extent that one is reminded of an episode from the Keystone Kops of comic book fame/infamy. Since NATO had publicly ruled out a ground invasion from the beginning, Serbian forces were relieved of the necessity to position their tanks to cut off roads and other avenues of attack, where they could have more easily been targeted by NATO air power. Instead, they dispersed and hid their tanks and armored personnel carriers (APCs), leaving paramilitary units free to pursue ethnic cleansing. After 6 weeks of bombing, there were more Serb forces in Kosovo than when the campaign began.[65] The planning process was described as lacking a plan, and two parallel chains of command caused additional difficulties. In terms of hardware, there were interoperability problems and shortages of precision-guided weapons. At congressional hearings held a few months after the conflict ended, there were scathing criticisms of the DoD failure to create a

61

littoral naval force, the fact that 95 percent of the air forces' refueling fleet was deployed elsewhere when they were needed to support the Kosovo operation, the fact that pilots lacked adequate flying hours, and that the kill chain—the time between identification of a target and the delivery of weapons—was too long.[66]

Although examining past conflicts is in the abstract, and often in reality, a valuable exercise, there are pitfalls to be avoided. The first is that one may learn the wrong lesson and not discover it until attempting to apply it in the next confrontation. A second is that, although the lesson learned may be correct, it may not be applicable to subsequent conflicts, because of different factor inputs such as political circumstances, terrain, and changes in technology. A third caveat is that different entities within one's defense establishment may not agree on what lessons have been learned. Finally, one may have learned the correct lesson but be unable to apply it for political and ideological reasons. As noted above, all of these problems can be seen to some degree in the PLA's assessment of the war in Kosovo. As PLA sources have pointed out, China is not Kosovo, nor is it Yugoslavia. But were there no parallels between Kosovo and the type of military operation that the PLA anticipates fighting, there would be no reason for it to have so closely examined the conflict in Kosovo, or to have repeatedly used them as guides for defense planning. In August 2010, the British Broadcasting Company (BBC) reported that the PLA had staged night drills to repel Kosovo-like air raids by the United States.[67]

Implications for the United States.

American policy planners should be aware that the PLA scrutinizes the combat performance of the U.S. military in minute detail, and that it will seek to adapt its weapons and strategy to counter, match, or exceed those of the United States. However, Chinese analysts are selective in their choice of factors to emulate. Assuming that they are saying privately what they say publicly — an important caveat — this selectivity shows several flaws in the lessons they have learned that U.S. planners should take note of.

First, the analyses seem to ignore many of the deficiencies that U.S. military and civilian critics cited in their post-Kosovo assessment. Some of this is understandable, since they are unlikely to be relevant to a war fought by the PLA. China would presumably not have to try to placate numerous members of a fractious coalition, and would therefore have no need to fetter the PLA with rules of engagement that make targeting difficult, Nor would Beijing publicly rule out a ground invasion, thereby avoiding the disadvantageous consequence of freeing an adversary from positioning its tanks at probable lines of attack where they could be easily targeted. But the PLA's publications do not evince awareness of the shortages of munitions, in the types of munitions available, and in personnel whose skills levels were adequate for the jobs they were asked to do. This indicates that the PLA may overestimate the capabilities of the U.S. military.

A second implication that U.S. authorities should be aware of is the Chinese penchant for sanctifying misinformation from its own military history to justify its use in the present day. The aforementioned admonition not to abandon tried-and-true tactics, since doing so led to the defeat of communist forces during the Encirclement Campaigns, is based on a falsified account of what happened that party historical accounts have accepted as truth. This apparent unwillingness to challenge shibboleths constitutes a potential vulnerability that U.S. planners should take into consideration.

A third factor to be aware of is that a desire to overestimate the role of the population in helping to defeat an invader could lead the Chinese into another dangerous blind alley. Although it is true that the Serbian population initially supported President Milosevic's defiant actions, civilian support for the war eroded under the bombing campaigns to an extent that Milosevic, fearing that he might be overthrown by his own people, capitulated.

A related instance that also reveals a vulnerability the United States should be aware of is the apparently uncontested belief that the downing of the F-117 fighter was a triumph of inferior weapons and or people's war.[68] NATO experts have pointed out that, had the FRY military had an adequate integrated air defense system and more soldiers who were properly trained to use the equipment they had, many more NATO planes might have been brought down. American planners should carefully monitor whether such mis-assessments are distracting attention from creating of a stronger defenses, in this case an upgraded integrated air defense system (IADS).[69]

A fourth factor to be aware of is that the Chinese, in identifying themselves in the role of the FRY government, and people do not appear to recognize that they are likely to be in the position that NATO was in the FRY if they fight the sort of informationized war on China's periphery that has been the focus of the

PLA's strategy since Kosovo. In a confrontation in Tibet, Xinjiang, or Taiwan, it is the PLA that will have to contend with people's war resistance.

Fifth, Chinese commentaries do not acknowledge that the same dependence on high technology that they believe to be the Achilles heel of the American military may become a comparable vulnerability that the United States can use against the PLA as its own weaponry becomes increasingly sophisticated.

Finally, U.S. planners should be aware of the PLA's tendency to interpret actions that the United States sees as reactions to particular events, such as the decision to intervene in Kosovo to halt ethnic cleansing, through the prism of a conviction that it is part of an American grand strategy to maintain and extend U.S. global hegemony. Its analysts appear to see no contradiction between this and an equally strongly held belief that the United States has entered a period of rapid decline.

ENDNOTES - CHAPTER 2

1. Michael R. Gordon, "Weeks of Bombing Will Aim to Break Milosevic's Grip," *New York Times*, April 1, 1999. Additionally, the palace itself, formerly the residence of a king, was considered of historical value.

2. Bernard Gordon, "U.S. Warns Russia: Don't Provide Help to Serbian Military," *New York Times*, April 10, 1999, pp. A1, A8.

3. Yue Xuanyi (岳宣义), "科索沃战争对我军政治工作的警示" ("Warnings and Enlightenments Provided By Kosovo War For the Political Work of Our Army"), 解放军报 (*PLA Daily*), August 24, 1999, p. 6.

4. Jin Tao (金涛) , "'多来诺骨牌'谬论土重来" ("'Domino Theory' Stages a Comeback"), 解放军报 (*PLA Daily*), April 9, 1999, p. 4.

5. Zhang Zhaozhong (张召忠), "北约会出动地面部队马" ("Will NATO Dispatch Ground Forces?"), 解放军报 (*PLA Daily*), April 5, 1999, p. 4; Hu Wenlong (胡文龙), "北约空袭将作战略调整" ("NATO To Make Strategic Readjustment To Its Air Strikes"), 解放军报 (*PLA Daily*), April 15, 1999, p. 4.

6. Tan Baoping (谭保平), "在科技练兵的聚焦点上着力新三大三防：训练引发的思考" ("Make Efforts to Focus of Science and Technology Troop Training—Thoughts on the New 'Three Offensives and Three Defensives' Training"), 解放军报 (*PLA Daily*), November 23, 1999, p. 6.

7. Wang Hui (王辉), "掀起信息化作战的盖头来" ("Lifting the Cover From Information Operations"), 中国国防报(*China National Defense News*), December 11, 2008, p. 3.

8. Ma Ling (马玲), "U.S. Strategy for the 21st Century as Viewed From Kosovo—A Conversation With Strategist Yao You-zhi" ("姚有志"), 大公报 (*Ta Kung Pao*), Hong Kong, May 3, 1999, p. A1.

9. *Ibid.*; Dong Guozheng (董国政), "军事因素回潮因由何在" ("Causes of the Reversion to Military Affairs"), 解放军报 (*PLA Daily*), September 10, 2008, p. 7.

10. Liu Huadi (刘化迪), "冷战思维仍在影响当今世界" ("Cold War Thinking Still Influential in Today's World"), 解放军报 (*PLA Daily*), February 28, 2005, p. 11.

11. See, among many other such references, Bi Changhong (毕长虹), "单极化图谋与战争危险" ("Polarization Plot and Danger of War"), 解放军报 (*PLA Daily*), May 21, 1999, p. 4.

12. Qin Yonghua (秦勇华), "从科索沃战争看战役后勤保障" ("Looking at Logistical Support in the Kosovo War"), 解放军报 (*PLA Daily*), August 17, 1999, p. 6. The "third line" refers to a project undertaken under Mao Zedong to relocate defense assets to caves and other concealed locations in the PRC's hinterlands to shield them from destruction in case of attack by the Soviet Union or some other enemy. The remoteness of their locations also reduced the bases' usefulness, and the project is generally considered to have been a failure. See Barry Naughton, "The Third

Front: Defence Industrialization In the Chinese Interior," *China Quarterly*, No. 115, September 1988.

13. Tan Baobing (谭保平), "Stressing the Focus of Science and Technology Troop Training—Thoughts on the New 'Three Offensives and Three Defensives' Training," 解放军报 (*PLA Daily*), November 23, 1999, p. 6; see also Tian Long (天龙), "中国军力报告与中美关系" ("Chinese Military Strength and Sino-American Relations"), 镜报 (*The Mirror*), September 1, 2003, pp. 42-44.

14. Hu Jian (胡坚), "反空袭不可忽视反救援" (Anti-Rescue' Operations Necessary"), 解放军报 (*PLA Daily*), June 22, 1999, p. 6.

15. Tang Liehui (唐列辉), "努力探人与战器结合的优解" ("Make Efforts to Find Best Solution to Man-Weapons Integration"), 解放军报 (*PLA Daily*), June 15, 1999, p. 6.

16. Zhu Wenquan (朱文泉) and Zhao Taizhong (赵太忠), "提高针对性增强坚迫感—从科索沃局再谈入特久学习高科技知识" ("Focus on the Key Aspects, Enhance a Sense of Urgency—Viewing the Profound and Protracted High-Tech Knowledge Lessons of the Kosovo Situation"), 解放军报 (*PLA Daily*), May 25, 1999, p. 6.

17. Cary Huang, "Beijing Sets Up Panel on High-Tech Weapons," *Hong Kong Standard*, June 11, 1999, p. 6.

18. Fu Quanyou (傅全有), "大兴科技练兵强　固钢铁长城" ("Vigorously Conduct Military Training in Science and Technology to Strengthen the Great Steel Wall"), 求是 (*Qiushi, Seeking Truth*), No. 15, August 1, 1999, pp. 12-17.

19. Duan Zhiming (段志明), Mei Lijin (梅里金), Liu Jianmin (刘建民) and Xiang Zihui (项子辉), "科索沃销烟的警示—广州军区某集团军 '从北约空袭南联盟看科技练兵' 座谈会纪要" ("Warning From the Flame of War in Kosovo—Summary of Forum Held By a Group Army of Guangzhou Military Region Under the Theme of Implications of NATO Bombing of Yugoslav Federation for Military Training With Science and Technology"), 解放军报 (*PLA Daily*), April 20, 1999, p. 6.

20. Sha Lin (沙麟), "Two Senior Colonels and 'No-Limit Warfare'," 中国青年报 (*China Youth Daily*), June 28, 1999, p. 5, FTS 19990728000697.

21. Qiao Liang (乔良) and Wang Xianghui (王湘穗), 超限战 (*Unlimited War*), Beijing, China: PLA Literature and Arts Press, 1999.

22. Sha Lin, p. 5.

23. Zhu Xiaoning (朱小宁), "袭断 '非对称战场'" ("A Monopoly on the 'Asymmetrical Battlefield'"), 解放军报 (*PLA Daily*), November 23, 1999, p. 6.

24. Yue Xuanyi(岳宣义), "Warnings and Enlightenment Provided by Kosovo War for the Political Work of Our Army," 解放军报 (*PLA Daily*), August 24, 1999 p. 6, FTS 19990919000018.

25. Lo Ping, "Zhu Rongji's Visit to U.S. and Internal Struggle Within Top Hierarchy," 动向 (*Tung Hsiang*), No. 164, April 15, 1999, pp. 6-10, FTS19990427001937. According to Lo, a veteran correspondent for the respected Hong Kong magazine 争鸣 (*Cheng Ming*), the demonstrations took place March 22-24.

26. Willy Wo-Lap Lam, "Urgent U.S. Action Needed to Soothe Beijing and Prevent Collapse of Ties," *South China Morning Post*, May 1, 1999, p. 1. Lam hypothesized that the reason military hard-liners were able to gain the upper hand is that Beijing saw patriotism as a means to divert attention from social problems such as unemployment.

27. Yü Ching-sheng, "Jiang Zemin Repeatedly Expounds China's Domestic and Foreign Policies in Three Internal Speeches Giving a Quick Response and Winning the Support of the Public," *Ching Pao*, July 1, 1999, pp. 24-26, FTS19990703000863. Article is dated June 3, 1999, based on Jiang's speeches prior to that; hence Pan's article of June 8 can be considered a response to Jiang.

28. Agence France Presse, "'Forget Bombing, Court Investment'," *South China Morning Post*, May 19, 1999.

29. Pan Shunrui (潘顺瑞), "战争离我们并不遥远" ("War Is Not Far From Us"), 解放军报 (*PLA Daily*), June 8, 1999, p. 6.

30. Xiong Guangkai.

31. Cheng Dezhi, "由美国成立网络司令部想到的" ("Thoughts on the American Military's Establishment of a Cyberwar Command"), 火箭兵报 (*Missile Force Daily*), June 22, 2010, p. 3.

32. U.S. Department of Defense, *Annual Report to Congress, Military and Security Developments Involving the People's Republic of China 2010*, available from *www.defense.gov.pubs/pdfs/2010_CMPR_Final.pdf*; ibid., *Annual Report on the Military Power of the People's Republic of China* 2009, available from *www.defenselink.mil/pubs/pdfs/ China_Military_Report_09/pdf* .

33. Ajey Lele, "China's Posture in Space and Its Implications," *Strategic Analysis* (New Delhi), Vol. 21, No. 4, July 1-August 31, 2008, pp. 605-620.

34. This summarizes the assessments found in several articles such as (no author) "超限戰的第一線專訪林勤經中將" ("The First Line of No-Limit Warfare: Conversation with LTG Lin Abe"), 國防政策評論 (*Taiwan Defense Affairs*), Vol. 1, No. 4, September 2001, pp. 125-143; Chung Chien (鐘堅), "共軍高技術犯台戰爭如何以戰逼降" ("PLA's High-tech War Preparation: Taking Taiwan Without Bloodshed"), in *ibid*, Vol. 1, No. 1, October 2000, pp. 140-147; Cheng Jung-mai (鄭君邁), "無人飛行載具之運用與前景" ("Use and Prospects of Unmanned Aerial Vehicles"), 空軍學術雙月刊 (*Air Force Bimonthly Journal*), January 7, 2006, pp. 1-6.

35. Lin Guoli (林国利) and Zhu Jingcheng (朱竟成), "反思拉氏的'七十天" ("Reflecting on Rumsfeld's 'Seventy Days"), 中国国防报 (*China National Defense News*), January 12, 2006, p. 3.

36. An Weiping (安卫平), "立足现有装备谋打赢" ("Rely on Existing Weapons to Win"), 前進報 (*Forward Daily*), March 27, 2006, p. 4.

37. Liao Keduo (廖可铎), "好战法也是撒手剑" ("Good Tactics Are Also A Trump Card"), 战友报 (*Soldiers*), March 10, 2009, p. 2.

38. Zeng Fanxiang (曾凡祥) and Chen Yongbo (陈永波), "直面全球气候挑战－军队应探索烟发展之路" ("Face Global Climate Change Directly: Military Should Examine Low Carbon Emission Development Path"), 解放军报 (*PLA Daily*), December 17, 2009, p. 12.

39. Lu Yuan *et al.* (路远), "卫星信息反抗研究" ("Research on Satellite Information Countermeasures"), 现代防卫技术 (*Modern Defense Technology*), Vol. 35, No. 5, October 2007, pp. 86-91.

40. Wei Liping, "Adept at Playing Hide and Seek with Reconnaissance Satellites: Interview With Camouflage Protection Expert and Senior Engineer Liu Baorong," 空军报 (*Air Force News*), April 19, 2007, FEA20070717231986.

41. Liu Jun (刘军), "战场魔术师" ("Battlefield Magician"), 火箭兵 (*Missile Force Daily*), April 4, 2006, p. 3.

42. Kuo Nai-jih (郭乃日), "商用衞星影像的衍生用途" ("Uses Derived from Commercial Satellite Imagery"), 看不見的臺海戰爭 (*The Invisible War Across the Taiwan Strait*), May 1, 2005, pp. 145-174.

43. Minnie Chan, "PLA Sets Up Centralised Cyber War Command," *South China Morning Post*, July 22, 2010, p. 6.

44. Medius Research, "Report Says China Military Likely Behind Cyber Espionage and Attacks," July 6, 2010, available from *www.prenewswire.com/news/releases/medius-research-report-says-chinse-military-likely-behind-cyber-espionage-and=attacks-97850_579. html* .

45. *Mobilization Law of the People's Republic of China* (中华人民共和国动员法), February 26, 2010, available from *www.npc.cn*.

46. James Mulvenon, "2010 National People's Congress Highlights: Defense Budgets and the New National Defense Mobilization Law," *China Leadership Monitor* No. 32, Spring 2010, p. 3.

47. Dennis J. Blasko, "Chinese Strategic Thinking: People's War in the 21st Century," *China Brief*, Vol. 10 No. 6, March 18, 2010.

48. Yin Bangxiong (尹邦雄), "信息战必修构建和利用畅通的军民通信网络" ("Information War: Must Smoothly Construct a Military-Civilian Communications Network"), 战士报 (*Soldier's Daily*), December 27, 2005, p. 3.

49. John Markoff and David Barboza, "Paper in China Sets Off Alarms in U.S.," *New York Times*, March 20, 2010.

50. Pan Chin-chang (潘進章), "Preliminary Examination of the Chinese Military's 'Political Warfare'," 國防雜誌 (*Defense Journal*), No. 1, Vol. 24, pp 31-43; citation from p. 37.

51. Shang Jinsuo (尚金锁) and Li Liming (李黎光), "党的空军建设指导理论的创新" ("Innovative Development of the Party's Guiding Theory for Air Force Formation"), 军事科学 (*Military Science*), October 20, 2007, pp. 42-48; citation from p. 48.

52. Jiang Xun (蔣遜), Wang Yawei (王亚伟), Xiong Wankui (熊万奎), "空军机动能力建设的启示" ("Lessons from the Establishment of Air Transport Power"), 现代军事 (*Conmilit*), August 2, 2008.

53. Jiang Shuli (江书立), "加强现代空军作战后勤核心保障能力建设" ("Strengthen the Building of Modern Air Force Logistics Core Capabilities"), 空军报 (*Air Force Daily*), February 17, 2009, p. 4.

54. Chang Long, "Grasp the Trend of New Military Changes—Review and Prospect from the Gulf War to the Iraq War," 解放军报 (*PLA Daily*), October 28, 2003, CPP20031030000061.

55. General Lin Abe.

56. Anatol Lieven reinforces this latter point in "Hubris and Nemesis: Kosovo and the Pattern of Western Military Ascendancy and Defeat," Andrew J. Bacevich and Eliot A. Cohen, eds., *War Over Kosovo*. New York: Columbia University Press, 2001, p. 103.

57. France was the putative culprit, with information deliberately concealed from it by the other allies due to concern that it might be passed on to FRY contacts. See, e.g., Hugo Gordon,

"France Kept in Dark by Allies," *London Daily Telegraph*, April 9, 1999, p. 1.

58. For a detailed analysis, see Stephen T. Hosmer, *The Conflict Over Kosovo: Why Milosevic Decided to Settle When He Did*, Santa Monica, CA: RAND, 2001.

59. General Short, interviewed on Frontline, February 22, 2000, available from *www.pbs.org/wgbh/pages/frontline/shows/kosovo/interviews/short.html*.

60. See, e.g, Hu Chi-hsi, "Mao, Lin Biao, and the Fifth Encirclement Campaign," *China Quarterly*, No. 82, June 1980, pp. 350-280. Hu bases his conclusions on an examination of the Yan'an archive, obtained by Kuomintang forces when they captured the CCP capital,

61. The rumor at the time was that the bombing was in retaliation for anti-NATO espionage being carried out by Chinese intelligence personnel that had caused heavy losses to the U.S. Air Force, and that two of the three reporters killed in the attack doubled as intelligence agents, as in fact Xinhua personnel often did. Su Lan, "Chinese Embassy Bombing Incident—China-US Espionage War Comes to Light," *Kaifang* [*Open*], Hong Kong, No. 152, July 2, 1999, pp. 17-19, in FBIS FTS19990720000639.

62. Su Size (苏思泽), "Kosovo War and New Military Theory," June 1, 1999, p. 8, FTS19990701000148.

63. Xie Wenqing (謝文悝) and Liu Wanping (刘万平), "'Humanitarianisn in Name But Hegemony in Fact'—Commenting Upon NATO and Denouncing Power Politics," 解放军报 (*PLA Daily*), May 23, 1999, p. 4, FTS19990601001918.

64. Benjamin S. Lambeth, *NATO's Air War for Kosovo: A Strategic and Operational Assessment*. Santa Monica, CA: RAND, 2001, pp. 2001-201, citing an interview with an unnamed American officer involved in the operation.

65. *Ibid*.

66. *Lessons Learned From the Kosovo Conflict — The Effect of the Operation On Both Deployed and Non-Deployed Forces and On Future Modernization Plans*, hearing before the Military Procurement Subcommittee of the House Committee on Armed Services, October 19, 1999, available from *commdocs.house.gov/committees/security/has292020.000/has292020_0.HTM*; see also Lambeth.

67. BBC, London, August 11, 2010, citing Minnie Chan, "PLA Carries Out Night Drills Near Yellow Sea Based On Scenario of An Attack By the United States," *South China Morning Post*, August 11, 2010.

68. The F-117 was actually brought down not by a mobilized population, but by the 3rd Battalion of the FRY's 250th Air Defense Brigade. The colonel who commanded it attributed his success to the F-117's stealthy radar signature being momentarily disrupted by its bombing doors being open.

69. It should be noted that the PLAAF's January 2011 test flight of the J-20 indicates that the denigration of the invincibility of the stealthy F-117s did not deter the PLA from developing its own stealthy plane.

CHAPTER 3

SINICA RULES THE WAVES?
THE PEOPLE'S LIBERATION ARMY NAVY'S
POWER PROJECTION
AND ANTI-ACCESS/AREA DENIAL LESSONS
FROM THE FALKLANDS/MALVINAS CONFLICT

Christopher D. Yung

EXECUTIVE SUMMARY

This chapter examines the lessons the Chinese military has drawn from the Falklands/Malvinas conflict of 1982 and applied (doctrinally, operationally, and in terms of procurement) to the expected contingencies of Taiwan and an "Out of Area" maritime campaign.

MAIN ARGUMENT

Chinese analysts highlight the following conclusions, which serve as guidance for the operations practiced and executed, doctrine being developed, and weapon systems and platforms procured. These conclusions are: "Know your enemy, know yourself"; the importance of tactical estimates and correct deployment/employment of forces; the importance of tactical and war-fighting guidelines (doctrine); the importance of effective systems of command and control; the importance of national mobilization and defense economy; "Take your protection with you"; the importance of bases and access to facilities; the paramount importance of air power; the important role of merchant shipping; the role of amphibious forces; and logistics as force multiplier or "Achilles Heel."

POLICY IMPLICATIONS

- Owing to their applicability to China's defense of the "Near Seas," the Chinese military are likely to continue procuring or developing into a mature capability diesel-electric submarines, modern surface combatants, land-based and sea-based maritime strike aircraft, anti-ship cruise missiles, anti-ship ballistic missiles, and maritime surveillance capabilities to track and target ships at sea.

- Owing to their applicability to China's "Out of Area" maritime campaigns, the Chinese military are likely to continue procuring or developing L-class amphibious ships, aircraft carrier capabilities, nuclear attack submarines, aerial refueling capabilities, and replenishment ships.

- Operationally, the People's Liberation Army (PLA) will continue participating in exercises that stress combined arms ground-sea-air operations; amphibious operations; coordination among surface combatants, air forces, and sub-surface forces; command and control of forces afloat, in the air, and ashore; and a combination of general purpose forces with ballistic missiles and other Second Artillery forces.

- The PLA will seek to gain access (temporarily or periodically) to a naval support facility far from China's shores, will continue to practice its operations far from Mainland China in conjunction with foreign partners, and will continue to operate "Out of Area" in the Gulf of Aden, the Indian Ocean, and in other foreign locations.

INTRODUCTION

Commentaries on China's PLA cite Operations DESERT SHIELD/DESERT STORM and the Kosovo Conflict as military conflicts to which the Chinese have paid particularly close attention. These commentaries correctly argue that these two conflicts played central roles in convincing the PLA that it needed to conduct an extensive modernization program and a thorough reevaluation of Chinese military doctrine.[1] While there is no question that Operations DESERT SHIELD/DESERT STORM and Kosovo played an important part in shaping Chinese perspectives on defense transformation, an often overlooked military conflict that had a profound impact on Chinese military thinking is the 1982 Falklands/Malvinas War between Great Britain and Argentina.

With the exception of the excellent article[2] written by Lyle Goldstein of the China Maritime Studies Institute (CMSI) of the Naval War College, the author can think of no other piece written by a non-Chinese author dedicated to the major lessons that the Chinese took away from that conflict. There are many reasons why this may have been the case. First, because Operation DESERT STORM and the Kosovo campaign loom large in Chinese writings and commentaries of western military campaigns, they have drowned out the fewer, but no less important, Chinese writings commenting on the Falklands/Malvinas. Second, because Operation DESERT STORM and Kosovo were conflicts involving the United States — the most advanced military in the world — western analysts and observers discussing those conflicts' major lessons on modern warfare may have themselves overlooked the importance of the Falklands/Malvinas campaign and what it offers to a modern military audience by way of lessons. Third, the Chinese have been very focused on the transformation of the PLA from a relatively backward, manpower intensive military to a joint, information-centered, mechanized, combined arms force. The Chinese have themselves claimed that the best recent examples of western campaigns to provide lessons on these larger transformational issues are the Desert Storm and Kosovo campaigns—not the Falklands/Malvinas campaign.

With the above commentary in mind, then, what does a chapter on China's lessons from the Falklands/Malvinas conflict add to our understanding of China's future military capabilities and China's concept of operations? As Lyle Goldstein pointed out, there is quite an obvious analogy between the situation the Argentineans found themselves in in 1982 and the possibility that the Chinese may be in a similar military situation sometime in the future; that is, the Argentineans had the task of preventing an outside power from interfering in a territorial dispute close to Argentina's shores.[3] This is not unlike a China-Taiwan-U.S. scenario. The lessons that the Chinese can take from the Falklands/Malvinas are directly applicable, then, to the Anti-Access/Area Denial (A2/AD) strategy that the Chinese are said to be preparing for in case of a Taiwan contingency.[4] But is it also true that the Chinese can learn from the British experience of that war? Are there naval, power projection, and expeditionary issues the Chinese are learning from when they examine that conflict? Since the PLA appears to be focused on two broad contingencies—a Taiwan scenario and an out of area contingency—it behooves us to examine closely the one case history that seems to offer lessons for both contingencies. What naval power projection and expeditionary lessons as well as anti-access/area denial lessons have the Chinese learned from the Falklands/Malvinas conflict? And what does this tell us about future Chinese naval and maritime capabilities and concepts of operations?

WHY THE CHINESE STUDY THE FALKLANDS/MALVINAS WAR

Thus far, the Falklands/Malvinas campaign represents the last major naval or maritime campaign of any tactical or operational significance. No conflict since then has involved so many elements of naval operations in a major theater of war—amphibious ships, submarines, surface combatants, naval aviation, and, of course, aircraft carriers. It is thus no wonder that the Chinese have spent some time paying attention to its lessons. In 2000 Vice Admiral Ding Yiping, the former PLA Navy (PLAN) Chief of Staff, wrote that "for the future of military theory, development of military units and of military equipment, [the Falklands/Malvinas] war produced a deep influence."[5] Lyle Goldstein points out that the Nanjing Naval Command College had dispatched research teams to "study naval forces, naval strategy, sea defence, and blockade operations in the Falklands/Malvinas War with the goal of understanding future naval warfare."[6]

The Falklands/Malvinas campaign also involves a conflict centered around sovereignty or territorial disputes—something that the Chinese are themselves heavily involved in. Therefore, Chinese commentators have periodically revisited the Falklands/Malvinas conflict not just to derive the military, tactical, and operational lessons that it offers, but also to obtain pearls of wisdom on the political and legal ramifications of the conflict.[7]

Finally, it should be recalled that the Falklands conflict preceded Operations DESERT SHIELD/DESERT STORM by 7-8 years, respectively, and it preceded the Kosovo conflict by 16 years. Before these two major conflicts were available for the PLA to derive lessons from, the most relevant instance of modern war that the Chinese could learn from prior to the 1990s was the Falklands/Malvinas campaign.

A BRIEF SUMMARY OF THE FALKLANDS/ MALVINAS CONFLICT

Before discussing at length what the Chinese took away from the Falklands/Malvinas conflict, it is important to briefly discuss what transpired in that conflict. This is not the place to present the legal and historical arguments that the British and the Argentineans have offered to support their claims to the Falklands/Malvinas. Suffice it to say that both the British and Argentina claims cite initial discovery, administration of the islands, colonization, uncontested sovereignty for significant periods of time, and the self-determination of the islands' inhabitants. As we now know, this unresolved dispute continued into the late 20th century when, after talks on the future of the Falklands between Argentina and Great Britain broke down, Argentina took the Falklands by force, prompting the formation of a British expeditionary task force, which sailed over 8,000 nautical miles to the south Atlantic, launched bombing raids against the defenses on the Falklands from the British base on Ascension Island, and used one of its nuclear attack submarines to sink one of the Argentinean navy's cruisers (the *Belgrano*). The British suffered serious losses from air attacks from the Argentinean air force, but finally in

May and June 1982 they conducted an amphibious assault against the Argentinean defenses on the Falklands and eventually compelled the surrender of Argentinean forces on the Falklands on June 14 and from the Argentinean forces on the South Sandwich Islands on June 20.

WHAT HAVE THE CHINESE WRITTEN ABOUT THE FALKLANDS/MALVINAS CONFLICT?

"Know Your Enemy, Know Yourself."

Although it has become a clichéd phrase lifted from the ancient writings of Sunzi, Chinese military thinkers actually take seriously the idea that in a conflict the central task of the military and the national security decisionmakers is to get the strategic policy absolutely right—that means having a very solid understanding of what the enemy is likely to do, his strengths and weaknesses, and understanding your own strengths and weaknesses. This has applications to Chinese strategy regarding actions meant to deny access to the United States during a Taiwan contingency. In 2007 the Chinese press (*Xinhua*) published an article on the Falklands/Malvinas conflict.[8] In it, the author—military historian Zhou Ming—argued that one of the reasons the British won that war and the Argentineans lost it was because British strategic policy was sound while Argentinean strategic policy was not. Although "the Argentinean side initially seized the initiative . . . they erroneously judged that England was not able to launch an expedition, and at the same time also overestimated their own nationalistic feelings and military capabilities."[9] The analysis continues that "this policy was built on the foundation of wishful thinking."[10] England, by contrast, though initially [had to] hastily retaliate, its strategic policy was accurately, objectively, and in clear headed fashion, able to estimate the situation, adopting resolute and vigorous guiding principles, giving priority to the military struggle, while simultaneously taking control of politics, foreign relations, and economics, and amply mobilizing international and internal factors.[11]

A Chinese assessment made 6 years earlier issued the very same arguments.[12]

The Importance of Tactical Estimates and Correct Deployment/Employment of Forces.

In the first article noted above, Zhou Ming wrote of the importance of tactical estimates (i.e., intelligence, surveillance, and reconnaissance), and of deploying the right forces for the right missions and tasks. The article states,

The Argentinean military, in considering the international situation, the (likely) British plans, and other strategic considerations made errors in judgment. After England dispatched its forces, they [the Argentinean military] thought England would attack Argentina's native territory (the mainland), and took a large quantity of troops and used them to defend the mainland; with regard to its border dispute with Chile, they [exercised] a deeply suspicious vigilance, and to its border dispatched a large quantity of armored units; in the Malvinas war zone . . . they failed to make ample use of that territory, barely deploying as occupation troops 3% of the total armed forces.[13]

Even when it came to deploying forces to the war zone, the Argentineans exercised poor judgment.

"[I]n East Malvinas they took the main force and concentrated them near ports and harbors, and in their defensive zones dispersed their defensive forces, and did not have ample enough motorized units in reserve, thereby giving the English military opportunities that could be exploited."[14]

The Importance of Tactical and Warfighting Guidelines (Doctrine).

The Chinese have observed that Argentina's defeat in the Falklands/Malvinas conflict can, in addition to the factors noted above, be explained by its military following poor tactical guidelines. "[T]he Argentinean military philosophy was passive, its tactics inflexible, and furthermore lacked real effective aircraft to attack the British defensive capabilities and, still further, to attack Britain's most important, yet most vulnerable supply shipping; this was Argentina's greatest mistake."[15] This failure to observe Great Britain's glaring weakness in the length of its logistical supply line is a particularly egregious fault of the Argentinean military. "From the perspective of the history of warfare, to not attack a very long and yet very vulnerable supply line, is extremely short-sighted."[16] England, on the other hand, had a correct tactical philosophy. Its "tactics were more agile, and its forces were good at snatching key links [objectives], and seizing the initiative."[17] By seizing the southern Malvinas, the British were able to rather quickly inspire the imaginations of the common British citizen, while at the same time establishing a foothold and an advanced base in the operating area. They gave their nuclear attack submarines the freedom to take the initiative and attack the Argentinean navy aggressively. The resulting sinking of the *Belgrano* by the nuclear attack submarine HMS *Conqueror* forced the fragile Argentinean navy into staying out of the war.[18]

The Importance of Effective Systems of Command and Control.

Argentina's joint command during the Falklands/Malvinas conflict, Chinese writings have observed, "was famously ineffective and unable to bear the burden of making strategy and policy and coordinating the action of the upper level echelons, including the president . . . with the [military] high command."[19] Lacking any real combat experience, the upper echelons of the Argentinean decisionmaking system did not accomplish anything significant in this conflict. The command and control system of the war zone was difficult for all involved to understand.[20] As a result, another Chinese assessment concludes, "[v]arious Argentine command elements were unaware of one another's orders and bungled the use of intelligence."[21]

The Importance of National Mobilization and Defense Economy.

Beyond what the two countries did on the battlefield and within the highest levels of national security decisionmaking, the Chinese have commented that Argentina was not particularly well-placed either economically or in terms of population morale for the conflict. "Although Argentina had determination to seize the Malvinas," Chinese authors have written, "there was not a long period of morale preparation and materiel [build up] preparation."[22] The Argentinean soldiers dispatched to the Malvinas were insufficient and their eventual situation (i.e., number of forces) did not improve. Added to this, Argentina itself,

> lacked the defense industry, and during peacetime with regard to the most important strategic goods and materials [it] failed to put these items in reserve. After the United States and the European Union launched an arms embargo, then usable aircraft, missiles and other wartime consumables were not able to be replenished.[23]

Take Your Protection with You.

In "The Union Jack Rises Again," one of a number of essays on foreign wars published in a book compiling the military history of foreign wars (1993), the authors Wang Shuangmei and Duan Guangda wrote that one of the most notable observations from the Falklands/Malvinas conflict was the military capability that the British were able to bring with them across long distances to settle the territorial dispute.[24] In particular, this essay, as well as other Chinese commentary on the war, focuses on the British ability to create a protective bubble by integrated sea and air forces formed around the military task force.[25] Chinese analysts note that there are a number of methods an expeditionary force may pursue to create a "blockade" of sorts. First, a submarine may keep outside forces at bay either through the indirect threat it poses to surface combatants or by stealthily attacking intruders; second, by maintaining a constant air and sea patrol around the task force; and finally, by direct confrontation by surface combatants to challenge or dissuade intruders from penetrating a protected area.[26] Chinese authors point out that the British ability to take its protection along also meant that the attacker's power was able to isolate the operating area from the interference of Argentina's armed forces from mainland South America. That is, the area around the Falklands/Malvinas could be isolated by a sea and air blockade and then it could be attacked and retaken. By contrast, the Argentineans failed to effectively use air power, submarines, surface combatants, and high-tech precision weaponry (e.g., anti-ship cruise missiles [ASC-Ms]) to keep the British task force out of the operating area. In addition, the British ability to export airpower through the Royal Navy's aircraft carriers was cited as one of the central elements of the British success in the Falklands/Malvinas dispute.[27] Similarly, the authors in "The Union Jack Rises Again" note that it was also important that the British brought long-range nuclear submarines, which were able to wreak havoc with the Argentinean naval surface forces—sinking the *Belgrano* and essentially forcing the Argentinean Navy to sit out the war.[28]

The Importance of Bases and Access to Facilities.

Chinese writings cite the importance of access to facilities and bases for British success in the Falklands/Malvinas conflict. In a recent essay on the Falklands/Malvinas conflict, one Chinese author noted that the Royal Air Force (RAF) was able to launch air strikes from Ascension Island against the defenses entrenched on the Falklands/Malvinas.[29] Those strikes would not have been possible if the British had not had access to that territory. Chinese authors have also correctly noted that bases and facilities are necessary for military forces to put themselves in order before being dispatched on expeditions and offensive operations.[30] This is akin to the U.S. Navy amphibious doctrine concept of Preparation, Embarkation, Rehearsal, Movement, Assault (PERMA). Owing to the fact that the task force had deployed in a hurry, some of the surface combatants and amphibious ships had been incorrectly loaded.[31] The task force was forced into re-loading equipment and supplies on Ascension Island. The "Preparation" aspect of the operation would not have been possible without access to the advance base on Ascension.

The importance of access to a base of operations is not restricted to an established, fully constructed facility. Chinese authors point out that the simple access to a firm and stable piece of territory or land from which to conduct operations is essential to military operations.[32] For the Falklands/Malvinas campaign, one Chinese author writes that the essential factor that enabled the British to attack Argentinean forces from a base of operations was brought about by successfully landing British ground forces on the Falklands/Malvinas themselves, and the establishment of a beachhead is the crux of the matter.[33]

The Paramount Importance of Air Power.

Chinese observers of the Falklands/Malvinas correctly point out that the correct application of air power was an extremely important factor explaining the success of the British expedition. One recent Chinese essay on the relevance of air power to this conflict pointed out that the tasks for which aircraft were used in this conflict were: to cooperate with the special task force fleet in conducting its operations; to conduct air combat to include air-to-air combat and strikes against land and sea targets; to conduct reconnaissance and gather intelligence on the disposition of the enemy's forces; to conduct air defense and "counterstealth" operations; and finally, to serve as a lead, guide, or navigation asset for the attack forces.[34]

Chinese observers note that British air power helped create a protective blockade around the British task force. These authors also note that it was Argentinean aircraft that alone were able to penetrate the blockade, attack British forces, and ultimately to sink the HMS *Sheffield* and other Royal Navy ships. Inadequate construction of airfields, Chinese authors point out, obstructed Argentina's air campaign against the British.[35] RAF access to Ascension Island, the creation of an air bridge from England to Ascension Island, and carrier aviation permitted British aircraft to feed the British logistics system, thereby permitting the British war effort in the Falklands/Malvinas.[36] Royal Navy landing ships and landing craft, Chinese authors note, sailed to the Falklands/Malvinas under the protective cover of British aircraft provided by the two carrier battle groups of the task force.[37]

The Important Role of Merchant Shipping.

Chinese commentators on the Falklands/Malvinas conflict point out the important role merchant or civilian shipping played. The Royal Navy lacked the sufficient number of ships to transport a steady stream of supplies to the theater of conflict. Chinese military historians note that the British brought 60 civilian merchant vessels to the Falklands/Malvinas conflict.[38] The Chinese essay speculates that reliance on merchant vessels, and by extension civilian crews, to conduct naval operations was what caused, in part, the British to have to expend close to 10 million pounds sterling per day over the course of the operation.[39] The heavy reliance on merchant shipping can also prove to be a risky course of action. When the merchant vessel (MV) *Atlantic Conveyor* was sunk by Argentinean aircraft, the Royal Navy lost valuable military assets necessary for the conduct of the landings on the Falklands/Malvinas.

The Role of Amphibious Forces.

Chinese observers of the Falklands/Malvinas conflict also took note of the importance of amphibious operations for the British success in that campaign. Chinese commentaries take note of the fact that the Argentineans completely underestimated Great Britain's ability to mobilize an expeditionary force, embark that force on amphibious ships, sail thousands of miles as part of a joint expeditionary force, and then land those forces for offensive operations against the Argentinean defenders.[40] Another military historian puts it this way, "the crucial or key element allowing [the British] to obtain a correct military campaign was its ability to conduct a successful amphibious campaign."[41] This campaign allowed the British to attack Argentinean military power and neutralize it, then at the point where the British landed on the Falklands/Malvinas to build or establish a solid base of operations, and thereafter to conduct offensive combat operations.[42] Amphibious operations also put the British in a position to assume a dominant position over the Argentinean defenders.[43]

Logistics as Force Multiplier or "Achilles Heel."

Chinese articles on the Falklands/Malvinas make much of the centrality of logistics to modern warfare. One article notes that the Argentineans did not have even one adequately sized airport or airfield to which additional forces or equipment could be flowed.[44] Consequently, on the Falklands/Malvinas islands themselves the Argentinean military lacked the necessary supplies to provide a sustained defense. By contrast, the article noted the British logistical system provided British forces with the supplies that they needed to wage their war. Although the logistical line was long and would have been vulnerable to a cunning and ruthless enemy had Argentina been more prepared, the British were able to piece together a logistical system that supported their operations for the duration.[45]

The flip side of this observation, Chinese authors note, is that the Argentineans should have focused on the British logistical system as its "Achilles Heel." Since British forces and equipment had to travel such long distances to get to the theater of operations, some attention should have been paid by the Argentinean military on how to attack that system.[46] The British logistical system would have been a "soft underbelly" against which Argentina could have made surgical cuts to disrupt the British war effort. Instead, Chinese articles note, the Argentineans seemed oblivious to this factor as anything important and having the potential to affect the outcome of the war.[47]

APPLYING THE LESSONS OF THE FALKLANDS/ MALVINAS CONFLICT

From the above account, it is clear that Chinese observers have paid attention to the Falklands/Malvinas conflict and have drawn specific lessons from it. Does it follow that China's military leadership has taken those lessons and applied them to the improvement and development of the PLA? In other words, do we see evidence of these lessons in doctrine, procurement or acquisitions, and in operations?

Doctrine.

As some observers of the PLA have noted, there is no equivalent to the English word "doctrine" in Chinese.[48] The PLA refers to practices, guidance, and theory. Within authoritative PLA documents attesting to the future practices, guidance, and theory of warfighting, then, do these reflect some of the lessons of the Falklands/Malvinas conflict? In a word, "Yes." Although it will be apparent later in this chapter that specific weapon systems and platforms and missions exercised or practiced will be more applicable to either a Taiwan contingency or an out of area power projection operation, by and large, the doctrinal lessons taken from the Falklands/Malvinas campaign generally apply equally to both. The first of these common lessons is the PLA guidance on the role of logistics both in support of PLA power projection operations and in support of the PLA's efforts to defend its territory in the "near seas." Jianxiang Bi has written that in authoritative PLA guidance:

> According to PLA assumptions, the most critical center of gravity is a support system located in an opponent's forward deployed and rear bases, which could not be defended against every attack in every place and at every conceivable time. Today, the military heavily depends on its logistics support system, so that the system itself becomes bloated, extremely visible and vulnerable.[49]

As we have noted above, one of the key lessons that Chinese observers have taken away from the Falklands/Malvinas conflict is that the Argentineans failed to recognize the vulnerability of the British logistics system and hence, passed up the opportunity to attack that vulnerability. In similar fashion, the Chinese have also recognized, partially as a result of the lessons derived from the Falklands/Malvinas campaign, that logistics is a "force multiplier" for one's own operational efforts. Here is what China's *Defense White Paper* of 2008 had to say on the issue of maritime logistics:

> Aiming at enhancing its integrated logistical support capabilities, the Navy has preliminarily built a logistical support system with shore-based logistical support as the foundation and sea-based logistical support as the mainstay, and meshes the two into an integrated whole. It has stepped up the building of ship bases, berthing areas, supply points, docks and airfields. As a result, a shore-based support system is basically in place, which is coordinated with the development of weaponry and equipment, and suited to war-time support tasks. The Navy has gradually deployed new types of large integrated supply ships, medical ships and ambulance helicopters, and succeeded in developing many types of maritime support equipment and a number of key technologies, leading to significant progress in the modernization of the maritime support force.[50]

The second area in which the Falklands/Malvinas conflict may have had a significant impact on PLA warfighting doctrine both for power projection and for A2/AD is in the employment of air power. Bi Jianxiang again writes:

> China's military leaders now call for substantial offensive air capabilities, with emphasis on developing joint hard-target kill weapons, warning and tracking system, and real-time (near real-time) C2. While [PLAAF] foreign acquisition programs aimed at achieving regional reach and a flexibility of opera-

tions and responses remain a top priority of the Air Force, F-11/Su-27 fighters and indigenous helicopter production is increasing. Within a decade, the air units have already acquired a status of notable importance, allowing the PLA to entertain a far wider operational option spectrum than ever before.[51]

As this chapter has pointed out previously, Chinese observers of the Falklands/Malvinas conflict clearly took away the importance of air power to the eventual outcome of that war. Argentina's failure to take full advantage of its airpower hampered its A2/AD efforts; Great Britain's ability to make use of aircraft carriers, access to Ascension Island, and aerial refueling, helped it project power far from its shores and snatch victory.

That the Chinese took to heart the important lesson from the Falklands/Malvinas campaign that an expeditionary force and an anti-access force has to operate in an integrated, self-protected manner is also illustrated in its 2008 *Defense White Paper*. The *Defense White Paper* clearly describes a naval force that is meant to create a protective bubble around a task force:

> Efforts are being made to build new types of submarines, destroyers, frigates and aircraft forming a preliminary weaponry and equipment system with second-generation equipment as the core and the third generation as the backbone. The submarine force possesses underwater anti-ship, anti-submarine and mine-laying capabilities, as well as some nuclear counter-attack capabilities. The surface ship force has developed a surface striking force represented by new types of missile destroyers and frigates, and possesses maritime reconnaissance, anti-ship, anti-submarine, air-defense, mine-laying, and other operational capabilities. The aviation wing has developed an air striking force represented by sea-attack aircraft, and pos-

sesses reconnaissance, anti-ship, anti-submarine, and air-defense capabilities.[52]

Another doctrinal lesson taken from the Falklands/Malvinas and that applies both to a Taiwan contingency and an out of area military campaign is the importance of establishing a firm strategic policy. Mark Stokes, in his observations of how China would undertake an air war, observes that:

> [p]reparations for a campaign begin with issuance of strategic direction in the form of a strategic policy development process called the *juece* . . . the *juece* first establishes a general game plan . . . for military action that explores all possible outcomes, develops stratagems . . . and analyzes centers of gravity.[53]

Given the criticism the Chinese have leveled at the Argentinean failure to establish a sound strategic policy, this process clearly was in part derived from the lessons of the Falklands/Malvinas conflict.

Additionally, current doctrine or guidance defining how the PLA should exercise command control, and which is applicable to both an A2/AD contingency and an out of area power projection operation, can also be argued to have been derived from the lessons of the Falklands/Malvinas. Stokes again points out what authoritative sources claim to be the proper organization of joint command and control headquarters. This organization is meant to make sure that all of the relevant warfighting and political decisionmaking bodies are involved, and that each layer of organization understands its decisionmaking role—a lesson clearly taken from the Falklands/Malvinas experience: "[T]his [Joint Force Headquarters] organization normally would consist of representatives from the Central Military

Commission, the four general departments, service headquarters, and the Chinese Communist Party. . . . [T]he primary mission of the command would be to plan and prepare for joint operations and exercise authority over each corps-level service branch . . . assigned to the Joint Theater Command."[54]

Finally, as far as doctrine goes, the PLAN's statements about what it expects future naval campaigns will look like seems to be a direct reflection of what they observed in the Falklands/Malvinas conflict. In China's *2008 Defense White Paper*, the PLAN expects intense conflict over control of the sea.[55] This means that the PLAN must strive for control of surface, subsurface, and air. The difficulty the Argentineans faced in integrating the different parts of the military to fight a comprehensive campaign suggests a Falklands/Malvinas influence upon Chinese doctrinal thinkers when in this same document, the PLAN argues that the naval campaign both in projecting power and in denying access to an invading force must involve the integration of sea, air space, and land operations. The PLAN's emphasis on the importance of high-tech, long-range, precision weapons may also be traced to the Falklands/Malvinas campaign if also reinforced by PLA observations of Operation DESERT STORM and the Kosovo Campaign. Despite all of the shortcomings of the Argentinean military, the Argentinean Air Force's successful use of the Exocet missile to sink the *Sheffield* is an immediate example of the power and effectiveness of high-tech, long-range, precision weaponry on the battlefield.

Procurement.

Additional evidence that the PLA is applying lessons learned from the Falklands/Malvinas conflict is found in the procurement record of the PLA. The most striking bit of evidence is that the PLA has consistently been procuring platforms, weapons systems, and capabilities that are applicable in an A2/AD context and that are directly related to the lessons of the Falklands/Malvinas. For example, according to Ronald O'Rourke,

> China reportedly is developing or deploying maritime surveillance and targeting systems that can detect U.S. ships and submarines and provide targeting information for Chinese ASBMs and other Chinese military units. These systems reportedly include land-based over-the horizon back scatter (OTH-B) radars, land-based over-the-horizon surface wave (OTH-SW) radars, electro-optical satellites, radar satellites, and sea-bed sonar networks.[56]

Additionally, the lessons taken from the Falklands/Malvinas on the importance of land-based aircraft applied to a maritime scenario seem to have had some (reinforcing) effect on Chinese acquisition priorities. O'Rourke points out that "ONI [Office of Naval Intelligence] projects that the numbers of land-based maritime strike aircraft, carrier-based fighters, and helicopters will almost triple between 2009 and 2020."[57] The Department of Defense (DoD) report to Congress on Chinese military power noted the Chinese interest in developing Anti-Ship Ballistic Missles (ASBMs) and ASCMs, and Admiral Robert Willard, the U.S. Pacific Command (PACOM) commander, stated that he believed the Chinese ASBM capability had reached

Initial Operating Capability (IOC).[58] The procurement of such hi-tech, long-range precision weaponry conforms to the value the Chinese originally saw in such hi-tech anti-ship weaponry as the Exocet missile during the Falklands/Malvinas conflict.

Both the Falklands/Malvinas and an A2/AD strategy suggest that there is great utility in an effective submarine force—especially a diesel submarine force. O'Rourke notes that:

> currently the submarine force consists of six nuclear [-powered] attack submarines [SSNs], three nuclear [-powered] ballistic missile submarines [SSBNs], and 53 diesel [-electric] attack submarines [SSs]. Over the next 10 to 15 years, primarily due to the introduction of new diesel-electric and [non-nuclear powered] air independent power (AIP) submarines, the force is expected to increase incrementally in size to approximately 75 submarines.[59]

Finally, both the lessons of the Falklands/Malvinas conflict and an A2/AD strategy call for the development of a robust surface combatant force. Again O'Rourke's analysis is pertinent here.

> China since the early 1990s has deployed five new classes of indigenously built destroyers, one of which is a variation of another. Compared to China's 14 remaining older *Luda* (Type 051) class destroyers which entered service between 1971 and 1991, these five new indigenously built destroyer classes are substantially more modern in terms of their hull design, propulsion systems, sensors, weapons and electronics. . . . Like the older *Luda*-class destroyers, these new destroyer classes are armed with ASCMs.[60]

An examination of the PLAN's order of battle also suggests that the PLA is thinking beyond the Taiwan contingency. Some of the procurement items that have recently stood out are the acquisition and the planned acquisition of L-class ships (e.g., the landing ship dock [LSD], amphibious transport dock [LPD], and landing helicopter dock [LHD]).[61] While it is tempting to believe that procurement of these amphibious assets is a reflection of the steady development of a Taiwan-contingency capability, the L-class ship is more suited for longer-range expeditionary operations. The procurement of scores of landing craft and Landing Ship Tanks (LSTs) makes more operational sense for Taiwan than the procurement of a large deck ship that can carry troops, aircraft, and vehicles hundreds of miles before off-loading them. It should also be noted that the most recent PLAN deployment to the Gulf of Aden for counterpiracy escort operations included for the first time the Kunlunshan—the PLAN's current LPD.[62]

L-class ships make sense more for a South China Sea or East China Sea dispute than they do for a Taiwan contingency because they are capable of transporting aircraft on their decks—much as aircraft carriers do.[63] Air power projected from China during a Taiwan contingency need not come from the flight decks of ships, but from PLA Air Force (PLAAF) bases on the mainland.[64] In fact, air cover and air strike operations in a Taiwan context make much more sense coming from mainland bases than from the flight decks of ships. That is because during war at sea those flight decks are much more vulnerable to air attack themselves and, of course, the ships that they are on are vulnerable to a whole host of threats from submarines, surface combatants, and mines. Therefore, if a military force can help it, it will usually prefer to operate under the cover of air coming from land bases. Of course, as naval history attests, countries operating far from their shores do not have that luxury and must rely on the flight decks of aircraft carriers and other aircraft carrying ships to provide protection for their expeditionary task force. Flight decks on L-class ships are much smaller than those found on aircraft carriers and accommodate fewer aircraft; nonetheless, they can still be used to provide air cover and defense of the task force for a limited conflict in the South or East China Sea[65] — a lesson the Chinese took away from the Falklands/Malvinas. Additionally, L-class ships do not have the associated potential political backlash that aircraft carriers do in the region.

Despite the potential backlash, recent Chinese commentaries and statements from high ranking PLA officials suggest that China will soon acquire an aircraft carrier and attempt to make it operational.[66] The push for a carrier, an associated air wing, and the ships to protect the carrier, is clearly descended from the lessons the PLA has taken from other navies and their campaigns — including the British experience during the Falklands/Malvinas conflict. China and just about every other navy in existence acknowledge that to operate far from coastal waters requires that the Navy in question "bring its protection with them." At one level, that means bringing an L-class ship with aircraft deployed on it; but it also likely means bringing an aircraft carrier with all of the air and fire power that that entails.

Bringing protection with you also implies a long-range submarine capability — particularly that found in nuclear attack submarines. The Chinese have a large number of diesel submarines;[67] however, one could argue that these would be used almost exclusively for a Taiwan contingency. Since they are extremely quiet and stealthy but do not have an especially long range, diesel subs are exceptionally suited for placement in choke points and other strategic locations, where they can lie in wait for approaching naval task forces—a situation very applicable to a Taiwan contingency.[68] The nuclear attack submarines are much more useful at greater distances from China's shores. The continued utility of long-range attack submarines with greater endurance explains why the Chinese continued to put money into a *Han* class replacement, even though diesel submarines—designed to lie in waiting in shallow water—are much more relevant to an A2/AD military strategy. The possible development, then, of the Type 095 class nuclear attack submarine speaks to the fact that the Chinese may be serious about developing a sustained long-distance attack submarine capability.[69] Such a capability would play a role similar to the Royal Navy's use of its submarines to attack the surface combatant force of the enemy during the Falklands/Malvinas dispute.

China's continuing interest in procuring air-to-air refueling assets (e.g., the reported purchase of IL-78 *Midas* tankers on order from Russia)[70] may also be a reflection of the lessons the British learned from the Falklands/Malvinas conflict. The British found that they lacked sufficient aircraft to sustain air cover for the Royal Navy task force. Even with the presence of an aircraft carrier and with air-to-air refueling allowing an air bridge to be formed between Ascension Island and the Falklands/Malvinas, the British still lacked sufficient air power. Similarly, the Chinese recognize that they may lack the air power from L-class ships and the one or two carriers that they develop down the road. At present, the PLAAF has in its inventory 10 H-6U tankers and the PLAN Air Force (PLANAF) has in its inventory four such aircraft.[71] Supplemental airpower could be derived from an aerial refueling capability that would extend the legs of PLAAF aircraft operating far from bases on the Mainland or off Hainan Island. The development of this capability is, as these numbers attest, slow. This suggests that for the present the Taiwan contingency remains a higher priority than out of area power projection, but that could change as the Taiwan contingency becomes remote.

While on the subject of the importance of air power, China's continual development of its jet aircraft program is in part a legacy of the lessons taken from the Falklands/Malvinas. No modern military or navy can be effective without modern aircraft. Thus, the PLAAF and the PLANAF remain embarked on a program of acquisition and development of the J-10, the Su-27, and Su-30 to ensure that the PLA has the most up to date aircraft that it can afford to buy or build.[72]

The arrival of China's most modern logistics and supply ships can also be argued to be at least partially the result of the lessons from the Falklands/Malvinas. Since logistics was a force multiplier for the British and an "Achilles Heel" for the Argentineans, the Chinese clearly recognize the centrality of logistics to out of area operations. The procurement of the newest class of comprehensive supply ships over the past half decade is illustrative of this viewpoint.[73] Again, like the pace of aerial refueling assets, the PLAN's acquisition of underway replenishment ships has been slow. This again may be a reflection of the fact that the Taiwan contingency remains a higher priority than out of area power projection.

Operations.

The China-watching community has had decades to watch the PLA and the PLAN exercising the Taiwan contingency. It should therefore not be surprising that many experts on the PLA have amassed evidence that Chinese military training is geared toward its most important contingency—a Taiwan scenario. But is it also the case that that training is based in some part on the lessons of the Falklands/Malvinas conflict? David Shambaugh noted that in 1995 and 1996 the "so-called East Sea (Donghai) exercises increased dramatically in scale, involving live-firing from ships, tanks, and bombers. Even more notably, in both years, the PLA's Second Artillery introduced a new element into the mix: short range ballistic missiles."[74] These exercises, which began in 1994, also involved "mock amphibious landings and combined air-ground-naval operations."[75]

Shambaugh also noted the combination of surface combatants and tactical aircraft with submarine and anti-submarine exercises beginning after 1998, which represented another "Falklands-like" evolution. Of particular note was the increasing length of both the diesel electric and nuclear powered submarines during these exercises.[76] The combination of surface combatants, amphibious operations, ground force operations, and the use of high-tech precision weaponry (e.g., ballistic missiles) are vintage lessons from the Falklands/Malvinas conflict.

Similarly, Captain (U.S. Navy, Ret.) Bernard Cole observed that in 1999 the PLAN's "naval-aeronautical-antisubmarine" exercise endeavored to practice "Command and control of forces ashore, in the air, and at sea" and "was exercised by the Fleets' Naval Air Force Command Center."[77] In June 2000, Cole noted, the East Sea exercises emphasized "securing beach heads, executing rapid maneuver along front lines, rapid establishment of air defenses, and securing logistics in conjunction with the use of antiaircraft artillery and landing vessels. Exercise goals included making an amphibious assault, ensuring logistics support, and moving inland, all in the face of enemy air superiority."[78]

Although China has not recently engaged in naval combat, its current operations out of area might reflect the lessons of the out of area operations of other navies — the Falklands/Malvinas conflict being one of them. The importance of civilian merchant shipping in support of out of area operations — a lesson directly passed down from the Falklands/Malvinas War — has been largely accepted by the PLAN. The Gulf of Aden deployment, the 2002 global circumnavigation by a PLAN task force, and port visits and exercises with the navies of Southeast Asia and South Asia all relied on a comprehensive supply ship that conducted underway replenishments, provided food stuffs and other consumables to the task force crews, and performed routine medical exams.[79]

The temporary support and access arrangements that the Chinese government has made with the governments of the countries with ports in the Indian Ocean, the Gulf of Aden, and South China Sea reflect the PLAN's long experience with out of area operations since the early 1970s. However, the importance of access to naval facilities and bases was definitely reinforced by the British experience in the Falklands/Malvinas War. In the wake of the PLAN Gulf of Aden deployment, Rear Admiral Yin Zhuo's recent interviews and articles[80] calling for the establishment of some kind of base or facility that could support the out of area deployers focused his arguments on the kinds of logistical difficulties such a facility would overcome: access to medical care, access to repair and other maintenance facilities, a site to load equipment, and easing a long and tenuous supply line. Although the admiral did not cite the Falklands/Malvinas as a supporting example—clearly the Falklands/Malvinas case supports the idea that advance basing eases the burden and makes possible out of area operations.

The PLAN has also recently conducted "show of force" or demonstration exercises in the East China and South China Seas that are slight reflections of the Falklands/Malvinas campaign. *The South China Morning Post* reported[81] that destroyers, frigates, and auxiliary ships from the North Sea Fleet passed between Taiwan and the Philippines (the Bashi Strait) to conduct large scale exercises in the South China Sea. This was followed up by another naval task force from the East Sea Fleet comprised of a *Sovremenyy* guided missile destroyer, frigates, and submarines passing through Japan's Miyako Strait to conduct anti-submarine warfare (ASW) exercises in the Pacific, near to Japan. These task forces representing a capability that "brings its protection with it" through the presence of submarines and guided missile surface combatants as part of a single multi-vessel force are obviously lessons the PLAN learned a long time ago from the Falklands/Malvinas campaign about what its navy task forces should look like.

CONCLUSION: WHAT'S NEXT FOR THE PLAN?

Given that the PLAN has learned from the Falklands/Malvinas conflict and given that it has applied these lessons to what it has procured and how it operates today, what does this suggest for the future operations, activities, and trajectories for the PLAN? As mentioned at the beginning of this chapter, there is a very strong analogy between the Falklands/Malvinas conflict and the anti-access/area denial operations the PLA is contemplating, should a Taiwan contingency arise. We should therefore expect the PLA to continue procuring weapon systems, platforms, and other capabilities that accord with the lessons of the 1982 conflict and fit in nicely with an A2/AD strategy. Therefore, the continued acquisition of modern diesel-electric submarines, ever improving surface combatants, an effective and operational ASBM and its attendant maritime surveillance capability to effectively survey and target ships at sea, as well as additional land-based maritime aircraft, can all be expected. The Falklands/Malvinas case, however, also provides lessons on how to project power over long distances to accomplish a nation's objectives. In the short-run, were China to apply its Falkland lessons to its power projection operations, it would first most likely negotiate for a more overt and consistent access to facilities far from Mainland China's shores. This would enable China to repair its ships at shipyards far from Chinese bases; it would allow its personnel access to medical care, and it would also permit its forces access to better communication support infrastructure. In short, it would go a long way towards helping China with its out of area logistical challenges.

Additionally, China will continue to procure replenishment or comprehensive supply ships. This will permit the PLAN to operate far from home waters and will ensure the PLAN's ability to operate far from home in the absence of a network of bases and facilities. To protect any task force operating far from home waters, the Chinese will continue to develop and build destroyers and other surface combatants until they have enough capacity to support missions deemed essential by the Chinese Communist Party (CCP), the Central Military Commission (CMC), and the PLA General Staff Department (GSD). The Chinese will continue to develop and procure air-to-air refueling assets in order to permit PLAAF and PLANAF aircraft to support Chinese naval forces operating further out from China's shores in such contingencies as a South China Sea or East China Sea dispute.

In the long-run, the PLAN will likely continue to develop and procure amphibious forces with a capability to operate out of area and far from China's shores (i.e., large deck amphibious ships). The purposes of such a force would not be meant to apply to a Taiwan contingency, but for a long-distance dispute in the South China or East China Seas. On the subject of the acquisition of new assets, the Chinese are likely to have developed or acquired (and made useful by the PLAN) an aircraft carrier purportedly for the purpose of meeting a mission in support of a sovereignty dispute with other countries in the region. Lastly, if the lessons of the Falklands/Malvinas campaign are any guide, China will continue to develop and directly procure long-range nuclear powered attack submarines that would act in support of out of area task forces.

China's future naval development, in terms of doctrine, procurement, and operations, can head in many directions as is true for any navy; fortunately, it would seem that the Chinese appear to have relied very heavily on a single case study as a model for its future navy — a single model that seems to apply both to a Taiwan contingency and an "Out of Area" power projection campaign. One of the unanswered questions regarding China's naval development is: despite the evidence that the PLA has learned from the Falklands/Malvinas case, why has it taken the PLAN so long to develop these capabilities? Despite the positive trends that this chapter has noted, the pace of some of these developments has been relatively slow. Of the five new classes of destroyers introduced by the PLAN, only one or two have been commissioned for each new class. In addition, the PLAN commissioned no new destroyers in 2008, 2009, and 2010. Despite the importance of underway replenishment ships and aerial refueling to Chinese power projection missions, the PLA and PLAN orders of battle for these platforms remain very modest. The reasoning behind this gradualist approach may lie in higher leadership decisions regarding tradeoffs, assignment of higher priorities to missions other than out of area power projection, and, yes, budget shortfalls. Despite the to-date glacial movement of the PLAN toward the development of a power projection capability, nonetheless, our observations of PLAN force structure development seem to suggest that the PLAN is applying the broader lessons of that 1982 naval conflict. It would be prudent here in the West to pay closer attention to the Falklands/Malvinas case.

ENDNOTES - CHAPTER 3

1. David Shambaugh, *Modernizing China's Military: Progress, Problems, and Prospects,* Berkeley, CA: University of California Press, 2002, pp. 1-6.

2. Lyle Goldstein, "China's Falklands Lessons," *Survival,* Vol. 50, No. 3, June-July 2008, pp. 65-82.

3. *Ibid.,* p. 66.

4. Anti-access and area denial are not Chinese terms. The Chinese tend to describe operations associated with Taiwan and operations related to the prevention of U.S. interference in Chinese internal affairs (e.g., Taiwan) in terms of "Near Seas" defense. The phrase "Anti-Access/Area Denial" — entirely a U.S. conception — was first introduced in the 2001 *Quadrennial Defense Review*. The terms are meant to characterize efforts to impede or prevent the U.S. military from intervening should China decide to attack Taiwan. The basic concept is to take operational steps to prevent approaching U.S. Navy carrier strike groups from getting within operating ranges of tactical aircraft. It has also been used broadly to mean preventing U.S. military forces from operating freely in the region without accepting high degrees of risk. For a fuller description and discussion of Anti-Access/Area Denial, see Jan Van Tol *et al.*, *Air Sea Battle: A point of Departure Operational Concept*, Washington, DC: Center for Budgetary and Strategic Assessment, May 2010, footnote 1, p. 1. See also Michael McDevitt, "The PLA Navy Anti-Access Role in a Taiwan Contingency" Paper written for the 2007 CAPS-RAND-CEIP-NDU Conference on PLA Affairs, November 2007.

5. *Ibid.*

6. *Ibid.*

7. "Isn't calling the islands 'Malvinas Islands' Violating International Law?" available from *webcache.googleusercontent.com/search?q=cache:QpOGjZ726NcJ:www.tianya.cn*. In interviews with at the PRC State Oceanic Administration and the China Society of Law of the Sea in September 2010, our interviewees noted that such cases as the Falklands/Malvinas conflict could possibly be relevant to China's sovereignty claims. The interviewees refused to speculate, however, on exactly how the two cases are similar.

8. Zhou Ming, "Argentina, England Malvinas Islands Conflict" (The Malvinas Problem), available from *news.xinhuanet.com/ziliao/2007-03/28/content_5906424_2.htm*.

9. *Ibid.*

10. *Ibid.*

11. *Ibid.*

12. Pan Pangui, "马岛战争的经验和启示" ("Experience and Insights from the Malvinas Wars"), 军事历史 (*Military History*), January 2001, p. 17.

13. Zhou Ming.

14. *Ibid.*

15. *Ibid.*

16. *Ibid.*

17. *Ibid.*

18. *Ibid.*

19. *Ibid.* For a similar assessment of Argentinean command and control, see also Fang Fang, "*Kuaisheng Nandaxiyang: Madao Zhizhanzhong Kongzhong Liliang Yunyong Fenxi*" ("Rapid Victory in the South Atlantic: An Analysis of Application of Airpower in the Malvinas War—Part 1 of 3"), *Guoji Zhanwang* (*World Outlook*), May 2006, p. 47.

20. Zhou Ming.

21. Fang Fang, p. 53, as seen in Goldstein, p. 68.

22. Zhou Ming.

23. *Ibid.*

24. Xie Jingfang and Duan Guangda, eds., "The Union Jack Rises Again," *International Famous Campaigns* (血溅奇谋: 中外著名战役实录), Harbin, China: Harbin Publishing House, 1993, pp. 1224.

25. *Ibid.* See also Wang Hongguang, ed., *Analyses of Classical Battles*, Beijing, China: Military Science Publishing House, 2009, p. 288.

26. "England-Argentina Malvinas Conflict: 1982, April 2 to June 14," Wang Hongguang, ed., *Analyses of Classical Battles*, p. 288.

27. Xie Jingfang and Duan Guangda, eds., "The Union Jack Rises Again," p. 1225.

28. *Ibid.*, pp. 1226-1227.

29. "England-Argentina Malvinas Conflict: 1982, April 2 to June 14," p. 288.

30. Xie Jingfang and Duan Guangda, eds., pp. 1225.

31. *Ibid.*

32. "England-Argentina Malvinas Conflict: 1982, April 2 to June 14," p. 297.

33. *Ibid.*

34. *Ibid.*

35. Zhou Ming.

36. *Ibid.*

37. Xie Jingfang and Duan Guangda, eds., p. 1230.

38. *Ibid.*, pp. 1224.

39. *Ibid.*

40. Zhou Ming.

41. "England-Argentina Malvinas Conflict: 1982, April 2 to June 14," p. 297.

42. *Ibid.*

43. *Ibid.*

44. Zhou Ming.

45. *Ibid.*

46. *Ibid.*

47. *Ibid.*

48. Shambaugh, p. 56. See also David Finkelstein, "China's National Military Strategy: An Overview of the 'Military Strategic Guidelines'," Roy Kamphausen and Andrew Scobell eds., *Right Sizing the People's Liberation Army: Exploring the Contours of China's Military*, Carlisle, PA: Strategic Studies Institute, U.S. Army War College, 2007, pp. 69-140.

49. Jianxiang Bi, "Joint Operations: Developing a New Paradigm," James Mulvenon and David Finkelstein, eds., *China's Revolution in Doctrinal Affairs: Emerging Trends in the Operational Art of the Chinese People's Liberation Army*, jointly published by Santa Monica, CA: RAND Corporation, and Alexandria, VA: Center for Naval Analyses, 2003, p. 64.

50. Full text: China's National Defense in 2008, available from *news.xinhuanet.com/english/2009-01/20/content_10688124_5.htm*.

51. Jianxiang Bi, "Joint Operations: Developing a New Paradigm," James Mulvenon and David Finkelstein, eds., *China's Revolution in Doctrinal Affairs: Emerging Trends in the Operational Art of the Chinese People's Liberation Army*, p. 66-67.

52. Full text: China's National Defense in 2008.

53. Mark A. Stokes, "The Chinese Joint Aerospace Campaign Strategy, Doctrine and Force Modernization," James Mulvenon and David Finkelstein, eds., p. 237.

54. *Ibid.*, pp. 239-240.

55. *Ibid.*

56. Ronald O'Rourke, "China's Naval Modernization: Implications for U.S. Navy Capabilities—Background and Issues for

Congress," Washington, DC: Congressional Research Service, February 2008, p. 22.

57. *Ibid.*, p. 23.

58. "Military and Security Developments Involving the People's Republic of China," Annual Report to Congress, Office of the Secretary of Defense, 2010, p. 30; Yoichi Kato, "U.S. Commander Says China Aims to Be "Global Military Power," *Asahi Shimbun*, December 28, 2010, available from *www.asahi.com/english/TKY201012270241.html*.

59. O'Rourke, p. 21.

60. *Ibid.*, pp. 17-18.

61. *Ibid.*, pp. 26-27.

62. See reporting from *Xinhua*, July 1, 2010.

63. O'Rourke, p. 26.

64. Ken Allen, "PLAAF Modernization: An Assessment," James Lilley and Chuck Downs, eds., *Crisis in the Taiwan Strait*, Washington DC: National Defense University Press, 1997, pp. 230-232.

65. Christopher Weuve, "PLAN CV Initial Thoughts," *Evolving Maritime Roles for Chinese Aerospace Power*, Conference paper presented at the China Maritime Studies Institute, U.S. Naval War College, Newport, RI, December 10-11, 2008, pp. 1-9.

66. In March 2007, a PLA General speaking to the press at the National People's Congress indicated that the Chinese carrier program was underway. That same month, an official of China's Commission of Science and Technology in National Defense (COSTIND) stated that China will soon acquire an aircraft carrier and the development program was underway. See Nan Li, "What Are Required for China to Acquire Aircraft Carriers," *Evolving Maritime Roles for Chinese Aerospace Power*, pp. 1-2.

67. O'Rourke, pp. 9-14.

68. Michael McDevitt, "The Strategy and Operational Context Driving PLA Navy Building," Kamphausen and Scobell eds., *Right Sizing the People's Liberation Army*, pp. 500-501.

69. *Jane's Defence Weekly*, April 24, 2009, available from *www.defence.pk/forums/china-defence/25667-china-publicly-displays-shang-class-ssns.html*.

70. Colonel (USAF) Gabe Collins, Mike McGauvran, and Lieutenant Colonel (USAF) Tim White, "Chinese Aerial Refueling Development," *Evolving Maritime Roles for Chinese Aerospace Power*, pp. 8-9. O'Rourke, pp. 9-14.

71. *Ibid.*

72. Phillip C. Saunders and Erik Quam, "Future Force Structure of the Chinese Air Force," Kamphausen and Scobell eds., pp. 392-393.

73. Bernard Cole, "Right Sizing the Navy: How Much Naval Force can Beijing Deploy?" Kamphausen and Scobell eds., *Right Sizing the People's Liberation Army*, p. 532.

74. Shambaugh, p. 100.

75. *Ibid.*, p. 102.

76. *Ibid.*

77. Bernard D. Cole, *The Great Wall at Sea: China's Navy Enters the Twenty First Century*, Annapolis, MD: Naval Institute Press, 2001, pp. 130-132.

78. *Ibid.*, p. 130.

79. Andrew Erickson, "Chinese Seapower in Action: the Counter-Piracy Mission in the Gulf of Aden and Beyond," Paper presented at the National Bureau of Asian Research, Strategic Studies Institute of the U.S. Army War College, and Texas A&M University's Bush School Conference, "The PLA at Home and Abroad," Carlisle, PA, September 25-27, 2009, pp. 8-18.

80. "Yin Zhuo: The PLAN Should Build a Long-Term Supply Base in Djibouti," China Gongying Shang, December 28, 2009, available from *cn.china.cn/article/n494656,fe393f,d2477_12053.html*.

81. Greg Torode, "Exercises off Japan and Taiwan Show PLA's New Prowess; Flotilla Practising off Japan and Taiwan,"*South China Morning Post*, April 18, 2010.

CHAPTER 4

THE PEOPLE'S LIBERATION ARMY'S SELECTIVE LEARNING: LESSONS OF THE IRAN-IRAQ "WAR OF THE CITIES" MISSILE DUELS AND USES OF MISSILES IN OTHER CONFLICTS

Christopher Twomey

The author wishes to thank Eric Heginbotham, David Shlapak, Thomas Christensen, David Lai, Roy Kamphausen, Travis Tanner, and Michael Glosny who provided invaluable guidance on both conceptual and empirical points. The author also gratefully acknowledges the research support of Daniel Alderman, Ginger Blanken, Eben Lindsey, Lyle Morris, and Chris Siegel.

EXECUTIVE SUMMARY

This chapter finds that China has "learned" few lessons from ballistic missile usage per se in other historic cases. Instead, it has engaged in a degree of doctrinal innovation that moves well beyond the traditional "terror" attack usages of ballistic missiles.

MAIN ARGUMENT

China has not imported lessons directly from Iranian and Iraqi use of ballistic missiles in the 1980s, or Iraqi use in either 1991 or 2003. It has certainly examined those cases, and portrays a relatively accurate assessment of the military role they played. That said, it does dress up those attacks in typical inflated language about their political utility for sowing terror and thereby attacking the adversary's morale. Nevertheless, these lessons are not then analytically extrapolated to China's strategic situation. Instead, the substantial innovation that China has undertaken with regard to its ballistic missile force, and apparently its missile doctrine, moves orthogonally away from such brute terror attacks. Thus, precision attacks on key nodes of military utility are the core of Chinese missile strike strategy. This suggests a degree of innovative doctrinal development. The Chinese appear to be extrapolating from American standoff precision strike campaigns in the 1990s and 2000s, to be sure, but nevertheless adapting these lessons to areas of their own relative technology competency.

POLICY IMPLICATIONS

This analysis raises some operational implications and calls for further research as well.

- The flexibility with which the People's Liberation Army (PLA) developed distinct technical answers to doctrinal demands is likely to be disconcerting for the U.S. military that uses a different approach, rendering problematic the anticipation of likely future such innovative developments by the PLA.
- China is likely to continue to emphasize and diversify the roles for its missile forces beyond traditional strategic roles.
- Further examination of the interaction of demand-pull of operational needs and the supply-push of existing bureaucratic and technical expertise is warranted. This would help anticipate future likely directions for emphasis

in deployment of capabilities and development of doctrine for the PLA.

INTRODUCTION

Conventionally-armed ballistic missiles (CABMs) are an important set of Chinese military capabilities today. The question of how China thinks about using them is of critical importance for the United States; regional partners including Japan, Taiwan, South Korea; and others. However, understanding how the People's Republic of China (PRC) sees this issue remains more contested than one might expect. This chapter will begin a preliminary examination of one set of influences on Chinese operational doctrine for CABMs: learning from abroad. First, it examines the limited lessons that China has drawn from the Iran-Iraq War of 1980-88 and Iraq's use of CABMs in 1991 and 2003. Then it turns to a characterization of the Second Artillery Force's (SAF) missile doctrine as best as it can be adduced. In so doing, the linkages and distinctions from U.S. precision strike attacks are noted. Finally, it concludes with some implications for how we understand the sources of doctrinal innovation in the Chinese system.

Clearly, the PLA values CABMs; at the very least, the increase in the number of CABMs indicates this. According the Pentagon's *Annual Report of Chinese Military Power*, Beijing has been engaged in rapid buildup of short-, and to a lesser extent, medium- and intermediate-range missiles. Most prominent of these are the DF-11 and -15 missiles that would be used as a primary means to threaten and engage in conflict with Taiwan in the event of a sharp deterioration of relations. According to the Pentagon's 2010 report, these have doubled in number from 2003 to 2007 — from 400 to 800 — and grew by nearly the same number of missiles over the next few years, to approximately 1100 today.[1] Other missiles, such as the DF-21, are also important, both as vehicles for anti-ship, anti-satellite, or anti-ballistic missile interceptor operations and possibly for attacking targets on U.S. military bases in Guam and Japan.

CABMs are widely believed to be at the core of China's strategy to deter or compel Taiwanese behavior. A recent RAND report emphasizes CABMs' potential utility in a coercive air campaign, for instance.[2] Other studies analyze the interaction of missile defenses (MD) against longer-ranged Chinese CABMs.[3] And, of course, CABM launches were the culminating points in the PLA Nanjing Military Region exercises of 1995 and 1996, although the effects of that crisis are much contested.[4]

Beyond its strict military utility, China's missile buildup has important political connotations as well. For instance, the growth in missiles is routinely highlighted as an important marker of China's aggressive intentions toward Taiwan, both in the United States and Taiwan. Even Taiwanese referenda criticizing China's missile buildup are viewed as problematic in Beijing, serving as a political challenge despite lack of tangible effects on the military balance. Consequently, the missile buildup rates and potential deployment locations are offered for consideration as early confidence and security-building measures (CSBMs) across the Taiwan Strait.[5] All of these emphasize the political role of missiles in the cross-strait relationship that transcends narrower military calculations.

Yet our understanding of the potential role that CABMs might play, in Beijing's hands in particular, but even more generally, is based on a somewhat thin historical record.[6] The Iran-Iraq War of 1980-88 provides the most intense example of such weapons being used.[7] The "war of the cities" in the later stages of that war began with aerial assaults on urban areas, but soon attrition of manned aircraft was found to be too costly. Thus, a moderate sized missile duel was carried out in the final years, beginning in 1985. The effect of the entire "war of cities" was relatively modest by the standards both of strategic conflict and even the more conventional battles in the Iran-Iraq War. Some 500 Iraqi missiles were launched, but only about 2,000 Iranians were killed in the campaign.[8] But the campaign had a broader effect than numbers alone show:

> The significance of the assaults was their psychological impact, as they provoked a panic among urban dwellers leading to mass exodus from cities such as Tehran. The regime had simply lost control of events, as it could neither offer assurances to a frightened public nor meaningfully retaliate against Iraq's latest act of aggression.[9]

Similarly,

> From a military point of view, the value of the attacks on Iranian population centers, the "war of the cities," has been virtually nil. The only real value of these attacks has been their effect on morale. Even an ineffective Iraqi raid on Tehran boosts Iraqi morale—in much the same way as the ineffective Doolittle raid on Tokyo boosted American morale in early 1942. The enemy capital is the preferred target in this kind of exchange.[10]

(The Iranian arsenal was smaller, with fewer than 200 missiles launched, causing even fewer casualties.)

There are other CABM campaigns one might draw upon for learning the relative advantages and disadvantages. Over 3,000 V-1 and -2 rockets were launched by Germany against London, United Kingdom (UK); Antwerp, Belgium; and other urban targets in the waning days of World War II. Additionally, Hezbollah and Hamas have used Katyusha rockets against civilian targets in Israel over a sustained period.[11] Hezbollah was reported to use longer range systems imported from Iran in the 2006 war against Israel.[12] The 1982 Lebanon War also saw the use of these shorter-range rocket systems. In all these cases, you have standoff munitions of somewhat limited accuracy: this is precisely the case for much of China's CABM arsenal.[13]

However, the most important other case to consider is the 1991 Gulf War, and to a lesser extent, the related 2003 campaigns in the current Iraq War. These modern cases also saw strategic use of CABMs both against U.S. forces and Israeli and other neighboring civilian centers.

Thus, it is worth asking the question, what has China learned from these campaigns? Since a similar terror campaign is often regarded as an important element of China's strategy against Taiwan, it is important to look at how these campaigns, the most substantial campaigns we have available, are viewed in Beijing and Wuhan, home to the Second Artillery Force's Command College. In addition to the question outlined by the editors of this volume regarding the observations and lessons drawn by the PLA and the implications of those observations and lessons for contemporary capabilities and doctrine, in this case it is also particularly interesting to ask what lessons were not learned that might otherwise have been. This gives us some ability to assess the relative importance of different sources of Chinese doctrine.[14]

A brief word on scope is warranted. While the Iran-Iraq War represents the largest usage of CABMs by both combatants, it is still a fairly narrow case. Thus, in contrast to the focus of some other chapters in this volume on a single historical case, this chapter will broaden its focus. It will consider the PLA's lessons regarding ballistic missile usage against ground targets in a number of cases. However, this chapter does not assess the more esoteric—and potentially revolutionary—weapons under development for the DF-21 platform in particular, such as the anti-ship ballistic missile (ASBM)[15] or the anti-satellite (ASAT) system[16] that China is fielding. (That said, as the conclusion suggests, this chapter finds SAF doctrine is influenced by bureaucratic factors, and the continued development of DF-21 variants is consistent with that finding.)

While other applications of the DF-21 are not considered in this chapter, what does emerge from an examination of the Chinese literature is the closely associated lessons one might draw from the employment of long-range cruise missiles. Similar to CABMs, these systems are challenging to defend against and can strike rear area targets. Additionally, in most cases, as with ballistic missiles, cruise missiles are more useful against static than mobile targets. They have been used in a wider range of recent conflicts and their inclusion in this study seems appropriate without excessively expanding the chapter's scope.

Beijing does not appear to see the launching of ballistic missiles against "soft" targets as its preferred model. Further, authoritative Chinese doctrinal documents make clear this is not how the PLA plans to use such weapons, despite the existence of some positive historical experience by others.[17] Instead, the primary driver for Chinese CABM usage seems to be a desire to emulate the effects of U.S. air-launched precision-guided munitions systems (cruise missiles and shorter ranged systems) using different systems.

Viewing the Iran-Iraq "War of the Cities" from Beijing.

Chinese military authors working on missile doctrine, asymmetric strategies, and strategic coercion have examined the Iran-Iraq War. However, the relevance of the lessons appears to be quite limited. The propagandistic tone in Chinese writings (i.e., missiles as powerful weapons of the weak and less developed combatants) colors the historic evaluations, as does an emphasis on political morale that is common to Chinese strategic thought. Still, there is little discernable carryover from those evaluations to contemporary Chinese doctrine.

In overview, Chinese analysts note that the war exemplified the potential utility of CABMs. Thus:

> From World War II up to today, although Surface to Surface tactical ballistic missiles have only been in existence for 50-plus years, their use in the Fourth Middle East War [of 1982], the Iran-Iraq War [of 1980-88], and Gulf War [of 1991], has made people appreciate their power.[18]

That article goes on to characterize the Iran-Iraq War as a particularly strong example of this phenomenon:

> The 'war of the cities' began when Iraq used ground-to-ground Tactical Ballistic missiles in their primary attack on Iran's capital...close to 10,000 people were

blown up, and 1,000 buildings and structures were destroyed. The huge power of the missile war of the cities amazed people all over the world.[19]

Another study noted Iraq's missile attacks were successful in "killing 1,700 Iranians and flattening buildings in the process." It went on to note that Iran's retaliation "was not as effective as Iraqi SCUD-B result," given accuracy issues.[20] The attacks were regarded as "the most impressive, influential and effective use of missiles ever seen since then [WWII]."[21] The *Jiefangjun Bao's* précis of the war emphasizes the economic costs that these strategic attacks imposed.[22]

Indeed, earlier CABM campaigns are assessed similarly; for instance, the German V-1 and -2 attacks:

> During the period between June 1944 and March 1945, the German military launched a total of 8,090 V1 rockets and 4,320 V2 rockets at the British capital London and continental Europe. The technology of these rockets was rudimentary, and their accuracy was very poor. Although they failed to completely change the fate of defeat for Germany, the V1 and V2 rockets did deliver psychological shocks to the Allied forces and badly terrorized the residents.[23]

A history web page on the Chinese Ministry of Defense web site echoes these conclusions about the coercive utility of the weapons.[24]

More definitive Chinese sources echo these conclusions but do little to extrapolate them forward to contemporary Chinese circumstances. The *Science of Second Artillery Campaigns* (SSAC) is regarded as the definitive official statement available to scholars to assess how China conceives of the role of its Second Artillery Force, the military element responsible for all land-based and strategic missiles.[25]

The SSAC notes that a range of limitations prevented a more substantial set of military effects from being achieved in the "war of the cities," but nevertheless, highlights the important *political and coercive* successes derived from the campaign.

> [In the campaign] several thousand buildings were destroyed. Iran also fired 60 "Scud-B" missiles which struck more than 20 cities centered around Baghdad. It killed and wounded several thousand people. Due to almost total destructions of missile warning and command control systems during the war, the missile forces lacking proper trainings, and many problems in target selections and applications of tactics on the missile strikes on both sides, they did not fully utilize the functions and power of the expensive and modern ground-to-ground missiles. However, by whatever element we use to assess, analyze, and judge this "Raids against cities" with missiles, it possessed significant campaign characteristics. *It not only brought both sides mentally, economically, and militarily insufferable pressure and great losses but also became the catalyst in ending the war between Iraq and Iran.*[26]

Thereafter, as will be seen below, SSAC spends little time focusing on the use of missiles against cities per se, and likewise does not much consider the coercive use of missiles against populations and — thereby — political will.

Nevertheless, there is some extrapolation of this sort of approach to the contemporary era. One analysis from the *Jiefangjun Bao* evaluates successes in both the Iran-Iraq War, and in the U.S. campaign against Yugoslavia over Kosovo's status. It concludes that rear area strikes seem to be viable against economic infrastructure targets and are able to achieve compellence:

In this type of no-contact war, the goal of launching air strikes is not just to eliminate the opponent's effective military strength but to weaken the opponent's integrated national strength through strategic air strikes, thereby causing the opponent to basically lose its resistance and confrontational ability.[27]

While that source was also evaluating air power more broadly, missile strikes were one component considered.

Still, beyond official channels, there are some sources that emphasize the limitations of such coercive strategies aimed at populations. In a glossy publication from the commercial press, *World Affairs* (世界知识出版社), a very pessimistic view of the utility of such attacks against cities is laid out:

During the Iran-Iraq War, many offensive strategies against cities and towns were used, but in actuality, this was a tactical mistake in the sense of putting the incidental before the fundamental. High ranking officers on both sides seem to delight in comparing themselves to those famous ancient generals, wanting was only to dominate a city, but this is only a superficial achievement of feeling completely "triumphant" and instead ignored the effectiveness of annihilating the enemy forces. They did not value concentrating the great amount of military superiority to annihilate enemy soldiers and focused on destroying cities. Because of this the battle was repeatedly stopped and started, creating a stalemate. The stalemate caused the war to drag out without a decision, and this situation, besides causing enormous consumption on each side, did not inflict heavy casualties on the enemy's strength. Therefore both sides' military strength remained in relative balance, and neither side was able to achieve decisive victory.[28]

Beyond the contested utility of a coercive effect achieved through missile attacks on urban areas, a range of nonauthoritative Chinese sources assert other direct implications of the Iran-Iraq war. One recurring, if erroneous, theme on internet sites and discussion boards is that actual combat operations have created greater interest in CABMs. Thus:

> the Iran-Iraq War saved China's tactical missiles . . . providing a few lessons: first, tactical ballistic missiles with conventional warheads are useful [up to that point], China had not considered that arming these with explosives had practical application other than intimidation.[29]

Other discussions on Chinese military web sites suggest the same linkage.[30]

However, such internet speculation is patently inaccurate, illustrating the importance of careful use of authoritative Chinese sources and evaluating those in the context of other empirically observable forms of Chinese behavior, procurement, and policy. To be sure, the earliest work on conventionally armed missiles does occur in the 1980s:

> Commercial interests served as the primary impetus for development of conventional tactical ballistic missiles. . . . During the mid-1980s, Beijing's senior leadership began to develop options for arming solid fueled ballistic missiles with conventional warheads.[31]

However, the emphasis on conventional missiles in the Second Artillery Force's own arsenal is a relatively recent phenomenon; linking the emphasis on CABMs solely to the Iran-Iraq War is simply not correct for several reasons. First, as Kenneth Allen and

Maryanne Kivlehan-Wise note, "it was not until 1998 that Second Artillery developed the concepts referred to in [their chapter] as the 'conventional missile attack campaign' and compiled its first instructional text-book."[32] Without such doctrine, it would have been hard to impute any causal element to a war a decade earlier. Moreover, Mark Stokes puts the shift in priority to developments at the end of the 1990s:

> A series of events that occurred between March and August 1999 sharpened PRC focus on the United States and Taiwan in its strategy and force planning. There is a large body of evidence that suggests an important high level decision was made in the early to mid-May 1999 time frame to accelerate key weapons systems R&D and production programs. After the initiation of the NATO air campaign in March 1999, media reporting suggests the CMC [Central Military Commission] lobbied for funding to accelerate several programs, including new ballistic missile variants, land attack cruise missiles, and other systems.[33]

Elsewhere he argues, "during annual meetings at Beidaihe in August 1999, China's senior leadership decided to accelerate the production and deployment of enough ballistic missiles to outfit four short-range ballistic missile (SRBM) brigades by 2002."[34] Additionally, the *Science of Military Campaigns* [战役学] of 2000 suggests an increase in importance of CABMS.[35] Finally, John Wilson Lewis and Litai Xue date the shift as beginning in 2001.[36]

As Figure 4-1 shows, the large increase in arsenal size also begins to occur around the turn of the century. Surges in 1999-2001 and in 2006-2009 seem consistent across the two data sets. As doctrine and increase in numbers of systems occur at the end of the 1990s, this suggests other key drivers beyond the Iran-Iraq "war of the cities" in the development of CABMs.

Chinese SRBMs by Year

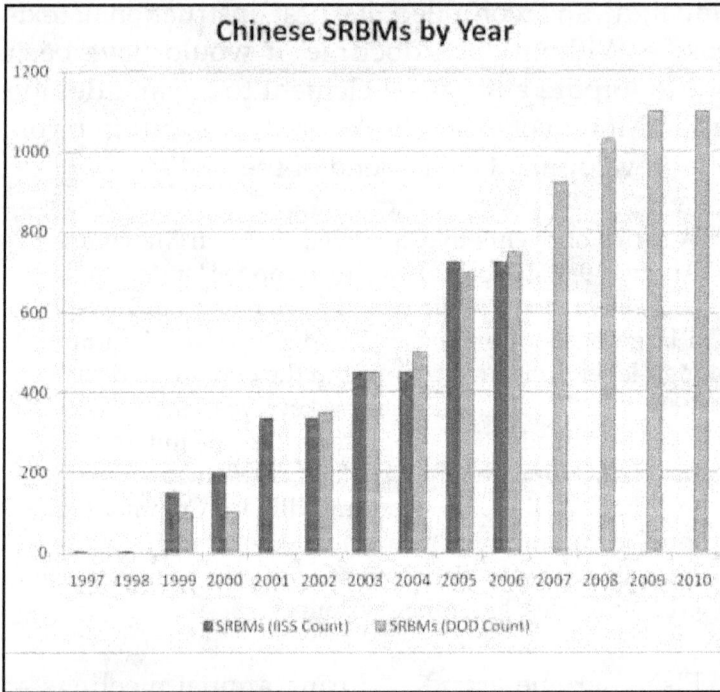

Source: International Institute for Strategic Studies (IISS), *Military Balance*, various years; U.S. Department of Defense (DoD) *Annual Report on Chinese Military Power*, various years. The DF-11 and -15 systems, those relevant to Taiwan and only Taiwan, are included.

Figure 4-1. Chinese SRBMs by Year.

Other Cases Teach More?

It does seem that other cases beyond the Iran-Iraq "war of the cities" use of missiles have been more influential in shaping PLA perceptions about the utility of CABMs. The Iran-Iraq war is not even mentioned in the 2006 edition of the *Science of Military Campaigns* (战役学) and receives only passing mention, as discussed essentially in its entirety above, in the *Science of Second Artillery Campaigns*. As noted above, the German experience receives occasional commentary, although again, its lessons seem rather limited.

The 1995-96 exercises in the Taiwan Strait likewise appear to have had little influence on these debates. This may be due to the politically sensitive nature of these exercises: since the handling of the crisis is generally viewed as a failure for Beijing, discussion of it is likely to be muted. (It is often viewed as a loss for Beijing since it provoked a clear signal of American support for Taiwan through the deployment of two carriers to the region.) Even fairly benign references were confined to the Hong Kong PLA-affiliated press, such as: the exercises were "intended to show that the Chinese communists have the capacity and the mastery to carry out attacks on, and blockade multiple targets." [37] The treatment of the crisis in authoritative military internal documents available outside of China is again exceedingly superficial: "In order to strike against the expansion of the Taiwan independence forces, the PLA organized missile training, launched joint campaign exercises in the vicinity of Taiwan, and effectively suppressed the rampant arrogance of the Taiwan independence forces." [38] This is essentially the only mention of the Taiwan Strait crisis in the aforementioned PLA National Defense University (NDU) report, [39] and hardly constitutes strategic analysis.

Similarly, interviews with Chinese analysts by Robert Ross emphasize similar broad-brush conclusions by Chinese interlocutors: "missiles may be the only weapon China can use to deter Taiwan independence, because it is the only Chinese conventional weapon that the United States cannot defeat."[40] That is far from a detailed assessment of how those missiles serve Chinese interests, what they threaten, what they can defeat and what that defeat means militarily. It is likely, as Ross notes, that such discussions are too politically sensitive to be evaluated, contested, and debated within the Chinese military system.

However, the Gulf War of 1991 and a few other American post-Cold War campaigns do serve as important fodder for PLA and civilian military analysts.[41] The two most important implications for the missile area — the coercive role of CABMs and the implications of precision-guided munitions (PGMs) for the utility of advanced, accurate, conventionally armed ballistic missiles — are discussed first.

Coercive Power for the Weak? One theme from Chinese analysis of the Gulf War is the role that CABMs served as a weapon of the weak, one of the few tools that Iraq had at its fingertips that it could use.

> According to incomplete statistics, in the Gulf War, Iraq launched 83 SCUD B missiles against multinational army stations and within Israel. Even though this kind of missile has only a 300 meter target precision and some were intercepted by American "Patriot" missiles, in the Iraq and multinational army mutual resistance process, they still were a huge deterrent....
>
> During the Gulf War, Iraq sustained an early attack by the American-led multinational forces, and under conditions whence the Navy forces could not dock, the Air Force jumped one by one to safety, and ground forces had no choice but to dig holes for cover, the only missile that could hit back was the SCUD missile.[42]

While such analysis seems to raise many unanswered questions (A huge deterrent to what? What value was there in "hitting back" at the end of the day?), similar assertions were made by others. Researchers at the PLA Air Force (PLAAF) Command College write such attacks "caused the multinational forces and allied countries tremendous psychological pressure."[43] Similarly, Lewis and Xue found that:

> Senior PLA officers maintained that a "huge psychological impact on the enemy" would result from even a conventional missile attack and that a conventional missile force could "deter the outbreak of a conventional local war in a time of peace and contain the expansion and escalation of a conventional local war after it had broken out."[44]

And indeed, within China there is some discussion of the role of positive utility for "backward weapons" within the Second Artillery units:

> Therefore, if the old-type missile forces are ready to use the weapons in their hands, train hard to become crack troops, tap into their potential in a scientific manner, and consistently keep the old armaments in perfect operating condition, they can also achieve the goal of "fighting and winning" a future war.[45]

Even here, and consistent with critiques of western militaries' faith in the coercive power of strategic bombing, the logic is not laid out precisely.[46]

This is a lesson that draws directly from the sort of assessment of the Gulf War:

> From the aforementioned war, we can see that even a small country without air or sea superiority, poor and weak countries, if they possess [ballistic missiles], can still pose a threat to powerful enemy countries. This is because in a war, ballistic missiles can attack population centers, industrial bases, and other economic and

political targets, inflicting psychological pressure on the opponent and acting as a deterrent. In terms of war tactics, you can strike a military's rear assembly positions, bridge positions, fuel depots, airports, and command/control centers, allowing you to complement or even replace aircraft missions. Therefore, large, small, strong, weak, rich and poor countries all scramble to obtain ballistic missiles. Ballistic missiles have turned into the modern weapons of the gods.[47]

While these sorts of arguments are indeed laid out regarding Iraqi use of ballistic missiles, as noted below, they find little manifestation in contemporary doctrinal statements from the Second Artillery.

Threatening to Expand the War through Terror Attacks. A second area of emphasis in Chinese writings is the Iraqi attempt to use ballistic missiles to expand the U.S.-Iraq War to involve Israel. This is mentioned pervasively.[48] For instance, an authoritative PLA history concludes:

> These missile attacks by Iraq not only created psychological fear for the people of Saudi Arabia and Israel, but also nearly led to a serious crisis which could have ruptured the multinational coalition. . . . From a military point of view, the 42 missiles that Iraq fired at Israel did not create many casualties, however, their political implications were enormous. Iraq's goal in firing missiles into Israel was to lure Israel into joining the war, to achieve the strategic objective of destroying and dividing the hastily established anti-Iraq coalition.[49]

Similarly, a TV military affairs news report on Phoenix TV updates the same point: It argued that Iran draws significant deterrent value from its ballistic missiles that could be used against Israel and that China, too, benefits from the deterrent value of its force.[50]

Again, one problem here for drawing any such positive conclusions for the Chinese is that these attacks, in the end, did not work. Thus, SSAC takes a rather defensive tone:

> The missile strikes did not reverse the fate of failure of the Iraqis, but it did demonstrate that the strike campaign of missile forces could have its functions in the modern high tech warfare. On the contrary, under the circumstances that the coalition forces had great superiority . . . the ballistic missile forces fought alone and implemented the "Sacred Orders" of Saddam Hussein from the beginning to the end. It also had frightened the enemy and displayed important status and functions of missile forces' strike campaign in future high tech localized warfare.[51]

Beyond that, another limitation is that this strategic context lacks any direct analogue for China. Drawing additional parties in does not have the same implication outside the Middle East; China would certainly prefer to contain any conflict (with Taiwan, Japan, or others) rather than expand it (to the United States or any other regional actor). Thus, this facet of the Middle East experience is simply irrelevant despite being frequently mentioned in the Chinese literature.

Tactical Lessons. Finally, and most promisingly from the perspective of this chapter, a few tactical lessons are both discussed in the military literature and seem to have some focus within Chinese practice. First, there is recognition among Chinese writings of the value of missile launcher mobility and on survivability more generally. This likely has fed into some of Beijing's emphasis on mobility of its own forces:

> Iraq's ability to launch its Scud missiles throughout the war despite repeated U.S. air strikes to destroy

them gave [Beijing's] leaders some confidence in the survivability of China's mobile missiles. That confidence in turn motivated the Second Artillery to concentrate ever harder on mobile operations.[52]

The 2006 edition of the *Science of Military Campaigns*, as well as other scholars of China's military, echo this point.[53] The Chinese writings also implicitly recognize the challenges these necessary changes (mobility, etc.) poses for command and control.[54]

Second, a related lesson was the need to achieve quick launching missiles, given the existent threat of air strikes. As discussed below, this concern played something of a circular role in shaping Chinese thinking about the utility of CABMs,[55] but nevertheless it was a driver of one particular element of technical development, namely the use of solid fuel propellants. There were other parallel drivers here as well, of course: "Thus in 1982, Zhang Aiping, speaking for the Central Military Commission at a gathering in Dalian, noted that there was a worldwide trend toward solid propellant missiles and called for a comprehensive development of these rockets in China."[56]

Finally, some Chinese analysts traced limitations in Iraq's ability to effectively use its missiles to Iraqi military limitations in training:

> But Iraq kept piled up a small mountain of common types of advanced guided munitions within its barracks up until the war ended. It is just that these advanced munitions didn't have anyone who knew how to use them. When the Iraqis charged enemy lines, they were still using hand grenades and Molotov cocktails. Why did this happen? Although they had much advanced equipment, they lacked the officers and soldiers trained to use it.[57]

The *Jiefangjun Bao* article goes on to note that China needed to do better. There is certainly substantial emphasis on improving the quality of training and technical capacity throughout the Second Artillery Force today.[58]

A strategic lesson of the importance of "seizing the initiative" also flows from the Gulf War in China's writings.[59] However, this is a broad lesson regarding modern warfare and is not drawn to the Gulf War missile campaign per se.

Core Tenets of Second Artillery Doctrine Are Different and Innovative.

The above "lessons learned" are rather thin gruel. The core elements of Chinese missile strategy today are, at least at first blush: precision attack, joint attack, and the missile's role in suppressing enemy strike capabilities. These components are essentially missing from the historic record and found nowhere in the discussion of historic ballistic missile usage described above. Nevertheless, they seem central to China's missile strategy today. This suggests that genuine internal innovation is a more important driver of doctrinal thinking in the PLA in this area.

As laid out by the SSAC, the goals of the missile force are: "penetrating the enemy's air defense system, striking the enemy's in-depth targets, and seizing air and naval dominance in future local wars under informationized conditions."[60] The 2006 edition of *Zhanyi Xue* (*Science of Campaigns*) writes of the role of missiles in attacking airfields and ports through "missile firepower blockades.[61] Civilian analysts in China explicitly link this to Taiwan:

But, if the fighting started across the Taiwan Straits, these planes will never get a chance to take off. Considering the narrowness of Taiwan Straits and the firepower from the Chinese mainland, their airports are so vulnerable. All airports will be destroyed in the first attack. Even if some of them can take off, they can't land.[62]

In order to achieve this, precision is key. This is clearly recognized within the Second Artillery. Again, SSAC makes the point forcefully:

Due to the transition from the industrial era to the information era, operational measures also start to develop toward the direction of large-scale operations to long-range precision operations. Precision operations are the objective requirements of the intense development of military technology and weapons and equipment. It is also the developmental trend of Second Artillery campaign operations.[63]

Similarly, in the PLA NDU's internal military text, *Intimidation Warfare*, the study's editorial board concludes the entire study with a section on the "rise of long range precision strike" in the final chapter on "Developing Trends in Military Deterrence using Missile Forces."[64] The point is made widely across the military literature.[65]

To emphasize the point, precision—or lack thereof—is rarely mentioned as an important limitation in the earlier ballistic missile campaigns (in World War II and Iran-Iraq, or even the Gulf War).[66] What is emphasized, repeatedly, is the importance of accuracy for *cruise* missile strikes:

Over the past 10 years, cruise missiles have been used many times in battle, acting as a first strike weapon that startles the enemy that has achieved many military successes. The below examples highlight their use in battle: During the Gulf War, America launched a total of 323 cruise missiles. On January 17, 1993, America launched 45 Tomahawk missiles from destroyers and cruisers . . . aimed toward 7 Iraqi nuclear development facilities in Baghdad. On June 27, America launched 23 Tomahawk missiles from destroyers, destroying Iraq's intelligence headquarters. On September 10, 1995, America launched 13 Tomahawk missiles from cruisers in the Adriatic Sea, destroying Serbian air defense radar, communication and command centers. . . . [5 additional similar examples are also listed].[67]

Beyond that, precision is regarded as the way of the future heading into the 21st century, and this is directly applied to the needs of China's ballistic missile forces at all levels.[68]

Another aspect addressed is the issue of the missiles' ability to penetrate tough air defense environments:

The PLA's conventional missiles will be used exclusively against the enemy's key military targets which the weapons of other services cannot reach. These targets include the communications hubs, weapons delivery platforms, and most practically, the aircraft carrier battle groups. Since these systems are under heavy protection, the demand for the conventional missiles is thus very high. Moreover, how to use these missiles is a matter of military art in solving the optimum timing and smart selection of targets.[69]

Clearly, missile defenses complicate this, leading to an emphasis on ensuring the penetrability of warheads.[70]

Closely related, there is an emphasis in Chinese writings on a new form of "noncontact warfare":

"Noncontact warfare will become the main style of air warfare for strong countries."[71] This depends on the role of precision (e.g., see the passages above), but also emphasizes long-range, stand-off attack. Thus, cruise missiles are seen as a useful means of attacking such air defense systems.[72]

Joint operations receive increasing focus in contemporary Chinese military affairs, and these two find little emphasis in the retelling of foreign countries' military experience with CABMs. The point here is that neither is the existence of joint and integrated operations trumpeted in assessing successful CABMs operations elsewhere historically, nor is their absence noted as a central cause of failure. Instead, they go unmentioned. But clearly, the role of integrating Second Artillery campaigns with the rest of China's military is an emphasis today.[73]

A final area worth mentioning is that the Chinese believe CABMs and long range cruise missiles give China an escalatory option short of nuclear weapons use, which would both be of limited credibility and would violate no-first-use rhetoric.

> One of the uses of conventional cruise missiles in long-range ground attacks is to attack the enemy targets that are far inland, which may help postpone or avoid using nuclear weapons in battle, thereby raising the nuclear threshold. Cruise missiles have the ability to intimidate as well as yield strategic advantages in battle. They have the ability to target most depths of targets, sometimes even having the ability to cover all depths of the enemy on the battlefield. The objective of cruise missile strategy is similar to nuclear strategy, in that when a battle starts, the target will be decapitation of the head organs of war, missile bases and economic centers, etc, and not the enemy army itself.[74]

A similar view about the utility of "long-range deterrent based missiles" is expressed by other Chinese authors at official research centers.[75] Lewis and Xue highlight a similar logic:

> Based on a review of [high tech] wars in the 1990s, senior PLA officers concluded that "strategic missiles had not played their predicted deterrent role in local wars," and the burning question for them was how to prevent or conduct a high-tech war. After investigating the outcome of recent armed conflicts, they understood that revolutionary increases in the destructive power and operating ranges of modern air-delivered conventional weapons could cripple an adversary's command-and-control system and destroy its war making potential. . . . However, China's plans for a high-tech local war contained a major flaw, the failed modernization of the PLA Air Force. . . . Despite a guiding principle that calls for air dominance, the PLAAF falls far short of its implementation even on its own territory. For the PLA, therefore, the only alternative is to adapt its strategic missiles to fight a conventional war. Caught between the doctrine and reality, the CMC has been forced to bet on the short- and medium-range missiles of the Second Artillery to fight and win a high-tech local war.[76]

The logic here is reminiscent of the recent U.S. emphasis on prompt global strike as providing additional options in dealing with "rogue states."[77]

Thus, the key elements in China's missile strategy today find little linkage to the main global experiences with such weapons. Instead, they represent something far more worrisome to Beijing's potential competitors: indigenous innovation and adaptation.

Sketching Implications for Understanding China and for U.S. Policy.

Given the paucity of data regarding the nature of doctrinal development in a military that lacks basic transparency, one must be modest in drawing conclusions. However, the tentative end points here are interesting and do raise important questions about the nature of doctrinal innovation.

In this case, thus, Chinese doctrinal development seems less affected by the direct lessons learned from similar militaries' ballistic missile usage patterns than from an extrapolation lessons from other military capabilities and an adaptation of them to areas where China has traditionally excelled in technology development. China has also adapted such lessons to its unique strategic environment. Rather than drawing on "terroristic" usage of ballistic missile campaigns in the 1980s and 1990s to inform the development of Chinese CABMs, Beijing looked elsewhere. That China studied and learned from American military interventions in the 1990s and 2000s in general is not contentious. What is interesting, however, is that Beijing appeared to adapt seemingly unrelated aspects of American lessons learned to Chinese strategic contingencies. One might infer that Beijing recognized it would be a decade or two before it was able to control the airspace over Taiwan to engage in an American-style coercive precision strike strategic campaign. This appears to have led China to move its missile force in the direction of serving that precision strike role in a way its air force will be unable to do for many years. This seems a deliberate choice to invest heavily in accurate guidance systems for precision-guided munitions with Chinese characteristics: Beijing is using expensive missiles to deliver its PGMs rather than cheaper guided warheads launched from reusable strike aircraft.

Beyond the strategic rationales for this shift toward a precision missile strike force, bureaucratic and organizational sources of doctrine may be important factors.[78] Lewis and Xue highlight a number of related dynamics in the case of the Second Artillery: reforms in the nature of science and technology development in the Second Artillery Force, a "budgetary bonanza," and domestic political changes.[79] Clearly, the lessons of U.S. military campaigns in the air delivery of PGMs are closely related to the Chinese innovations on the missile side. Disentangling the demand-pull of military expediency and supply-push of organizational and political options would be of great value for anticipating future developments in China's military. Given that China's missile force — both cruise and ballistic — has long been among the most advanced technologies fielded in China, it is not surprising that the PLA chose to take advantage of these technologies to respond to a new operational goal: precision strike. (Similarly, it is not surprising, through this lens, to find that when faced with an operational goal of holding at risk American carriers, China would again turn to missiles in its nascent anti-ship ballistic missile system.)

These multiple sources of causality suggest further examination of the interaction of demand/pull of operational needs and the supply/push of existing bureaucratic and technical expertise is warranted. This would help anticipate future likely directions for emphasis in deployment of capabilities and development of doctrine for the PLA.

Additionally, this analysis suggests that China is likely to continue to emphasize and diversify the roles for its missile forces. To some extent, there is a sound military rationale for this.[80] Nevertheless, China is likely to continue to rely on this area above and beyond that necessity. Even in cases where China's missiles might not be the optimal weapon, we should expect an over-reliance on such systems.

Most generally, this chapter also makes clear that the flexibility with which the PLA developed distinct technical answers to doctrinal demands is disconcerting for the U.S. military, which is often the explicit enemy of such development. While constrained in some dimensions, the PLA is displaying a degree of flexibility in innovation that is worthy of some admiration. While further examination of this process of innovation is challenging given the general opacity in the Chinese system and the high degree of classification of such issues in most countries; nonetheless, comparative study of Chinese doctrinal innovation in other areas might deepen our understanding of this process.

ENDNOTES - CHAPTER 4

1. Office of the Secretary of Defense, "Annual Report on the Military Power of the People's Republic of China: Report to Congress Pursuant to the FY2000 National Defense Authorization Act," Washington, DC: Department of Defense, July 28, 2003; "Military Power of the People's Republic of China: Annual Report to Congress," Washington, DC: Department of Defense, May 23, 2006; Office of the Secretary of Defense, "Military and Security Developments Involving the People's Republic of China: Annual Report to Congress," Washington, DC: Department of Defense, August 16, 2010.

2. David A. Shlapak *et. al.*, *A Question of Balance: Political Context and Military Aspects of the China-Taiwan Dispute*, Santa Monica, CA: RAND, 2009.

3. Thomas J. Culora, "The Strategic Implications of Obscurants," *Naval War College Review*, Vol. 63, No. 3, 2010; and Marshall Hoyler, "China's Antiaccess' Ballistic Missiles and US Active Defense," *Naval War College Review*, Vol. 63, No. 4, 2010, pp. 84-104.

4. Robert S. Ross, "The 1995-96 Taiwan Strait Confrontation: Coercion, Credibility, and the Use of Force," *International Security*, Vol. 25, No. 2, 2000, pp. 87-123; and Arthur Ding, "The Lessons of the 1995-1996 Taiwan Strait Crisis: Developing a New Strategy Toward the United States and Taiwan," Laurie Burkitt, Andrew Scobell, and Larry M. Wortzel, eds., *The Lessons of History: The Chinese People's Liberation Army at 75*, Carlisle, PA: Strategic Studies Institute, U.S. Army War College, 2003.

5. For discussion of the state of play in such confidence and security building measures (CSBM) discussions, see Bonnie S. Glaser, "Building Trust across the Taiwan Strait: A Role for Military Confidence-building Measures," *A Report of the CSIS Freeman Chair in China Studies*, Washington, DC: Center for Strategic and International Studies, January 2010.

6. One attempt to assess the utility of missile strikes in a Taiwan scenario can be found in Yitzhak Shichor, "Missile Myths: China's Threat to Taiwan in a Comparative Perspective," *CAPS Papers*, No. 45, 2008.

7. For a good overview of the war, including its diplomatic elements, see Ray Takeyh, "The Iran-Iraq War: A Reassessment," *The Middle East Journal*, Vol. 64, No. 3, 2010, pp. 365-83. For an earlier, more limitary focused assessment, see David Segal, "The Iran-Iraq War: A Military Analysis," *Foreign Affairs*, Vol. 66, No. 5, 1988, pp. 946-963.

8. Takeyh, "The Iran-Iraq War."

9. *Ibid.*, p. 380.

10. Segal, "The Iran-Iraq War," p. 598.

11. While the Katyushas are of very short range, more properly considered rockets than missiles, given the condensed strategic geography of Israel and the surrounding combatants, they play a similar role to the longer ranged systems in more expansive terrain.

12. For a good summary of the range of possible systems, see BBC, "Hezbollah's rocket force," July 18 2006, available from *news.bbc.co.uk/2/hi/middle_east/5187974.stm*.

13. Note that the technology level varies considerably between a Katyusha and a DF-21D variant. Nevertheless, the bulk of China's arsenal is not that advanced system, and instead serves a role similar to many of those earlier systems.

14. Thus, this chapter, and the broader project, speaks to the debates raised in an earlier generation of military affairs theorists who asked: What are the sources of military doctrine? Barry R. Posen, *The Sources of Military Doctrine: France, Britain, and Germany Between the World Wars*, Ithaca, NY: Cornell University Press, 1984.

15. See Andrew S. Erickson and David D. Yang, "On the Verge of a Game-Changer," *USNI Proceedings* 135, No. 5, 2009; and Craig Hooper and Christopher Albon, "Get Off the Fainting Couch," *USNI Proceedings*, Vol. 136, No. 4, 2010.

16. See the three articles in *China Security*'s special issue regarding arms races in space: "China's ASAT Test and Space Deterrence," *China Security*, No. 5, 2007.

17. See discussion in final section of this chapter.

18. Hou Yunli (侯云礼), "陆军地面战的'杀手锏'" ("Surface War's Assassin's Mace"), *PLA Daily*, August 22, 2001.

19. *Ibid*. The casualties claimed in this article are excessive relative to most accepted Western sources.

20. Lian Lujun (连鲁军), "波斯长矛: 伊朗流行弹道导弹家族" ("Iran's Shooting Star Clan of Ballistic Missile"), 国际展望 (*World Outlook*), No. 518, June, 2005. *World Outlook* is published by the Shanghai Institute of International Studies, which is associated

(from afar, but certainly administratively linked) with the Ministry of Foreign Affairs.

21. Zhou Yi (周义), Wang Zhongyi (王忠义), and Wang Ziyan (王自焰), "从飞毛腿到蜘蛛B" ("From 'Scud' to 'Spider B'"), 军事装备 (*Military Equipment*), Issue 1, 2004.

22. Zhong Jing (仲晶), "两伊战争" ("Iran-Iraq War"), *PLA Daily,* January 17, 2001.

23. Li Yuankui, ed., 高技术与现代战争 (High Tech and Modern Warfare), Beijing, China: Junshi Yiwen Chubanshe, January 1998, Open Source Center, CPP20061220320004.

24. Nie Yun (聂云), "看美国人怎么抢战利品" ("See How Americans Fight for War Spoils"), 中国国防报 (*China National Defense*), available from *www.mod.gov.cn/hist/2009-07/17/content_4004941.htm*.

25. *The Science of Second Artillery Campaigns* (SSAC) has a restricted circulation within China, but is publicly available elsewhere in Asia and the United States. It is apparently used to guide Chinese training on these and related issues.

26. 第二炮兵战役学 *(The Science of Second Artillery Campaigns)*, Beijing, China: PLA Publishing House, 2004, pp. 49-50. Emphasis added.

27. Xu Sining, "Analysis on New Characteristics of Rear Counter-Air-Strike Operations," *PLA Daily* (Internet Version), June 19, 2001, p. 6, Trans. by Open Source Center, CPP20010619000052.

28. 北京大陆桥文化传媒 (Beijing Continental Bridge Cultural Media), "中东战火" ("War in the Middle East"), Beijing, China: 世界知识出版社 (World Affairs Press), 2004, p. 223.

29. See essay entitled "中国战术弹道导弹的一些情况" ("The Status of Chinese Guided Missile Tactics"), available from a number of military bulletin boards. A clean copy can be found at *www.cnread.net/CNREAD1/jszl/y/yiming/zglj/122.htm*.

30. For instance, see essay entitled "两场战争与中国二炮的 '核常兼备'" ("The Two Wars and China's Second Artillery's 'Nuclear and Convention Preparedness'"), available from *www.360doc. com/content/09/1017/14/88979_7410637.shtml*.

31. Mark Stokes, "The People's Liberation Army and China's Space and Missile Development: Lessons From the Past and Prospects for the Future," Burkitt, Scobell, and Wortzel, eds., *The Lessons of History*, p. 212. Stokes draws on a wide range of published Chinese sources to come to this conclusion, including a range of official materials.

32. Kenneth Allen and Maryanne Kivlehan-Wise, "Implementing PLA Second Artillery Doctrinal Reforms," James Mulvenon and David Finkelstein, eds., *China's Revolution in Doctrinal Affairs: Emerging Trends in the Operational Art of the Chinese People's Liberation Army*, Washington, DC: CNA Corporation, December, 2005, p. 163. Note that if the debates above are correct, it is both interesting and disturbing that the political guidance to emphasize such strategy succeeded the development of doctrine rather than the other way around.

33. Stokes, "The People's Liberation Army and China's Space and Missile Development," pp. 215-216.

34. Mark Stokes, "Chinese Ballistic Missile Forces in the Age of Global Missile Defense: Challenges and Responses," Andrew Scobell and Larry Wortzel, eds., *China's Growing Military Power*, Carlisle, PA: Strategic Studies Institute, U.S. Army War College, 2002, p. 114.

35. See Chapter 14 in particular. Note this is an internally circulated document, suggesting it is more authoritative.

36. John Wilson Lewis and Litai Xue, *Imagined Enemies: China Prepares for Uncertain War*, Palo Alto, CA: Stanford University Press, 2006, p. 311, note 83.

37. Huang Tung, "M-Series Missiles and New Navy Equipment—New Weapons in Taiwan Strait Exercises," *Kuang Chiao Ching*, April 16, 1996, trans. by OSC, FTS19960416000022.

38. Zhao Xijin (赵锡君), 摄战: 导弹威慑纵横谈 (*Intimidation Warfare: A Comprehensive Discussion on Missile Deterrence*), Beijing, China: NDU Press, 2003, p. 166.

39. The other mention is no more analytic:

Determination in applying military deterrence by missile force is the most important factor in the power of deterrence. . . . It is built on the basis of objective strength, and also on the degree of self-confidence in applying that strength. . . . [For another example] when Taiwan authorities vainly attempted to proclaim "Taiwan's Independence" in 1995 and 1996, the Chinese government conducted test launches of missiles to the Taiwan Straits to defeat the strength of 'Taiwan Independence'.

Ibid., p. 253.

40. Robert S. Ross, "The 1995-96 Taiwan Strait Confrontation: Coercion, Credibility, and the Use of Force," *International Security*, Vol. 25, No. 2, 2000, p. 121.

41. See the other papers in this volume, in particular that by Dean Cheng, for an overview of some of these.

42. Hou Yunli (侯云礼), "陆军地面战的'杀手锏': 21世纪的地地战役战术弹道导弹" ("The Army's Surface War's Assassin's Mace: 21 Century Field Campaign Tactical Ballistic Missile"),中国军网 (*chinamil.com.cn*), June 18, 2008.

43. Zhang Jian (章俭) and Guan Youxun (管有勋), eds., 15场空中战争 (*15 Air Wars*), Beijing, China: Liberation Army Press, p. 262.

44. Lewis and Xue, *Imagined Enemies*, 269.

45. "Missile Brigade Commander On How to Win A War From An Inferior Position," *Huojianbing Bao* (*Rocket Forces News*) in Chinese, 07 Jul 2001, CPP20011126000202.

46. For one take on this, see Robert Pape, *Bombing to Win: Air Power and Coercion in War*, Ithaca, NY: Cornell University Press, 1996.

47. Li Chenglong (黎成龙), "现代武库中的佼佼者—弹道导弹" ("Leader in the modern arsenal—ballistic missiles"), *PLA Daily*, November 20, 1995.

48. In addition to the below, see *SSAC*, pp. 51-52; 世界传奇, 中东战火 (*War in the Middle East*), Beijing, China: 世界知识出版社 (World Affairs Press), 2005, pp. 234-235; and Yang Xuhua, Xin Zhan Ce, *Psychological Warfare Strategy*, Beijing, China: National Defense University Press, 2004, Open Source Center, CPP20100729658001001, pp. 14, 33, 94.

49. 军事科学院军事历史研究部 (Military History Research Department, Academy of Military Science), 海湾战争全史 (*The Complete History of the Gulf War*), Beijing, China: PLA Press, 2000, pp. 319-320.

50. See video clip from Phoenix TV available from *v.ifeng.com/mil/200902/ea41bb1c-f5f5-4232-8796-ec1600fcbf55.shtml*.

51. SSAC, p. 52.

52. John Wilson Lewis and Xue Litai, *China's Strategic Seapower: The Politics of Force Modernization in the Nuclear Age*, Palo Alto, CA: Stanford University Press, 1994, p. 190.

53. *Zhanyi Xue*, p. 178; You Ji, *The Armed Forces of China*, New York: I.B. Tauris, 1999, p. 88.

54. Allen and Kivlehan-Wise, p. 166.

55. See Lewis and Xue, *Imagined Enemies*, p. 243.

56. Lewis and Xue, *China's Strategic Seapower*, 187.

57. Lu Chen (鲁晨), "从一场'另类战争'说起" ("Perspective from A Different Type of War"), *PLA Daily*, May 24, 2003.

58. See Second Artillery Force chapter in Lewis and Xue, *Imagined Enemies*.

59. See both Chapter 12 in SSAC, which emphasizes the role of missile forces in doing so, and Lewis and Xue, *Imagined Enemies*, p. 42.

60. SSAC, p. 318.

61. *Ibid.*, pp. 94, 303.

62. "PRC Expert Tells Global Times: Taiwan's Military Strategy Naïve and Dangerous," *Global Times Online,* February 4, 2010, CPP20100205722007.

63. *SSAC, p.* 84.

64. Zhao (赵), 摄战 (*Intimidation Warfare),* Beijing, China: PLA Publishing House, 2005, p. 244ff.

65. Cui Jicheng (崔继承), Cao Xueyi (曹学义), and Ding Jun (丁军), "精确制导武器新发展" ("New Developments in Precision Guided Weapons"), *PLA Daily*, November 27 , 2002; Zhou Liang (周梁), Jiang Dong (姜东), and Zhang Limin (张利民), "导弹智能化新趋势" ("New Trends in Smarter Guided Missiles"), *PLA Daily*, July 17, 2002; Zhan Haoming (詹皓名), "陆战火龙" ("Fiery Dragon of Ground War"), 国际展望 (*World Outlook*), Vol. 16, 2000, p. 42; Hou Yunli (侯云礼), "陆军地面战的' 杀手锏': 21世纪的地地战役战术弹道导弹" ("The Army's Surface War's Assassin's Mace: 21 Century Field Campaign Tactical Ballistic Missile").

66. For an exception, although not one from a particularly authoritative source, see Zhou Yi (周义), Wang Zhongyi (王忠义), and Wang Ziyan (王自焰).

67. Yuan Jun (袁俊), "国外巡航导弹防御的发展动态" ("The Development and Cruise Missile Defense in Foreign Countries"), 中国航天 (*Aerospace China*), March, 2000. *Aerospace China* is licensed by the PRC Ministry of Aerospace, and Yuan Jun, the author, is an analyst at its China Aviation Combined Technology Institute in Beijing.

68. Xu Hong (徐宏) and Li Wei (李伟), "21世界战略导弹是啥样?"("What Will Strategic Missiles Look Like in the 21st Century?"), 环球军事 (*Global Military*), Vol. 5, 2001. *Global Military* is published by the PLA Press in Beijing.

69. Quoting a 1997 PLA National Defense University (NDU) report, You Ji, *The Armed Forces of China*, p. 99.

70. Hou Yunli (侯云礼), "陆军地面战的' 杀手锏': 21世纪的地地战役战术弹道导弹" ("The Army's Surface War's Assassin's Mace: 21 Century Field Campaign Tactical Ballistic Missile").

71. 军事科学院军事历史研究部 (History Research Department, AMS), 海湾战争全史 (A Comprehensive History of Gulf War I), p. 337.

72. Yuan Jun (袁俊), "国外巡航导弹技术发展综述" ("Summary of Cruise Missile Technology in Foreign Countries"), 航空兵器 (*Aviation Weaponry*), Vol. 6, 2000. The military-affiliated China Aviation Missile Research Institute publishes *Aviation Weaponry*.

73. SSAC, p. 72. Also see Lewis and Xue, *Imagined Enemies*, pp. 134, 137, 200-201, 262; and Allen and Kivlehan-Wise, "Implementing PLA Second Artillery Doctrinal Reforms, p. 166.

74. Yuan Jun (袁俊), "现代巡航导弹的威胁特点及其对作战的影响" ("Modern Cruise Missiles' Specific Effects on Coercion and Operations"), 中国航天 (*Aerospace China*), January 1999.

75. Qu Dongcai (曲东才) and Zhou Shengming (周胜明), "战争中的开路急先锋: 讯航道" ("The Vanguard of Battle: The Cruise Missile"),中国航天 (*Aerospace China*), July 2000.

76. Lewis and Xue, *Imagined Enemies*, p. 212. Interestingly, later, the two authors turn this argument on its head. Above, the weakness of the air force is a reason to develop conventional ballistic missiles. But subsequently, Lewis and Xue note:

> the CMC [Central Military Commission] would prefer to threaten or "blockade" Taiwan by the use of missiles fired in measured numbers close to but not on the island itself. PLA generals hold that for such a calculated demonstration to force to work, the missile bases would have to be protected. That military requirement in turn would make the PLAAF [People's Liberation Army Air Force] Taipei's first target. If Taiwan's planes could easily destroy the air based protecting China's missile bases, the missile forces would face the fearsome use-it-or-lose it predicament. . . .

Ibid., p. 243.

77. As well as time sensitive terrorist targets. On the potential here, see Bruce M. Sugden, "Speed Kills: Analyzing the Deployment of Conventional Ballistic Missiles," *International Security*, Vol. 34, No. 1, 2009, pp. 113-146.

78. Christopher P. Twomey, *The Military Lens: Doctrinal Differences and Deterrence Failure in Sino-American Relations*, Ithaca, NY: Cornell University Press, 2010.

79. Lewis and Xue, *Imagined Enemies*, pp. 179-181.

80. Again, this author is persuaded by the cost benefit and strategic calculations in a number of studies suggesting offensive missiles have advantages over missile defenses. Culora, "The Strategic Implications of Obscurants"; and Hoyler "China's 'Antiaccess' Ballistic Missiles and US Active Defense." For a broader assessment of these issues, see Paul Bracken, "Technology and the Military Face of Asian Security," Sheldon Simon, ed., *The Many Faces of Asian Security*, New York: Rowman and Littlefield Publishers, 2001.

CHAPTER 5

CHINESE LESSONS FROM THE GULF WARS

Dean Cheng

EXECUTIVE SUMMARY

This chapter analyzes Chinese military writings about U.S. wars with Iraq to determine what possible lessons the Chinese People's Liberation Army (PLA) may have learned from them.

MAIN ARGUMENT

PLA writings suggest that these two wars have been very influential, affecting Chinese tactical, operational, and strategic thinking. Not only have these wars affected Chinese military doctrine, promoting greater jointness, but they have also underscored the impact of information technology. This is reflected not only in an emphasis on increasing access to information within all aspects of Chinese military operations (the "informationalization" of the PLA), but also has led to renewed emphasis on political warfare, as embodied in the concepts of psychological warfare, public opinion warfare, and legal warfare.

POLICY IMPLICATIONS

The PLA, given its lack of combat experience, seems to be trying to compensate through the close study and analysis of other nations' wars — especially those of the United States. Especially influential have been the two Gulf Wars between the United States and Iraq.

PLA analysis of American military experience includes examination of the tactical, operational, and strategic levels of war. The resulting lessons learned affect the full range of Chinese military activities, including not only weapons acquisition, but doctrinal development and training. As important, it is leading Chinese military leaders to rethink their strategic approach to conflict.

PLA writings suggest that they consider political support from both elites and the public to be a key strategic center of gravity. These writings also suggest that the Chinese are likely undertaking measures in peacetime to influence domestic, American, and third-party elite and broader perceptions. This includes trying to create a legal environment that will be supportive of Chinese positions in the event of conflict, as well as influencing public opinion through media and public diplomacy.

INTRODUCTION

In thinking about the lessons the People's Republic of China (PRC), and especially the PLA, are likely to have derived from other nations' major wars, perhaps two of the most influential wars are those conducted by the United States in the Middle East: Operation DESERT SHIELD/DESERT STORM in 1991 and Operation IRAQI FREEDOM in 2003.

These two wars, set almost exactly 10 years apart, provided indications of what war in the post-Cold War environment, unconstrained by the superpower stand-off, might entail. They marked how the leading military power, the United States, fought what the Chinese term "local wars," and showcased modern military technology, not only in terms of long-range, precision strike weapons, but also command, control, communications, computers, intelligence, surveillance, and reconnaissance (C4ISR). Indeed, the two wars highlighted for the PLA the evolving role of information, not only at the tactical level, but also at the operational and strategic levels.

In examining the two wars, there is a wide range of Chinese discussions of the potential lessons that might be derived from each of these wars. To reduce this problem to manageable size, this chapter will focus on the high-intensity phase of operations in Operation IRAQI FREEDOM, lasting from March to April 2003 (sometimes termed "the march to Baghdad" in American writings). This will allow for some degree of comparability, since the problems of counterinsurgency are very different from those of high-intensity conflict; consequently, potential lessons learned are also likely to be less comparable with each other.

This chapter will examine these two major American wars in the Middle East and what lessons Chinese analyses would seem to have derived from these wars. It will begin with a brief survey of the two wars. It will then discuss some of the lessons that the Chinese military seems to have derived from both wars. It will then focus what the Chinese may have learned from the second Gulf War (Operation IRAQI FREEDOM), focusing on those lessons relating to the "three warfares."

Background: Two Clashes Between America and Iraq[1]

The first Gulf War began after Iraq invaded its neighbor, Kuwait, on August 2, 1990. Iraq's forces rapidly overwhelmed the small Kuwaiti military, and Iraqi president Saddam Hussein announced the incorporation of Kuwait into Iraq. On August 7, U.S. President George H. W. Bush decided that the Iraqi invasion required a U.S. response, and U.S. forces began to deploy to Saudi Arabia the next day.

Meanwhile, a series of 12 United Nations Security Council (UNSC) resolutions were passed, beginning on August 2 (UNSC Resolution 660), condemning the Iraqi invasion and culminating with UNSC Resolution 678, passed on November 29, which authorized all necessary means to drive Iraq out of Kuwait.[2]

With Iraq refusing to withdraw from Kuwait, the U.S.-led coalition commenced hostilities on January 17, 1991. After 38 days of aerial bombardment, Coalition ground forces (dominated by American units) began the ground offensive on February 24, 1991. After approximately 100 hours of ground combat, Iraq agreed to a cease-fire on February 27.

For the United States, victory was achieved at very low cost. U.S. casualties amounted to only 148 killed in action.[3] By contrast, most of the Iraqi forces that had been in Kuwait were shattered. Only five to seven of the 43 Iraqi divisions were still capable of offensive actions.[4] Iraqi casualties in the 6-week air and ground war were proportionately higher than those suffered in the Iran-Iraq War, which had lasted 464 weeks.[5]

According to the *PLA Encyclopedia*, the first Gulf War showed the importance of:

- Securing dominance of the electromagnetic spectrum.
- Aerial attacks as a strategic factor.
- Deception, coordinated operations among different services, and deep attacks in the rapid attainment of campaign objectives (战役目的).
- Fortifications and minefields.

- Logistical support to sustain high-technology weapons.[6]

Twelve years later, and a year and a half after the attacks on the World Trade Center and the Pentagon, the United States and Iraq found themselves again at war.

In the wake of the al-Qaeda attacks, the United States had toppled the Taliban in Afghanistan. Planning began soon thereafter for war with Iraq. In January 2002, U.S. President George W. Bush labeled Iraq, Iran, and North Korea as an "Axis of Evil."[7] American officials began to enunciate the argument that, in the face of potential terrorist threats, nations had a right to preemptive self-defense, with the clear implication that Washington would be justified in attacking Iraq for fear of the latter's support for terrorism.

Washington sought to garner international support for action against Iraq, while Baghdad attempted to forestall any such coalition. In January 2003, Saddam Hussein decided to allow United Nations (UN) weapons inspectors back into Iraq, to demonstrate his compliance with UN resolutions mandating his surrender of all weapons of mass destruction (WMD).[8]

Saddam's offer did not satisfy the U.S. Government, and in February 2003, U.S. Secretary of State Colin Powell addressed the UN to make the case for war. Despite his eloquence, the UNSC refused to approve a U.S.-United Kingdom (UK)-Spanish proposal to authorize force should Saddam and his sons refuse to depart Iraq and enter into exile.[9] The United States then chose to proceed anyway, forming a "coalition of the willing" to invade Iraq (composed primarily of itself and the UK). This coalition ultimately did not include Turkey, which foreclosed the possibility of a "northern" front of operations.

On March 20, 2003, U.S. forces bombed Dora Farms, where it was reported that the top Iraqi leadership, including Saddam Hussein, had gathered.[10] This effort, which was planned and executed in 6 hours, was intended to decapitate the Iraqi leadership.[11] It failed, as the reports of Iraqi leaders gathering at the site were false.

Unlike the first Gulf War, the ground war in Operation IRAQI FREEDOM began on March 21, after only a day of preliminary aerial bombardment. The U.S. 3rd Infantry Division (Mechanized) led a force ultimately totaling some five divisions (three Army, one Marine, one British) from Kuwait into Iraq. The 3rd Division advanced to An Nasariyah, then turned left towards Karbala and onwards to Baghdad, following the west bank of the Euphrates. Supporting it was the Marine 1st Division, which advanced along the east bank of the Euphrates. Despite massive sandstorms and sometimes fierce resistance, U.S. forces rapidly advanced on Baghdad. Saddam International Airport fell on April 3. On April 5, elements of U.S. Army units rolled into Baghdad. The move startled many Iraqi commanders, who had no idea that the U.S. ground forces had advanced so rapidly. The relative lack of resistance led U.S. commanders to abandon plans for a protracted siege of Baghdad, and instead push harder into the city. A subsequent incursion on April 7 resulted in U.S. forces occupying downtown Baghdad and led to the city's capitulation on April 9. By May 1, high-intensity combat operations in Iraq had ended.

PLA Lessons from the First Gulf War.

According to General Wang Baocun, "the Chinese military followed the progress of the [first Gulf] war closely. . . . It had a great effect on the PLA."[12] From this war, the PLA appears to have derived a range of lessons, from the strategic, through the operational, to the tactical.

At the strategic level, perhaps the most fundamental lesson is that the nature of warfare had radically changed. Whereas previous conflicts had been industrial wars that, like World War II, entailed the application of masses of manpower and equipment, the advent of new technologies had brought about Local Wars Under High-Technology Conditions (高技术条件下局部战争), also referred to as High-Technology Local Wars (高技术局部战争).

Such wars are marked by several characteristics, as evidenced in the first Gulf War:

- They are the product of advances in a broad range of scientific and technical fields. They generally involve the large-scale use of information technology, advanced materials, aerospace systems, and other advanced technologies in weapons systems.[13]
- These weapons systems do not operate in isolation, but instead are integrated with each other. Combat operations involve the linkage of reconnaissance, communications, command, weapons, and logistics systems into an integrated or unified combat system (一体化作战系统).[14]
- Local wars under high-tech conditions often cover vast expanses, which requires much more extensive command and control capability.[15] Chinese writings note that the Gulf War involved forces spread over some 140,000,000 square kilometers.[16]

- The rate of expenditure of weapons is much higher in such wars. In the Gulf War, the expenditure of munitions is assessed as 10 times that of the Korean War, and four times that of the Vietnam War.[17]

In order for the PLA to prepare for such wars, there was set forth in 1993 a new national military strategy, embodied within the "Military Strategic Guidelines for the New Period" ("新时期国家军事战略方针"). In addition to assessing the international security situation confronting the PRC and clarifying the role of the military in the context of overall national development, the Military Strategic Guidelines for the New Period laid out an assessment of the new nature of modern war and how the PLA should deal with the resulting challenges.[18] Embodied within these new Military Strategic Guidelines were the main areas for PLA modernization and reform. These included the incorporation of more science and technology within the PLA; enhancing the quality of PLA personnel; improving the PLA's organization and logistical infrastructure; and continued emphasis on ideological and political work.[19]

The 1990s then saw the PLA moving to fulfill these reforms. One essential achievement for the PLA was the incorporation of *the operational level of war*, embodied in greater thinking about campaigns, into their overall approach to conflict. The operational level of war is the linkage between the tactical level of war (where battles occur) and the strategic level of war (which sets out ultimate war aims). For the PLA, the operational level of war is comprised of campaigns, which are not simply large battles, but a series of battles, undertaken to achieve ends that are strategically significant.[20] In some cases, an entire local war may be resolved in one or a few campaigns.[21]

The importance of campaigns can be seen in the new combat regulations published in 1999, generically referred to as the "New Generation Operations Regulations" ("新一代作战条令"). These represented a wholesale change to PLA doctrine, placing campaigns at the forefront of the conduct of future operations. Furthermore, the capstone of these new operational directives is *The Essentials of Joint Campaigns of the Chinese People's Liberation Army* (中国人民解放军联合战役纲要). These regulations make it clear that the PLA must be prepared to fight future wars through the interplay of all of its services and the Second Artillery, rather than primarily relying on the ground forces. That is, for the PLA, future wars would be *joint* wars, fought at the campaign level.

Chinese interest in joint operations did not begin with the Gulf War. The PLA had already begun to adjust its organization in the mid-1980s, in light of what it had observed in the Fourth Middle East War, the American war in Vietnam, and the British experience in the Falklands.[22] Moreover, the PLA had also twice convened all-army conferences to discuss campaign-level theory (战役理论研讨会) in 1986 and 1988 and had also introduced the concept of joint operations as a topic of study in August 1987.

But the first Gulf War raised the prominence of joint operations. One PLA officer wrote that "the form of joint operations appearing in it [the Gulf War], of coordination among all service arms, will undoubtedly be a key trend of future war developments."[23] Another PLA analyst notes that the "characteristics of a joint operation of all branches of the military displayed in that war [the Gulf War] gave us a glimpse of things to come in the early 21st century."[24] This was echoed by the then-deputy director of the Academy of Military Science (AMS):

The Gulf War marked a big step forward in both military theory and practice. For instance, strategy and the battles were closely interwoven, with the latter playing a major role, sometimes overlapping with strategy and tactics.[25]

Joint operations are essential given the much expanded modern battlefield. Local Wars under High-Tech Conditions includes not only operations on land, at sea, and in the air, but also in outer space and the electromagnetic sphere. Similarly, they require not only traditional land, sea, and air forces, but also missile forces, special operations forces, and psychological warfare units.[26]

Within this context, the Gulf War also led to a variety of *tactical* and *technological shifts*. One is the establishment of a new "three attacks, three defends." In the 1970s, the "three attacks, three defends" referred to fighting against tanks, aircraft, and paratroopers while defending against nuclear, chemical, and biological weapons. By 2001, this had evolved to fighting against cruise missiles, stealth aircraft, and attack helicopters, while defending against precision strike, electronic interference, and enemy surveillance and reconnaissance.[27]

Just as the 1970s "three attacks, three defends" were a reflection of the greater importance of focused training, the new "three attacks, three defends" are described as reflecting the new situation confronting the PLA and represent an essential means of fighting and winning Local Wars Under High-Tech Conditions through joint operations.[28] In particular, the first Gulf War displayed the heightened importance of electronic and intelligence warfare, and of stratagem, as they "permeate campaigns and battles from beginning to end."[29] Similarly, General Wang Baocun suggests that a key PLA lesson from the first Gulf War was the focus on destroying Iraqi military command, control, communications, and intelligence (C3I) systems, in pursuit of the "decapitation principle."[30] This included strikes against military and civilian communications sites in both Iraq and Kuwait, as part of the opening salvo.[31]

A technological lesson from the first Gulf War was the enormously greater importance placed upon precision guided munitions (PGMs). While representing only 8 percent of the weapons expended, PGMs are said to have destroyed 40 percent of the high-value targets.[32] Such weapons, using a variety of guidance systems, may be launched from a variety of platforms, often at great distances. They are a fundamental reason why the battlefield is more expansive and more deadly.[33]

A final tactical and technological lesson was the enormously greater importance of space and electronic operations. In the Gulf War, for example, it is noted that the United States brought some 70 satellites to bear against Iraq. By PLA estimates, these satellites provided the United States with about 90 percent of its strategic intelligence and a substantial portion of its targeting information. Space systems also carried about 70 percent of all transmitted data for allied forces.[34] The ability to exploit space is seen as a major contributing factor to the Coalition's victory.[35]

PLA Lessons from the Second Gulf War.

In some ways, the second Gulf War served to reinforce and refine the lessons from the first Gulf War. Thus, *at the strategic level*, Chinese assessing the significance of the Iraq War seem to conclude that the world marked by "Peace and Development" is not very peaceful. Instead, the war against Iraq is seen as a warning to both the "Axis of Evil" nations and near-peer competitors not to challenge American leadership and dominance.[36]

Furthermore, according to a group of PLA officers drawn from the Academy of Military Sciences and the National Defense University, weakness or backwardness means that one will be beaten (落后就要挨打). In this regard, weakness refers not only to military capabilities, but to the full range of factors comprising comprehensive national power. At the onset of the first Gulf War, the American-led coalition isolated Iraq by imposing what amounted to a global cut-off of its trade. These sanctions remained in place even after the end of the war, limiting Baghdad's access to modern technology and weapons. Iraq was therefore badly outmatched in every way, economically and diplomatically as well as militarily, even before hostilities began in the second Gulf War.[37]

In addition, the second Gulf War further refined the PLA's understanding of local wars. From Local Wars Under High-Tech Conditions, the PLA transitioned to viewing future conflicts as Local Wars Under Informationalized (or Informationized, or Informatized) Conditions (信息化局部战争). This was reflected in the 2004 PRC *Defense White Paper*, which observes, "The forms of war are undergoing changes from mechanization to informationalization. Informationalization has become the key factor in enhancing the warfighting capability of the armed forces."[38] In a sense, the PLA has sharpened its focus from high-technology writ large to those that are associated with information.

At the operational level, this means a greater emphasis on information and the range of technologies associated with it, as well as operations to exploit the related advances that information technology has generated. As with the earlier interest in joint operations, this increased PLA attention to the potentials of information technology predates the second Gulf War. Wang Baocun, writing in 2001, notes five areas the PLA was already investigating:

1. Command, control, communications, computers, and intelligence (C4I) modernization;
2. Network-based wargaming;
3. Training of personnel in information warfare;
4. Conduct of information exercises;
5. Introduction of informationalized equipment.[40]

The second Gulf War highlighted the major advances the United States had already taken in these areas, and demonstrated how they had been operationalized and incorporated into U.S. forces. In particular, American forces seem to be operating in a more integrated, rather than just coordinated, form of joint operations. "With the arrival of informationalized warfare, integrated-style has already become a necessary form of joint operational command development."[41]

Subsequent Chinese writings also began to emphasize that PLA joint operations needed to move from multi-service planning to actual multiservice operations. That is, jointness was previously discussed in terms of creating a thorough joint campaign plan that would allow the disparate services to maximize their contribution. In the wake of the second Gulf War, though, the discussion shifted to joint forces actually operating together (rather than each simply contributing individually to the overall operation), as a function of shared information.

To achieve this greater jointness, PLA authors wrote that command and control structures should exploit the advances in information technology. One PLA analyst observed that, by virtue of more capable telecommunications equipment, the Anglo-American coalition forces in the second Gulf War were able to operate even more jointly than their predecessors had a decade earlier.[42] This was enhanced by the development and adoption of common software, standards, and engineering, which allowed both weapons and command systems across services to operate as a relatively seamless whole, and behave more like a truly joint organization.[43]

Reports suggest that the PLA began to increase both informationalization and integrated jointness after the second Gulf War. The Nanjing Military Region (MR), for example, "organized a war-zone joint-combat communications training" event in July 2004 to discuss army, navy, air force, and Second Artillery combat communications requirements.[44] As the news report observed, this is only part of the overall effort undertaken throughout the Nanjing MR to transition from *coordinated* joint operations towards *integrated* joint operations (从协同性联合作战向一体化联合作战方向发展).

Informationalization does not only benefit joint command and control, however, but assists decision-making in general. According to Chinese analyses, the Iraqi battlefield was virtually transparent — for the Coalition forces. U.S.-led forces had unrivaled access to space systems for reconnaissance, communications, navigation, weather forecasting, and global positioning. This allowed Coalition forces to accurately understand the battlefield situation, especially enemy dispositions, and then strike at essential targets with great precision. As a result, Iraqi forces could not hide, while Coalition forces could apply precision-guided munitions to maximum effect.[45] Recent Chinese military articles suggest that there is some effort underway to apply these lessons in their military exercises.[46]

Improvements in information technology have also accelerated command decisionmaking, allowing for more rapid actions and responses. Whereas the United States had needed 72 hours in the first Gulf War to establish targets for air strikes, this had been substantially reduced in the more recent war. The time required for selecting targets, gathering targeting information, transmitting it to strike units, and actually implementing an attack is measured in seconds, so that even mobile systems could now be targeted.[47]

Not surprisingly, reliance on informationalized weapons is increasing. Whereas only 8 percent of weapons used in the first Gulf War were precision munitions, in the second Gulf War, this had risen to over 90 percent, with over 7,000 PGMs fired in the first week alone.[48] Moreover, these weapons were generally more accurate and more powerful than their predecessors. As a result, what required 16-18 aircraft to destroy in the first Gulf War could be eliminated with one in the second; similarly, a carrier air wing could strike four times as many targets in the second Gulf War as in the first.[49]

In the view of the PLA, precision munitions will only become more important in the future, given their accuracy and lethality. Employed against an enemy's command and control infrastructure, as they were in the second Gulf War, an enemy's defenses will be rapidly disrupted, reducing their ability to resist and shortening the length of the conflict.

Why Did Iraq Do So Poorly?[50]

Given the imbalance of comprehensive national power, including economic strength, diplomatic access, and military capabilities, PLA analysts would seem to agree that Iraq's loss was a foregone conclusion. Iraqi strength was further sapped by nearly 20 years of war (including the Iran-Iraq War), and 13 years of economic sanctions. Iraq's military forces suffered from a "generation gap," when comparing their equipment with that of the Anglo-American coalition.

But some PLA analyses nonetheless conclude that Iraq could have waged a better defense. In particular, a more resolute resistance might have inflicted more losses on the American forces. Some believe that a more effective defense might have led to more American deaths, striking at the American "center of gravity (重心)," which is the desire to limit casualties.[51] Consequently, the Iraqi failure to inflict greater losses on Coalition forces, due to their half-hearted defense efforts, has attracted further PLA analysis.

Some of the Iraqi failures are attributed to conditions unique to their political situation. For example, Iraq clearly had not engaged in sufficient preparations for war. As the Coalition had required 3 months to build up their forces, the Iraqis could have taken advantage of that period to improve their own defenses, yet failed to do so. Most glaringly, they failed to convert their urban centers into defensive bastions. They did not construct fortifications and obstacles inside or outside the cities, nor did they lay minefields or build tunnels and other underground facilities to undergird their defenses. Even after the war began, the Iraqi military did not engage the American forces with heavy concentrations of firepower; instead, they dispersed their forces and assets (partly in order to avoid destruction by allied airpower).

Much of this failure to prepare is attributed to Saddam Hussein. As the dictator of Iraq, his strategic decisions hampered the defense. His underestimation of the Anglo-American intent to go to war retarded Iraqi war preparations, as well as defensive measures once the war had begun, such as the destruction of key bridges across the Tigris and Euphrates rivers.

Furthermore, Saddam himself was a problematic figure. His actions against the Kurdish and Shi'ite populations ensured that the nation would not be unified when confronted with an external threat. His imposition of a dictatorship and a cult of personality also detracted from his domestic legitimacy.[52] Moreover, his previous invasions of Iran and Kuwait had both failed, resulting in a 20-year legacy of military defeat, yet it also meant that he was seen as a regional hegemon by many other nations.[53] This resulted in a lack of support for his regime, even from nations that opposed the U.S. decision to go to war.

These weaknesses were exacerbated by allied efforts at undermining the will of the Iraqi military, population, and leadership. According to PLA analysts, the United States paid special attention to this "soft" form of warfare (软战). It sought, through a variety of means, to coerce Iraq to separate the government from the military, and both from the people, and to demoralize the military. American military operations were linked, in the Chinese view, to this "soft" war, engaging in "shock and awe" tactics once the decapitation effort had failed.[54] Thus, if the Iraq War was an opportunity to test advanced physical weaponry, it also provided an opportunity to test soft measures aimed at attacking an opponent's will.

THE THREE WARFARES AND THE SECOND GULF WAR

If information technology contributed substantially to both Gulf Wars (and markedly more so during the second than the first), the role of information shifted from the tactical and operational to the strategic in the second Gulf War. Informationalized warfare is marked by the struggle of stratagem, of policy, of morale, of thought, and of psychology. The ability to mold how information is perceived is now integral to warfare. As a result, both sides sought to weaken their opponent's will and support, maintain their own popular and military morale, and influence global views and positions.

These efforts to influence the popular will and shape perceptions, according to PLA writings, constitute "political combat styles under informationalized conditions" ("信息条件下的政治性作战样式\"). That is, they are forms of operations or campaigns.[55] They involve the use of national and military resources, consistent with military strategic guidance, to secure the political initiative and psychological advantage over an opponent, through strengthening one's own will, gaining allies, and debilitating an opponent.[56] Broadly speaking, these "styles" may be categorized as psychological warfare, public opinion warfare, and legal warfare, which are generally referred to as the "three warfares (三战)."

The PLA's interest in the three warfares predates the second Gulf War. In 2003, the PLA had set forth the "Chinese People's Liberation Army Political Work Regulations" ("中国人民解放军政治工作条例"). Among the tasks of political work, in Chapter 2,

Section 18, is conduct of the "three warfares" of psychological warfare, public opinion warfare, and legal warfare. The "three warfares" were not established due to the second Gulf War, but it would seem that additional impetus was imparted to their development by the recently concluded conflict.

Psychological Warfare.

The most basic of the "three warfares" is psychological warfare (although it is intimately linked to public opinion warfare and legal warfare). Psychological warfare is defined as conflict in the spiritual and psychological area (精神心理领域) and may be implemented at the tactical, operational, or strategic level. It operates with real and potential military power in the background, and employs various types of information as the main weapon. The purpose is to influence, constrain, and/or alter an opponent's thoughts, emotions, and habits, while at the same time strengthening friendly psychology.[57]

> There are myriad targets and objects of psychological warfare; it is applied against the enemy, but also against friends; it is targets externally, but also internally; it must deal with allied countries, but also the entire globe, and one must rely on the media acting in multiple directions jointly, with effective coverage of many areas, in order to comprehensively realize the various goals.[58]

Although much of the focus is on commanders and key decisionmakers, psychological warfare is also aimed at the broader civilian and military populations. It includes, but goes beyond, public opinion warfare and encompasses the range of actions that

171

will affect an opponent's population, social groups, military, government, and/or leadership, in terms of their beliefs and attitudes, including their will to resist. Thus, psychological warfare is seen as more than simply military propaganda, but is a reflection of comprehensive national power and overall national strength in psychological terms.[59]

In general, psychological warfare efforts can either narrowly focus on battlefield operations (e.g., through leaflets and broadcasts), or can operate more broadly, through propaganda measures and news and public opinion warfare. The narrower, tactical application requires understanding an opposing military's strengths and weaknesses, focusing on eroding the enemy military's psychology. The broader, more strategic forms of psychological warfare involve all the elements of national power, and are employed not only to bolster one's own military and population, but also seek to secure confidence and support from third parties and friendly states, and ideally to convert opponents to one's own cause.[60]

The strategic forms of psychological warfare have especially benefited from the proliferation of information technology, especially telecommunications and the Internet, as these allow one side to directly address the other side's civilian population and decisionmakers without having to first defeat their armed forces. Modern psychological warfare operations can have a real strategic impact, and have therefore grown from being a supplement to being a full partner for conventional military operations.[61]

Political mobilization of the populace is intimately linked with psychological warfare. Mobilization of the masses is one of the tools of strategic psychological warfare; conversely, enemy psychological warfare measures can obviate efforts at mobilizing the masses to support one's own efforts. For this reason, one PLA analysis concludes that it is essential to emphasize the justice of one's cause in order to secure both domestic and potential foreign popular support.[62] An opponent's psychological warfare efforts will conversely seek to call this justice into question.

To maximize effectiveness, Chinese writings suggest that psychological warfare will often begin before the formal commencement of open hostilities. This is based in part on the assessment that the purpose of psychological warfare measures is to influence the audience's emotions and assessment capacity, which will eventually influence their actions.[63] In order to do so, it needs to operate not only in the military and diplomatic realms, but also the political, economic, cultural, and even religious arenas, which cannot easily be done on short notice.

Psychological Warfare in the Second Gulf War. In the view of PLA analysts, the second Gulf War saw psychological operations conducted at an unprecedented scale and intensity, from the tactical to the strategic level, and engaging a range of both military and nonmilitary measures. In particular, the United States factored psychological warfare into all of its thinking from strategic decisions to operational plans, to actual tactical employment and military battles.

In the Chinese view, the United States began psychological warfare operations long before March 2003. The incessant claim that Iraq possessed WMD helped isolate Iraq from the rest of the international community. President Bush's description of Iraq as part of an "Axis of Evil" further linked Iraq with Iran and North Korea in the minds of many as a threat to global peace.[64] (These measures were also effective examples of public opinion warfare.) Meanwhile, the United States used a variety of diplomatic and economic means to try and isolate Iraq.[65]

As the onset of open hostilities drew closer, the United States directly called senior Iraqi officers on their personal cell phones and sent emails to their personal accounts, trying to induce them to surrender or otherwise not operate at full effectiveness. In other cases, the United States threatened Iraqi officers, should they employ WMD. Such measures sought to sow seeds of discord and mistrust within the senior Iraqi leadership, thereby dissipating solidarity at the very top.[66] The American government ensured that Iraq could not respond in kind by limiting Iraqi access to international media. For example, the United States pressured international satellite communications companies to limit Iraqi access, effectively implementing a strategic information blockade.[67]

Once the war began, the United States tried "decapitation" ("斩首行动") against Iraq by eliminating Saddam Hussein at the very outset. Having failed to kill Saddam, they then moved to "shock and awe operations" ("震慑作战"), bombing a range of Iraqi targets.[68] Unlike previous wars, however, the United States did not engage in a protracted aerial bombardment, but commenced ground operations within a day of the start of the bombing campaign. In doing so, it further underscored the massive scale of force being applied against Iraq. All of these efforts were intended not only to create military gains, but also sought to cripple Iraqi resistance by undermining their will to fight.

Psychological warfare was not one-sided, however. Chinese authors observe that, within the more constrained resources available to it, the Iraqi government also sought to employ psychological warfare, both to inspire greater resistance against the invaders and also to garner more support from abroad—or at least condemnation of the Anglo-American leaders of the coalition.

Once the war started, Saddam regularly appeared on television to show that he was, in fact, still alive and regularly exhorted the populace to resist the invaders. Iraqi Information Minister Muhammed Saeed al-Sahhaf, meanwhile, would highlight any American casualties or setbacks in his regular news briefings, and warned that if U.S. forces did not surrender, they would die in Iraq. These efforts not only countered American propaganda and helped stiffen Iraqi resistance, but in the Chinese view also gave the impression globally of stubborn Iraqi resistance and held forth the potential of major allied losses.[69]

However, in the end, the preponderance of coalition resources told, even in the psychological warfare arena. While Iraqi efforts could highlight credibility gaps in the American message, Iraq simply did not have the wherewithal to make its own message heard.

PLA lessons. For the PLA, the employment of psychological warfare operations in the second Gulf War offers a number of lessons. On the one hand, as PLA writings note, the human factor, the focus of psychological warfare efforts, remains the center of gravity. The Coalition forces, through their various psychological warfare efforts, caused the Iraqi military and civilian populace to lose faith in their ability to win.[70] Despite advances in technology, the human factor has not been eclipsed, and the failure to mobilize the masses, a crucial part of psychological warfare operations, can still lead to defeat.

On the other hand, popular support cannot be taken for granted. Despite fighting a defensive war against an external aggressor, the Iraqi government was not able to successfully mobilize the larger populace and sustain their support against the Anglo-American coalition.[71] This implies a continuing importance for political mobilization measures, a defensive component of psychological warfare.

Public Opinion Warfare.

Public opinion warfare (舆论战) refers to the use of various mass information channels, including the Internet, television, radio, newspapers, movies, and other forms of media, in accordance with an overall plan and with set objectives in mind, to transmit selected news and other materials to the intended audience. The goal is to generate public support both at home and abroad for one's own position and create opposition to one's enemy. It seeks to guide public perceptions and opinion so as to affect shifts in the overall balance of strength between oneself and one's opponent.[72] Although public opinion warfare employs the media and news organizations, in the Chinese context the two are distinct areas of study and have been since the 1990s.[73]

Just as advances in information technology allow one side to apply psychological pressure without having to first defeat the other side's military, it also significantly improves the ability to influence public opinion of both sides and of neutrals. Consequently, the media's role has advanced from being a strategic supplement, focusing on battlefield reports, to a type of "combat multiplier" that can help affect and decide the outcomes of conflicts.[74] In this view, public opinion is now a distinct, second battlefield, almost independent of the physical one.[75]

Public opinion warfare is linked to the issue of values; faced with the pressure of public opinion, few nations or political authorities would risk the opprobrium associated with being an aggressor. Instead, both sides will seek to employ various forms of media, including news broadcasts, to guide public opinion, obtain popular support, and try to influence third parties for support and sympathy. This is true not only in the pre-war phase, but even during a war, as modern media will subject every military action to close scrutiny.[76]

Public opinion warfare has already been employed in a number of local wars. When Mohammed Aideed's men dragged the bodies of American troops through the streets of Mogadishu, Somalia, in front of television cameras, this was an effective form of public opinion warfare, turning the American public against the war.[77]

Public opinion warfare was used by both sides, to some extent, in the first Gulf War. Iraq sought to justify its invasion of Kuwait by charging the Kuwaitis with siphoning oil illegally from disputed oil fields that underlay both countries. It also claimed that Kuwait was engaged in unreasonable territorial demands, referring to the disputed islands of Warbah and Bubiyan.[78] Both of these claims were used to influence global and regional public opinion.

The Coalition engaged in extensive public opinion warfare in the first Gulf War. An initial example is the claim that Iraqis had killed infants in Kuwaiti hospitals, taking them out of incubators.[79] Then, the Coalition obtained overwhelming UN support for the use of force to eject Iraq from Kuwait, signaling that Iraq was isolated and universally condemned and clearly calling into question the legitimacy of Iraq's actions. Once the conflict began, the U.S. side effectively flooded the airwaves with their version of developments. Although the war only lasted 42 days, the U.S. side held 98 news conferences.[80] Meanwhile, western news media constantly reported on the capabilities of advanced western weapons and munitions, further undermining Iraqi confidence.[81]

PLA Lessons. The second Gulf War demonstrated to the PLA how much further the state of the art had advanced in public opinion warfare. On the coalition side, public opinion warfare began long before hostilities were formally initiated. Since the first Gulf War, American media had constantly bombarded the U.S. audience, and much of the world, with messages demonizing Saddam Hussein and Iraq.[82] These negative messages had embedded themselves throughout the American body politic, and even in the larger international consciousness. President Bush's charge that Iraq was part of an "Axis of Evil" thus fell on fertile ground, after nearly a decade of acclimatization. To further support these efforts, in August 2002, the United States, with the help of Iraqi dissident groups and exiles, created a satellite television station.[83]

Once the decision was made to go to war, the media aspect of public opinion warfare intensified further. An "Office of Global Communications" was established in the White House to plan, coordinate, and manage news and information. This office helped create a public opinion and propaganda plan, based on, and in coordination with, the evolving war plans.[84] American spokesmen regularly provided talking points to both American and foreign news organizations, while senior officials regularly took to the airwaves.

Meanwhile, the United States also deployed a variety of assets to influence Iraqi public opinion. One is the EC-130E aircraft, an airborne television and broadcasting station capable of transmitting across a wide spectrum of frequencies including shortwave and television. These aircraft were deployed outside Iraq in December 2002, 3 months prior to the initiation of open warfare.[85] In addition, the U.S. Air Force (USAF) also engaged in massive leaflet drops, employing 158 aircraft to scatter 81 different types of leaflets.[86] Many Iraqi troops deserted their posts, after being warned by some of the leaflets that only areas that resisted would be bombed.

An especially effective means of influencing the global perception of the war was the "embed" program, and specifically the inclusion of foreign correspondents. On the one hand, there was a heavy presence of American journalists, whom Chinese analysts presumed will take a more pro-American stance. But by incorporating foreign journalists, including Chinese and other press who were skeptical of the United States, American public opinion warriors were able to project an image of objectivity and transparency. The United States effectively exploited these foreign voices, which as outsiders would be more readily accepted, to effectively speak on their behalf.[87]

Once hostilities began, public opinion warfare actively complemented military operations. The American media regularly aired claims that Saddam had been wounded, or that senior Iraqi leaders had been killed or had surrendered. These reports served to undermine Iraqi morale and helped precipitate the desertion or surrender of Iraqi troops, often without having to fight them.[88] This served the larger goal of eliminating Iraqi resistance with minimal bloodshed.

Similarly, when the U.S. advance slowed, there was extensive reporting by the press that this was rooted in Anglo-American concern about creating civilian casualties. "American media used reality to disguise their real goals and perspective, and invisibly guided public opinion."[89] Thus, one PLA volume concludes, given "the American military ability to easily take Baghdad, and the 'evaporation' of several hundred thousand Iraqi troops, it should be noted that American broadcasting strategy had achieved fairly good results."[90]

This complementarity was not one-way, however. Military operations were apparently at times undertaken in order to provide suitable material for public opinion warfare. Thus, Chinese observers note that, unlike in previous wars such as the Balkan conflict, the United States in this conflict did not immediately destroy the Iraqi communications and broadcasting infrastructure, even as it did interfere with Iraqi broadcasts. Instead, these facilities were allowed to remain on the air, so that the United States could exploit their frequencies to broadcast false messages and inaccurate information to further sap Iraqi will and foment societal disruption. Preserving Iraqi broadcast facilities also allowed the United States to claim that it was fighting a "clean" war, since Iraqi broadcasts aided in "transparency."

Iraqi efforts at public opinion warfare were effective, albeit limited. Indeed, Iraq made adroit use of its limited resources, as well as third party assets such as al-Jazeera, to access the Arab and Muslim world in the effort to win more public support.[91] One author observes that, when Iraqi chemical warfare experts appeared on television on March 27, the resulting images of American troops putting on their protective gear was greatly embarrassing, as no chemical or biological attacks were forthcoming. Meanwhile, Iraqi officials regularly appeared on television, not only to present the Iraqi version of events, but also to disprove American allegations that some had been killed or had defected.[92] Both sides were engaged in a struggle for credibility, an essential element of public opinion warfare.

Ultimately, however, Iraqi efforts were insufficient. Part of this was because of the capabilities available to the United States. Images and information were now digitized and easily transmitted and were often passed in real-time. Western media organizations, exploiting advances in modern technology, provide unprecedented reach for public opinion warfare efforts. The United States employed dozens of satellites to transmit information globally so as to influence both public opinion and the psychology of foreign leaders and populations while denying the Iraqis the ability to counter their efforts.[93] Indeed, at times the *only* source of information was British or American sources.

Not only was Iraq over-matched, but also their efforts were mostly concentrated at the tactical level. Unlike the Americans, the Iraqi leadership lacked the broader vision to undertake strategic level public opinion warfare.[94]

PLA lessons. From observing the second Gulf War, PLA analysts emphasize that it is essential that public opinion warfare be undertaken carefully and with a strategic perspective that looks at the overall objectives of a conflict. Public opinion warfare should complement psychological warfare, as well as general military operations. Similarly, military operations, or leaks of information relating to them, may be undertaken to support psychological and public opinion warfare efforts. Overall, public opinion warfare strategy should incorporate and address political, diplomatic, military, economic, scientific and technical (S&T), and other aspects. It should also take into account Party interests.[95]

Within this perspective, Chinese analyses suggest that public opinion warfare must follow an established plan and operate under a command structure. Only an integrated policy and unified command approach can allow such a complex piece of systems engineering to succeed. But the actual decisionmaking needs to be rapid and flexible, because in the world of public opinion, the first impression is key. Public opinion warfare must therefore assume a more offensive stance.

Moreover, as seen in the second Gulf War, "before the troops and horses move, public opinion is already underway (兵马未动，舆论先行)."[96] The leadership and coordination structure for public opinion warfare needs to be put in place prior to the outbreak of hostilities, because the scale of planning, as well as implementation, of public opinion warfare cannot be achieved on the fly.

The creation of the Ministry of National Defense Press Affairs Office (also known as the Ministry of National Defense Information Office) in 2008 was potentially motivated, in part, by the interest in shaping domestic and foreign views of China's military, including in peacetime. PLA officers assigned to this office now regularly give press briefings, answer questions, and release official statements.[97] The formation of this office may constitute an organizational response to lessons learned from the second Gulf War. Similarly, courses that teach Chinese military officers how to talk to the foreign press are being incorporated into Chinese professional military education (PME).[98]

Another lesson that PLA analysts seem to have drawn is that the United States, with its media strength, has an overwhelming advantage in the ability to shape public opinion to its own ends. "American media has strong real strength, operates on a large scale, and advanced technology."[99] In the recent war, the United States rapidly put those strengths to work by rapidly creating a public opinion warfare campaign plan and implementation structure.

These strengths and advantages were further magnified because, as Chinese writings consistently suggest, the Western media, especially American and British news organizations, were aligned with, if not actively subordinate to, the Anglo-American authorities. The U.S. Government is described as employing CNN and NBC to influence both American and global public opinion in support of the war with Iraq.[100] Another volume describes the American media as attacking Iraq and accusing Saddam of possessing WMD because it was under the control of the government and the military (美国媒体又在政府和军方的操控下).[101]

This is not necessarily described in pejorative terms. Rather, crafting public opinion is seen as an essential role of the media.

> In the period of preparing for war . . . not only do media make it appear to the masses/public that there are few choices, but also inevitably will describe the enemy as posing a serious threat, so that one's own nation has no choice but to engage in self defense. Clear evidence of this is that after the "9-11" incident, the U.S. government and the media both widely discussed the "Axis of Evil."[102]

For developing nations, not only must they research how to counter the *military* advantages of a hegemon, but also how to handle the *public opinion* and *broadcasting* advantages of a hegemon. As one Chinese article puts it, wartime news and propaganda guidelines should seek to establish news dominance (新闻权), and information dominance (信息权), on the path to obtaining psychological dominance (心理权).[103]

In this regard, it is therefore interesting to consider the recent Chinese decision to create a 24-hour English-language global news service under the aegis of *Xinhua*.[104] Given the concern about shaping public opinion, and the belief that such news organizations as CNN and Fox News are in the service of the U.S. Government, it may well be that this new news entity reflects a major "lesson learned" from the Gulf War.

Legal Warfare.

Legal warfare (法律战) is defined as the use of both domestic and international law, as well as the laws of armed conflict (武装冲突法), to garner international and domestic support by presenting oneself as the more just or virtuous side in legal terms.[105] The basic form (基本样式) of legal warfare is described as arguing that one's own side is obeying the law, accusing the other side of violating the law (违法), and making arguments for one's own side in cases where there are also violations of the law. Legal warfare appears to have gained more prominent public attention beginning in 2003, although it is not clear whether this is linked to the second Gulf War.[106]

The essence of legal warfare, as with the other two warfares, is political warfare, with the aim of helping one's own side to secure the initiative in wartime. Legal warfare also seeks to gain greater support, both at home and abroad, by helping one's own side claim to be in the right.

Implementing "legal warfare" is to gain the right in warfare. Regardless of whether a war is just or not (正义与否), the two sides in a war will both make every effort to develop "legal warfare," and seek out means of constructing legal bases for undertaking the war, and confirm that they themselves are the reasonable and legal side.[107]

Also as with the other two warfares, legal warfare is seen as closely linked with typical military operations. Military conflict encompasses legal warfare, while legal warfare permeates the entire course of military conflict. However, legal warfare often precedes military conflict, and will frequently be sustained after the military conflict has concluded.[108]

In its recent local wars, the United States has sought to use international law to explain and justify its actions. This was evident in the first Gulf War, where the United States exploited its reputation as a nation that abides by international law to justify its involvement in the Iraq-Kuwait conflict. Thus, the United States sought UN authorization at the very outset of that conflict, and by gaining it, fought the war under putative UN, and not simply American, auspices.[109]

The tables were turned in the Kosovo War, when, in the Chinese view, the United States bypassed the UN in implementing a military solution. However, the United States employed the North Atlantic Treaty Organization's (NATO) common defense stipulation to address the legal issue. It broadly propagandized that this action was "consistent with the law" ("合法性"). It deluded many people in the Western nations and caused the Kosovo War to be considered a "legal" war in the West.[110]

185

Legal warfare in the second Gulf War. In the second Gulf War, the United States linked legal warfare to psychological and public opinion warfare. It began by demonizing the Iraqi regime as part of the "axis of evil," and exploiting the media to develop popular support for war with Iraq. It also began to promulgate the doctrine of "preemption" ("先发制人"), which it claimed was legal. The right of preemptive self-defense to counter terrorism thus was inserted into the American consciousness, which the administration exploited to persuade the American Congress to pass an authorization of the use of military force. The Americans then used this domestic construct to seek support from other nations.

When the United States was nonetheless unable to secure UNSC approval for war, it then claimed that Iraq was in violation of previous UNSC resolutions regarding weapons inspections. These prior resolutions were portrayed as justifying the American issuance of an ultimatum to Iraq prior to commencing hostilities.

By contrast, Iraq was much better able to engage in legal warfare, at least in the pre-war phase. In particular, by agreeing to UN inspections during the debate over UNSC Resolution 1441, Iraq short-circuited UN approval of the United States going to war. It therefore effectively frustrated American legal warfare efforts. Subsequently, when the United States demanded UN authorization to issue an ultimatum to Baghdad, the Iraqi diplomats at the UN rebutted that demand with reference to the UN Charter.[111]

It was during the war, however, that the American use of legal warfare came into its own. For example, the United States contacted senior Iraqi officers to warn them that any use of WMD would result in war crimes trials after the conflict, and that "I was only following orders" would not be a defense. U.S. officials also implied that Iraqi deployment of forces in urban areas endangered civilian lives, and therefore also potentially violated the laws of armed conflict. Such measures, it is suggested, may have not only provided legal cover for U.S. actions, but also sapped the will of Iraqi military officers.

Meanwhile, the United States also used legal warfare to defend its own actions. For example, Coalition forces claimed that they had minimized collateral damage by employing PGM. At the same time, citing exceptions to various international laws, Coalition forces at times also attacked other civilian targets on the grounds that Iraq had exploited civilian facilities or hidden weapons in residential areas.

PLA lessons. One of the lessons that PLA authors mention is the need to integrate legal warfare efforts into the broader psychological warfare effort and with military operations.[112] The tenor of some of the Chinese writings on this subject seems to imply that legal warfare is less of an independent military operation than psychological warfare or public opinion warfare, although it supports both of those other forms of political warfare. This is not to denigrate the importance of legal warfare, however.

Indeed, considerations of legal warfare may have been a fundamental motivation for the creation of the PRC Anti-Secession Law of 2005. This law essentially argues that any attempt at seceding from China is fundamentally illegal. The creation of such a law would seem to be consistent with one PLA analysis that emphasizes the need to "pay attention to legal warfare requirements, and then promptly supplement domestic laws in key areas where there are gaps, so that legal warfare has laws it can rely upon."[113] Indeed, the publicity China accorded this piece of legislation suggests that they were also conforming with the recommendation that domestic laws be publicized to the world, "so that domestic laws' relevant regulations are recognized by the international community."[114] China has essentially informed both Taiwan and the world of the consequences of attempting to secede. It may be that Chinese claims to various territories such as the South China Sea and the Arctic, in addition to setting out Chinese interests, may also constitute a form of legal warfare, as other nations are notified of China's interests and, to some extent, their intentions.

INTERIM CONCLUSIONS

The two U.S.-Iraq wars have been key milestones for PLA analyses of the state of the art of local wars. The first Gulf War provided key contributions for the development of the current *gangyao* (纲要) that govern PLA operations. It is likely that lessons from the 2003 march to Baghdad have provided further material for PLA analyses, and those conclusions will be incorporated into the next iteration of Chinese regulations — if they have not been already.

Both wars, in the Chinese estimation, were decisively affected by high technology. In the second Gulf War, this aspect was brought into higher relief. The key form of high technology is information technology. The collection, control, management, transmission, and exploitation of information is the key to modern warfare — and not just by military authorities, but by the strategic decisionmakers and the masses.

The impact of information at the tactical and operational levels was the most visible, with video images of precision-guided munitions striking various targets, and American forces advancing incessantly, even in the face of massive sand storms. But PLA writings suggest that an essential lesson for Chinese officers is that information warfare is as much a strategic level action with tactical effects as it is tactical or operational level efforts that may lead to strategic consequences. Thus, what seems to bind Chinese analyses of the two Iraq Wars together is an evolving understanding that the true "key point" ("重点") of Local Wars Under Modern Conditions is information at the tactical, operational, and strategic level. Each of the "three warfares" represents a different way of exploiting and manipulating that information for a variety of audiences.

One of the interesting implications of this emphasis on information manipulation (and at some level, perception management) is that it could jeopardize the efficacy of People's War. As one PLA volume notes, the most outstanding characteristic of people's war is the broad participation of the masses.[115] Modern technology offers the masses more ways to participate in local wars, as well as to express their support. But the willingness of the masses to participate in a conflict, to lend their support, assumes a population that is and remains supportive of the conflict.

The very focus of the three warfares is to generate divides within the population and between the population and the leadership and to demoralize the population as it fragments, also through the use of modern information technology. Successfully applied against a population, the three warfares are, in some ways, antithetical to the concepts of People's War. One would therefore expect the PRC to develop counters to the three warfares. It may be that the reputed "Great Fire-

189

wall of China" and the recent controversy involving Google reflect precisely such efforts.

Policy Implications for the United States.

At this point in time, there is no reason to believe that the Chinese military or political leadership *seek* a conflict with the United States, but, like any rational politico-military leadership, they are almost certainly hedging against that possibility. Given what the Chinese seem to have learned from American military operations in Iraq over two wars, it is important for American policymakers to recognize that the Chinese are likely engaging in "combat preparation" in not only the physical and cyber arenas, but also the political. Therefore, American military and political planners should not only be engaging in traditional military planning for conflict (including continued research and development into the next generation of advanced weapons), but as important, should be considering how they will engage China in the political realm.

In this light, American policymakers, both military and civilian, must recognize that, in the event of a conflict with the PRC, the ability to gain domestic and international support can no longer be taken as a given. Indeed, China seems to already be taking steps to ensure international neutrality, if not support, and will be seeking to influence American opinion, both elite and popular, while safeguarding their own public from foreign influence. By contrast, American public diplomacy, much less psychological warfare and "military information support to operations (MISO)," are subject to a variety of laws such as the Smith-Mundt Act of 1948. Formulated in the heyday of print and radio journalism, these laws and regulations inevitably fail to take into account the realities of today's far more interconnected world, much less the Internet and social media. Modernization of the equipment of the American armed forces should therefore be complemented by updating both policies and legislation regarding political influence and outreach.

ENDNOTES - CHAPTER 5

1. In order to differentiate between the two wars, the first war, comprising Operation DESERT SHIELD/DESERT STORM, will be referred to as "the Gulf War," or "the first Gulf War." The second, Operation IRAQI FREEDOM, will be referred to as "the Iraq War," or "the second Gulf War."

2. Bruce W. Watson, Bruce George, Peter Tsouras, and B. L. Cyr, *Military Lessons of the Gulf War*, Novato, CA: Presidio Press, 1991, p. 223.

3. Frank N. Schubert and Theresa L. Kraus, eds., *The Whirlwind War*, Washington, DC: Center for Military History, 1995, p. 201. More Americans died in accidents during the war than in combat. Dilip Hiro, *Desert Shield to Desert Storm*, New York: Routledge Press, 1992, p. 397.

4. Schubert and Kraus, eds., p. 201.

5. Hiro, p. 396.

6. PLA Encyclopedia Committee, *Chinese Military Encyclopedia*, Vol. VII, Beijing, China: Academy of Military Science Publishing House, July 1997, p. 404.

7. Michael R. Gordon and Bernard E. Trainor, *Cobra II*, New York: Pantheon Books, 2006, p. 36.

8. *Ibid.*, p. 119.

9. *Ibid.*, p. 165.

10. Thomas E. Ricks, *Fiasco*, NEW YORK: Penguin Books, 2007, p. 118; and Gordon and Trainor, pp. 169-177.

11. Gordon and Trainor, p. 169.

12. Major General Wang Baocun, "China and the Revolution in Military Affairs (1)" *China Military Science*, No. 4, 2001 (English language Ed.), p. 151.

13. Gao Hongchun, ed., *National Defense Knowledge*, National Defense Teaching Materials, Vol. III, Beijing, China: AMS Publishing, January 2003, p. 120, 124.

14. *Ibid.*, p. 125.

15. *Ibid.*, pp. 125-126.

16. Wang Houqing and Zhang Xingye, *The Science of Campaigns*, Beijing, China: NDU Publishing House, 2000, p. 400.

17. Gao Hongchun, ed., p. 127.

18. For a full discussion of the Military Strategic Guidelines for the New Period, including what is encompassed within them, see David Finkelstein, "China's National Military Strategy: An Overview of the 'Military Strategic Guidelines," in *Right-Sizing the People's Liberation Army: Exploring the Contours of China's Military*, Roy Kamphausen and Andrew Scobell, eds., Carlisle, PA: Strategic Studies Institute, U.S. Army War College, 2007, pp. 69-140.

19. Finkelstein, Kamphausen and Scobell, eds., pp. 118-123.

20. Xue Xinglin, ed., *Campaign Theory Learning Guide*, Beijing, China: National Defense University Publishing House, November 2001, p. 36.

21. Wang Houqing and Zhang Xingye, Chief eds., *The Science of Campaigns*, Beijing, China: National Defense University Publishing House, May 2000, p. 9.

22. He Tiaoqing, chief ed., *Campaign Teaching Materials*, Beijing, China: Academy of Military Sciences Press, 2001, p. 71.

23. Gao Yubiao, chief ed., *Joint Campaign Teaching Materials*, Beijing, China: Academy of Military Science Publishing House, 2001, pp. 11-12.

24. Lieutenant Colonel Wu Jianchu, "Joint Operations – The Basic Form of Combat on High-Tech Terms," *China Military Science* , No. 4, 1995, *Foreign Broadcast Information Service - China* (FBIS-CHI), April 1996.

25. Colonel Zhou Xiaopeng, "On the Development of Joint Operations Theory," *China Military Science*, May, 1996, in FBIS-CHI, May 1996.

26. Shi Yukun, "Lt. Gen. Li Jijun Answers Questions on Nuclear Deterrence, Nation-State, and Information Age," *China Military Science* , No. 3, 1995, in FBIS-CHI, August 1995.

27. Gao Hongchun, ed., pp. 127-130.

28. "PLA Displays New 'Three Attacks, Three Defends,'" *Chen Bao*, Hong Kong, August 1, 2001, available from *military. china.com/zh_cn/head/83/20010806/10073959.html*.

29. Tan Wenhu, "Large Scale Joint Use of Forces for Disaster Relief Leads to Military Training Innovation and Development," *People's Liberation Army Daily*, July 1, 2008, *www.chinanews.com.cn/ gn/news/2008/07-01/1298392.shtml*.

30. Guo Meichu, *Discussion of High-Tech Local Wars*, Beijing, China: AMS Publishing, 2003, pp. 174-176.

31. Wang Baocun, "China and the Revolution in Military affairs (1)," p. 151.

32. Ma Yu, "Informationalized Warfare and Communications Mobilization," *China Defense Newspaper*, September 29, 2003.

33. Wang Baocun, "China and the Revolution in Military affairs (1),"p. 151.

34. Li Yinglian, Hong Xiangsheng, Gao Zhen, "The Categories

of Forms of High-Tech Operations," *China Military Science*, No. 2, 1995, pp. 104-109.

35. Gao Yubiao, chief ed., p. 54.

36. Chang Xianqi *et al.*, *Military Astronautics*, 2nd Ed., Beijing, China: National Defense Industries Press, January 2005, p. 249.

37. He Zhu, *Experts Discuss the Iraq War*, Beijing, China: AMS Publishing, January 2004, pp. 176-177.

38. *Ibid.*, pp. 141, 144.

39. PRC State Council Information Office, *China's National Defense in 2004*, Beijing, China: State Council Information Office, 2004.

40. Wang Baocun, "China and the Revolution in Military Affairs (2)," *China Military Science*, No. 5, 2001, p. 149.

41. Ren Haiquan, "Exploring the Path of Integrated-Style Joint Operations Command," *People's Liberation Army Daily*, September 20, 2005.

42. Li Daguang, "Space Dominance: The Basis for Victory in Information War," *China Defense Newspaper*, January 6, 2004.

43. Li Yingming *et al.*, "An Analysis of Integrated Joint Operations," *People's Liberation Army Daily*, April 12, 2005.

44. Sun Xi'an and Wang Xiongli, "PLA Nanjing MR Conducted Tri-Service Communications Exercise in July," *People's Front Line*, July 15, 2004, FBIS-CHI.

45. He Zhu, *Experts Discuss the Iraq War*, pp. 82-83.

46. See, for example, Li Yandong *et al.*, "PLA Exercise Involves Real-Time Intelligence Collection, Involving 20+ Types of Recon Techniques," *People's Liberation Army Daily*, December 27, 2010; and "Jinan PLA Exercise Greatly Successful," *People's Liberation Army Daily*, January 25, 2011.

47. Chang Xianqi, *Military Astronautics*, p. 261.

48. Fang Qiumin, "Four Major Aspects of Lessons from the Iraq War for Modern Warfare," *National Defense*, No. 9, 2003.

49. Chang Xianqi, *Military Astronautics*, p. 261.

50. This section draws heavily upon He Zhu, *Experts Discuss the Iraq War*, pp. 93-96, 141-146.

51. *Ibid.*, p. 111.

52. *Ibid.*, pp. 143-144.

53. *Ibid.*, p. 142.

54. *Ibid.*, p. 86.

55. He Diqing, chief ed., *Campaign Studies Teaching Materials*, Beijing, China: AMS Press, 2001, p. 50.

56. Academy of Military Sciences Operations Theory and Regulations Research Department and Informationalized Operations Theory Research Office, *Informationalized Operations Theory Study Guide*, Beijing, China: AMS Press, November, 2005, p. 403.

57. *Ibid.*, p. 404.

58. Nanjing Political Academy Military News Department Study Group, "Study of the Journalistic Media Warfare in the Iraq War," *China Military Science*, No. 4, 2003, p. 30.

59. National Defense University Research Section, *New Concepts of the Military Transformation*, Beijing, China: PLA Press, 2004, pp. 196-197.

60. *Informationalized Operations Theory Study Guide*, pp. 404-405.

61. National Defense University Research Section, *New Concepts of the Military Transformation*, Beijing, China: PLA Press, 2004, p. 199.

62. Wang Yongming *et al.*, *Research on the Iraq War*, Beijing, China: AMS Publishing, June 2003, p. 229.

63. *Informationalized Operations Theory Study Guide*, p. 405.

64. Nanjing Political Academy Military News Department Study Group, "Study of the Journalistic Media Warfare in the Iraq War," *China Military Science*, No. 4, 2003, p. 28.

65. Fan Gaoming, "Public Opinion Warfare, Psychological Warfare, and Legal Warfare, the Three Major Combat Methods to Rapidly Achieving Victory in War," *Global Times*, March 8, 2005.

66. Nanjing Political Academy Military News Department Study Group, "Study of the Journalistic Media Warfare in the Iraq War," *China Military Science*, No. 4, 2003, p. 30.

67. Fan Gaoming.

68. He Zhu, pp. 73-74.

69. *Ibid.*, p. 111.

70. Liu Gaoping, *Study Volume on Public Opinion Warfare*, Beijing, China: NDU Press, 2005, p. 197.

71. Tang Qunshen *et al.*, "Why Did We Not See People's War in Iraq?" *Guofang*, No. 8, 2003.

72. *Informationalized Operations Theory Study Guide*, p. 405; and Liu Gaoping, pp. 16-17.

73. Liu Gaoping, p. 5.

74. *Ibid.*, p. 68.

75. Nanjing Political Academy Military News Department Study Group, "Study of the Journalistic Media Warfare in the Iraq War," *China Military Science*, No. 4, 2003, p. 28.

76. Academy of Military Sciences Operations Theory and Regulations Research Department and Informationalized Opera-

tions Theory Research Office, *Informationalized Operations Theory Study Guide*, Beijing, China: AMS Press, November, 2005, p. 406.

77. "In Modern Warfare, Public Opinion Warfare, Psychological Warfare, and Legal Warfare Are All Frenetically Developing," *People's Liberation Army Daily*, April 1, 2004.

78. Those islands were at the heart of the 1961 conflict between Iraq and the then newly independent state of Kuwait.

79. Liu Gaoping, pp. 160-161.

80. *Ibid.*, p. 69.

81. *Ibid.*

82. Nanjing Political Academy Military News Department Study Group, p. 28.

83. *Ibid.*, p. 29.

84. *Ibid.*

85. Liu Gaoping, p. 71.

86. Fan Gaoming.

87. Nanjing Political Academy Military News Department Study Group, p. 32.

88. Liu Gaoping, p. 107.

89. Nanjing Political Academy Military News Department Study Group, p. 31.

90. Liu Gaoping, p. 70.

91. Nanjing Political Academy Military News Department Study Group, p. 32.

92. Liu Gaoping, pp. 72-73.

93. Fan Gaoming.

94. Nanjing Political Academy Military News Department Study Group, p. 29.

95. Liu Gaoping, pp. 87-93.

96. Nanjing Political Academy Military News Department Study Group, p. 28.

97. For further discussion of this office, see Matthew Boswell, "Media Relations in China's Military: The Case of the Ministry of National Defense Information Office," *Asia Policy*, No. 8, July 2009, pp. 97-120.

98. Thomas Bickford, "Trends in Education and Training, 1924-2007: From Whampoa to Nanjing Polytechnic," in *The "People" in the PLA: Recruitment, Training, and Education in China's Military*, Roy Kamphausen, Andrew Scobell, and Travis Tanner, eds., Carlisle, PA: Strategic Studies Institute, U.S. Army War College, 2008, p. 38.

99. Nanjing Political Academy Military News Department Study Group, p. 33.

100. Fan Gaoming.

101. Liu Gaoping, p. 27.

102. *Ibid.*, p. 161.

103. Nanjing Political Academy Military News Department Study Group, p. 30.

104. "Xinhua Launches CNC World English Channel," *Xinhua*, July 1, 2010, available from *news.xinhuanet.com/english2010/china/2010-07/01/c_13378575.htm*.

105. *Informationalized Operations Theory Study Guide*, p. 406; and Cheng Hui, "China's Military Begins Research and Training in Public Opinion Warfare, Psychological Warfare, and Legal Warfare," *Xinhuanet*, June 22, 2004.

106. Han Yanrong, "Legal Warfare: Military Legal Work's High Ground: An Interview with Chinese Politics and Law University Military Legal Research Center Special Researcher Xun Dandong," *Legal Daily*, PRC, February 12, 2006.

107. Fan Gaoming.

108. Cheng Hui.

109. Fan Gaoming.

110. *Ibid.*

111. Liu Kexin, chief ed., *Legal Warfare Knowledge Study Volume*, Beijing, China: National Defense University Press, 2006, pp. 298, 310-311.

112. Liu Jiaxing, "General's Views: Legal Warfare — Modern Warfare's Second Battlefield," *Guangming Daily*, November 3, 2004.

113. *Ibid.*

114. *Ibid.*

115. Luo Youli, *National Defense Theory*, National Defense Teaching Materials, Vol. II, Beijing, China: AMS Press, 2003, p. 112.

CHAPTER 6

PEOPLE'S LIBERATION ARMY LESSONS LEARNED FROM RECENT PACIFIC COMMAND OPERATIONS AND CONTINGENCIES

Frank Miller

EXECUTIVE SUMMARY

This chapter highlights lessons learned by the People's Liberation Army (PLA) from its studies of and interactions with the U.S. Pacific Command (PACOM), including their evolving motivations and areas of interests.

MAIN ARGUMENT

China's main purpose for interacting with the U.S. military was to assist in the modernization of the PLA. As the combatant command responsible for the Asia-Pacific Region, PACOM is the face of the U.S. Military to the PLA. The PLA readily engaged with PACOM when its interests could be met, or when PACOM offered entrée to more strategic, national-level lessons resident elsewhere in the United States. As the PLA's *shi*, or strategic positioning increased, other factors detracted from their desire to engage, but not their need to study, PACOM and its subordinate forces. These factors include a shared sense of competition for military primacy in Asia and the need in Beijing to protect the viability of their strategic message, even within the PLA's own ranks. Thus, the bilateral military relationship entered a phase of downward spiraling to the point now where the primary lessons the PLA wants to learn from PACOM is how to defeat it.

POLICY IMPLICATIONS

- Pacific Command and its forces, are increasingly seen by the PLA as a tool for surrounding and containing China's peaceful development. The PLA will engage with PACOM only when Beijing feels its strategic position in a particular issue is weak, when their studies assess PACOM can offer them lessons of value, and when engaging does not undermine another, seemingly unrelated but no less important, issue.
- The reduction of PACOM's voice in the bilateral relationship is a loss to Washington of a key component of the Department of Defense (DoD) global engagement strategy in dealing with China.
  - Where PACOM used to be a source for cooperation, it is now seen more as a potential enemy.
  - Where proponents of PLA modernization and transformation used to seek best practices and lessons from the U.S. military through PACOM, they are increasingly turning to other sources for the same information, not willing to pay the political price for dealing directly with the United States.
  - Where Washington used to have the ability to dial up or down the rhetoric in bilateral communications, the loss of PACOM as an accepted component in the relationship

has forced an unhealthy formality in what should be normal messaging between two militaries.

- Washington can no longer depend on PACOM to send objective messages to the PLA, because Beijing is too busy studying how to counter their operations to listen.

Traditional Chinese strategy is based on relative strengths and positions between antagonists. Given a known set of their own capabilities, the Chinese seek to learn everything possible about a potential rival's capabilities, and then modify their strategic approach accordingly.[1] China's preferable application of their foreign and security policies traditionally relies on the demonstration of a capability to coerce or force militarily other parties to adopt measures favorable to China.[2] When they cannot achieve a "Strong State" balance of power for lack of *shi*, they fall back on "weak state" strategies of delay, deceit, and development of domestic capabilities along with foreign allies.[3] China currently sees itself in this latter state and has been taking diplomatic[4] steps to achieve easy solutions along its periphery while delaying the harder issues. This diplomatic approach is designed to buy time for their economic and informational strategies to establish friendly (and in some cases, dependent) ties around the world, build deceptive perceptions of a China deserving of reestablishing its past glory and set the conditions for a return to the preferred strong state *shi*. The military dimension of this strategic shift requires completely overhauling a backwards, domestically-focused, and politically-driven military to meet the conditions of a modern deterrent force capable of influencing potential threats both along their periphery and in global areas of interest. It is this overhaul that is being seen by western and Chinese observers at all levels of the PLA over the past 40 years, but which seems to have accelerated in the last decade.

While other chapters of this volume will outline the global nature of China's studies, this chapter will focus on what they may have learned specifically from watching PACOM contingency and engagement operations in their own neighborhood. The author will attempt to answer why the PLA would seek to learn anything from an organization that has such a different structure and which they seemingly have no interest in emulating, are continuously complaining about, and whose every action seems to violate all of the Chinese principles for foreign relations. Following the pattern that whatever is adopted from external sources will be modified to have "Chinese characteristics," which parts of PACOM's organization and operations are they interested in, and why? And what evidence is available to make a direct linkage?

The short answer for the first question is obvious. PACOM is the face of the strongest military China sees every day, and whether the lessons they seek are for better understanding of a potential rival or for further development of their own armed forces, it is natural to pay attention to PACOM forces in the Asia-Pacific. Of course the PLA does not just watch PACOM; they watch all of the U.S. military,[5] but for purposes of this chapter, the author assumes PACOM is the model being studied.[6] To answer the other questions, though, requires a quick look at the PLA itself.

PLA Today.

The PLA is a learning organization[7] in that it is constantly searching itself and looking externally for the "best practices and efficiencies in its personnel, command and control, acquisition, training and operations systems." It is, however, a learning organization with Chinese characteristics, meaning it does not create an environment conducive to the upward flow of new ideas. The legacy of the Confucian taboo against correcting one's senior[8] prevents it from becoming a true learning organization in the Senge definition.[9] Instead, the PLA created two high-level organizations with the charter to advise the Central Military Commission (CMC) on external and internal army building issues of interest. These two institutions are located next to each other in northwest Beijing and report directly to the CMC. When studying what and how the PLA learns, these two organizations are key.

The Academy of Military Science (AMS) has hundreds of staff scouring military issues globally for anything of interest. AMS is not as much an educational academy as it is a research think tank. It offers no undergraduate programs and its graduate-level fellows are hand-picked to study in detail a specific topic.

The National Defense University was formed in December 1985 to develop and oversee the instruction of military theory and PLA doctrine to high-ranking officers,[10] specifically at the group army level or above for ground forces and army level for air and sea forces. Following an April 1998 Enlarged Meeting of the CMC to discuss decisions of the 15th CPC National Congress, the National Defense University (NDU) was tasked to support the CMC plan for the "Fostering of High-Ranking Officers of the 21st Century," which included a 30 percent reduction of the PLA's educational institutions.[11] The focus of NDU's mission planning broadened to ensure the PLA officer corps was both trained and educated at all stages in their career.

To expand the instruction to its officer corps at all levels, the PLA has thousands of officers and civilian instructors throughout a Professional Military Education (PME) system disseminating all that was learned and adapted. This PME system was one of the first to modernize into the "informationized" era through the consolidation of unit-run military academies into universities that direct studies at several regional colleges and schools, complete with distance-learning programs for remote units unable to attend a formal campus-based course of study.[12]

The manner in which AMS and NDU take lessons and develop doctrine or direct equipment development makes it hard to make any direct linkage to specific lessons. It is not only hard to determine exactly what may be learned from PACOM, but just as hard to determine what is being learned by the PLA at all. Many Chinese writers who are willing to discuss potential lessons are not directly linked to the military, while those who are often feel constrained by secrecy laws. So despite the assertion by Ministry of Defense Foreign Affairs Office Director, Major General Qian Lihua, that the PLA is "more transparent than the U.S. military,"[13] outside observers have a difficult time seeing though the opaqueness of PLA modernization.

There seems, however, to be a recognizable pattern of reform that matches the focus of People's Republic of China (PRC) leadership. The decision to change was first promulgated by Deng Xiaoping's recognition of China's *need* to modernize, though defense modernization was placed lowest among his four modern-izations. [14] Under Deng, strategic issues were tackled first, such as China's version of the Revolution in Military Affairs (RMA),[15] along with the 4-year project to update the AMS 1987 version of *The Science of Military Strategy*. Not completed until 2001, this study clearly shows that the PLA studies all sources globally available for lessons that can be applied to Chinese objectives. AMS published an official English translation in 2005.[16] Deng's modernization goals intersected well with U.S. means of engagement in the early stages of the bilateral relationship, primarily through arms sales and joint development programs. All three services assisted the PLA in upgrading their weapons systems, including the Air Force Peace Pearl project avionics upgrade for the F8-II, the Navy's provision of Mk 46 torpedoes and the Army's support to the PLA's artillery capabilities through the sale of the AN/TPQ-37 Firefinder counterbattery radar system and upgrades to their large-caliber ammunition. According to Lieutenant Colonel Jer Donald Get, the Chinese were also interested in man-portable anti-tank and anti-air missile systems and helicopters of all types.[17] The sale of Sikorsky "*Blackhawk*-like" S-70C medium lift transport helicopters was conducted through Direct Commercial Sales. PACOM-specific contacts during the Deng era included port calls to Qingdao and Shanghai, while hosting PLA Navy (PLAN) port calls twice; and tactical demonstrations by the 25th Infantry Division to high-level PLA visitors to Hawaii.[18]

Under Jiang Zemin, who sought to regain central control of Deng's openness and reform programs, the PLA developed *how* to modernize. He began making the PLA more professional by forcing them to divest of all commercial entities, promising a greater share of the central budget, and later making the PLA more available to the outside world through his 1997 New Security Concept. That he backed off of this concept a mere 2 years later does not negate the progress made in the PLA's acceptance that transnational problems belonged in their mission set.[19] Under Jiang's sponsorship and encouragement, the PLA embarked on an intensive two-track modernization program by attempting to upgrade their hardware and software simultaneously. Major weapons systems for all services were planned, either for purchase or development. While the United States was no longer a viable partner in the hardware track, the PLA decision to gain knowledge (software) when hardware is not available allowed significant increases in contacts with PACOM, such that, had the 1999 bombing of the Chinese Embassy in Belgrade not occurred, the potential to conduct more than 8 of the 81 planned and agreed-to contacts for that year was high.[20] The mid-to-late 1990s saw a significant increase in PLA attendance at multilateral conferences sponsored by PACOM or its subordinate commands.[21]

The recovery in engagement following the double dip in contacts caused by the Embassy bombing in Belgrade, Serbia, and the J-8/EP-3 collision, combined with a mutual concern that then Taiwan President Chen Shui-bian was going to cross the PRC's red line toward independence, all spurred a mutual desire to increase contacts and mutual understanding. Hu Jintao's "harmonious world" approach seems to have brought PLA modernization out of the Jiang-era crisis mode and under a long-term planning construct, described in the 2008 *Defense White Paper* as "the new stage in the new century."[22] Residual programs that began under Jiang, however, especially in support of equipment and capability development, will remain in effect through at least 2020. Still, as the PLA sought to modernize its organizational structure in this period, the United States was more than happy to offer advice and assistance where doing so did not raise legal and policy concerns.[23] PACOM led the way for the U.S. side, maintaining contacts through the Military Maritime Consultative Agreement (MMCA), lowering the level of interaction with the Mid-Level Officers Exchanges, and conducting multiple humanitarian relief efforts throughout the region, including in China.

But all actual changes have been dutifully anchored in Chinese traditional strategic thought, including the avoidance of war if possible, and when it is not possible to avoid war, to use every effort available to minimize the expenditure of resources and manpower to achieve a quick victory. Lessons that can be applied to their acquisition or development tasks are largely a "Title 10" issue for the United States, meaning the lessons come from the individual services, rather than from an operational command like PACOM.[24] Despite the comment attributed to Jiang Zemin that he would "prefer a good soldier waiting for good equipment over good equipment waiting for a good soldier," it was the acquisition and development of better equipment that allowed the lessons sought to shift in focus from the hardware begun under Deng and accelerated under Jiang, to the softer operational and tactical concepts the PLA is seeking around the world today.

To learn joint operations from the United States would require more focus on PACOM and its subordinate commands' operations. So where are they now? In this author's opinion, they are on the verge of fielding a comprehensive defense mechanism designed to prevent conventional interference in the maintenance of their security policies all along their periphery; focused primarily on their eastern coastline and borders, but deployable to any border region if needed. Doctrinally called the anti-access air defense (A2AD) strategy, it is designed to keep PACOM as far from the Chinese coast as possible, thereby negating the perceived strengths of a maritime littoral presence strategy. What they intend to learn from PACOM, therefore, is how to defeat it at the least possible cost.

The PLA last saw major combat during their attempt to force Vietnam out of Cambodia, 1979 to 1987.[25] For China watchers trying to ascertain the extent of modernization and whether doctrinal lessons have been learned, the lack of conflict means no direct demonstration of lessons learned. They have conducted very few deployments, often unhelpfully to this study by following the United Nations (UN) flag and standards, but there are some significant ones to note. The ongoing naval deployments to the Gulf of Aden are perhaps the most notable for both their duration and distance. Both attributes were honed through multiple ship visits to U.S., Canadian, and South American Pacific ports. A 4-month round the world cruise conducted in 2002 offered the PLAN excellent opportunities to develop long-range logistics and communications procedures.[26] Equally of interest, though, is the inclusion of the UN Convention on the Law of the Sea's Article 95, "Immunity of warships on the high Seas" on the website dedicated to the PLAN Anti-Piracy deployments. Though probably intended to support the legality and "just-operations" aspect of their deployment, this posting highlights the lesson learned that working outside of one's territorial waters requires adherence to international law.[27] Participation in bilateral and multilateral exercises such as Pakistan's AMAN (Peace) series of multinational maritime exercises offered them experience in multi-ship formations and tactical operations.[28]

Peacekeeping Operations (PKO) deployments, while promoting peace for the antagonists, also offer international prestige. As Chinese peacekeepers continue to become ever more useful (meaning lethal — which offers a greater deterrent to breaking the peace and is more useful in a peace building mission), China's voice grows in the leadership of the UN PKO Office.[29]

Chinese planners have received opportunities to learn how a large operation is planned, coordinated, and managed through Shanghai Cooperation Organization (SCO) Peace exercises, such as with Russia in 2005, 2007, 2009, and the latest in September 2010. The Chinese have often requested to observe U.S. exercises and did observe the Valiant Shield naval exercise in June 2006, but have expressed disappointment in the relative lack of access to U.S. operational activities, increasing their paranoia that U.S. exercises target China.

But some lessons that have applicability to army building can be loosely tracked chronologically, based on the PLA's history of engagements with PACOM since 1990.[30] In general, an initial focus to improve training regimens led to the realization that their personnel and education systems did not allow for expected benefits from modernized training concepts. This study led further to the realization that cooperation and coordination, both domestically and with regional neighbors, are essential to gaining greatest efficiencies in both deterrence and defense. The below case studies will follow in rough chronological order.

Organization.

The Chinese recognized in the mid-1980s that their bloated personnel system and top-heavy officer corps detracted from the professional military they sought to establish. Personnel management had to improve, including development of a noncommissioned officer (NCO) corps, officer education, and targeted recruitment of college graduates with high-tech degrees. They needed to find a model. West Point, which has long been popular both to visit and study, embodied all the PLA wanted; a high-technology curriculum in direct support of the U.S. Army's officer recruitment needs that attracts top tier high school graduates.[31] The establishment of a Cadet Exchange between West Point and the Nanjing Polytechnic Institute under the sponsorship of China's Ministry of Education has helped solidify this relationship, and demonstrates its importance to the Chinese by protecting it somewhat from the ups and downs of the overall bilateral military relationship. Additionally, the PLA dispatched numerous study teams to the United States and other countries to learn how modern societies attract, recruit, and retain the human capital required to run a modern military.[32] These trips included numerous visits to U.S. military NCO academies and hosting of NCO-led PACOM delegations to China.

A second organizational restructuring idea centered on PACOM itself—the regional command's war zone concept. This concept has been widely debated in China since the 1980s as a potential replacement for their military regions, but has yet to be fully implemented. The term took off in popularity around 1995-96, according to research by the Center for Naval Analysis (CNA).[33] Interestingly, this is about the time that

PACOM engagements with the PLA began to grow. One of these PACOM engagements offered a unique look at a newly-refurbished Guangzhou Military Region Command Center in December 1997, where the Commander, General Tao Bojun, noted his span of control was similar to that of the visiting PACOM Commander and that he saw himself as PACOM's counterpart.[34] This assessment seemed unusual at the time since the host for this visit was Lieutenant General Kui Fulin, whose position as Deputy Chief of the General Staff was seen in Hawaii as the appropriate counterpart for the PACOM commander.[35]

The PLA now considers PACOM's protocol rank as equivalent to a military region. Whether the reason for this downgrade in counterpart status was an internal determination of where PACOM fit into the overall U.S. National Defense hierarchy or whether it was in response to the increased access to the civilian leadership in the Office of the Secretary of Defense is unknown. The pattern is clear though, that since the passage of the National Defense Authorization Act (NDAA) in 2000, the rank of China's interlocutors with DoD has dropped proportional to the rise in U.S. interlocutors' ranks, and the opportunities for the PACOM commander to interact with the PLA leadership have been significantly reduced. This author believes the resultant loss of interaction, while unintended by the drafters of NDAA 2000, has lessened the cooperative nature of PACOM's relationship with the PLA, undermined a key component of PACOM's regional engagement strategy, and thereby impacted negatively on the way in which the PLA leadership views PACOM and its activities in the region.[36]

Equipment.

PLA studies of PACOM no doubt include the assigned equipment and how it is employed. PACOM operations that could be applied to the modern (in this case mechanized) era began during World War II. A lesson the Chinese clearly have taken from this conflict is the importance of the aircraft carrier when seeking to extend one's operational reach beyond the range of land-based bombers. The Chinese observed that until the U.S. Pacific Fleet developed and employed carrier-based attack capabilities, the Japanese carrier-based fleet dominated the Western and Central Pacific. The lesson learned then, was that aircraft carriers were essential to shift the fight away from one's own shores to the open ocean or even to the opponent's home waters. This is a lesson they teach as early as university-level military studies.[37] But as they teach the need for a more modern military, they also study the need to defend it. In some cases, by studying how the United States defends its ships from various threats, they also study ways to defeat the U.S. systems. This is perhaps easiest to see not by the studies themselves, but by the source of the studies. Two studies of U.S. shipborne weapons systems (precision-guided missiles by the PLA Air Force [PLAAF] Engineering University's College of Missile Engineering and optical-electronic anti-ship missile countermeasures by the PLA Electronic Engineering Institute) show direct correlations to development of PLA strategies to defeat these systems.[38]

Training Centers.

The PLA sought information on the establishment and use of the Army's National Training Centers, Combined Arms training, Opposing Forces, and the development and use of Laser Engagement systems. Engagement with PACOM, specifically the subordinate service commands, gave the PLA entrée to the national-level U.S. military, their ultimate counterpart and learning platform.[39] Today, the PLA has multiple large training centers with maneuver room for Brigade-size mechanized units, centrally controlled and monitored using remote sensors and cameras that enable precision feedback on the effectiveness of unit rotations.

Regional Engagement.

The PLA has also learned a great deal from PACOM's Security Cooperation Operations, which they call Military Diplomacy.[40] PACOM's exercise series with allies and partners throughout the area of responsibility (AOR) may have inspired a similar approach with their Shanghai Cooperation Organization (SCO) partners. Building peacetime bilateral relations through engagement in Central Asia, for example, not only supports China's counterterrorism goals, but also helps support a goal to prevent U.S. encirclement of China by maintaining close ties with Central Asian counterparts. It was through this series of exercises that the PLA deployed officially its first units abroad, demonstrating another trait common in PACOM engagement strategies—the importance of presence.

Multilateral engagements by the PLA support both diplomatic and modernization goals. They avidly participate in all key security forays in the region, including the Association of Southeast Asian Nations (ASEAN) Regional Forum (ARF) and Shangri-La Dialogues. Unlike their Foreign Affairs Ministry, however, the PLA rarely matches the ranks of the other attendees, citing a wide range of other responsibilities as the reason their principal invitee could not attend.[41] Whether this common decision is portfolio related or intended to send a diplomatic message of superiority in the region is unknown. Their attendance at the functional multilateral conferences is usually both professional and participatory, indicating a strong interest in the subject. This author's hypothesis is that conference attendance shows not only which subject areas the PLA is interested in learning, but where they are in their own development. The AMS seems to be tapped if they are seeking new ideas. As stated earlier in this chapter, their NDU develops the lesson plans and instructional packets for new doctrine, so if an NDU fellow attends a multilateral conference, it will usually be the second and subsequent years, and indicates the need to confirm, update, or build on the AMS report from the previous year.

If no expertise exists in either of the schools, however, the attendees usually hail from the appropriate general departments or service. The Pacific Area Special Operations Conference (PASOC) is a prime example of this phenomenon; since no Special Operations curriculum seems to exist in their central schools — probably due to the lack of a national level Special Operations Command structure — doctrine and training both are developed in the General Staff Department's (GSD's) Training and Doctrine Bureau.[42] One unknown is whether the end of conference attendance signals a shift in interest on the subject or a rebalancing of interests against concerns that the United States has lead for the issue. Stated differently, other than when attending a conference for diplomatic reasons, do they pre-plan a finite period of attendance or base the decision on some other external factor? This author believes the case of the PLA's attendance at the Asia Pacific Center for Strategic Studies supports the latter, though not depending on the external factor often cited by the PLA themselves.

Military Diplomacy/Global Relations.

Nothing demonstrates better the PLA's use of PACOM's multilateral conference opportunities as models for future behavior than their attendance at the Asia Pacific Center for Strategic Studies (APCSS). Established in 1996 as an engagement tool to encourage regional awareness and cooperation on issues of common concern, APCSS continually hosts conferences and seminars in their Waikiki, Hawaii, facility, inviting defense and security professionals from around the Asia-Pacific Region to venues lasting from 1 day to 9 weeks. The PRC at first resisted attending the seminars, and only started sending fellows about the time their NDU first offered its own International Symposium Course (ISC) in late 1999 (U.S. Fiscal Year 2000). Besides serving and former attachés, the PLA participation alternated between AMS and NDU faculty. The timing of their attendance, and the choice of fellows, points strongly to their intent to learn from APCSS how to better develop their own ISC.

The purpose of the ISC is, according to its introductory class, to introduce China's perspectives on the regional and global security issues of the day.[43] The PLA's simultaneous development of the ISC, which included adjusting its length and scope each year for

217

the first 4 years, matches well with their attendance at APCSS. Although they would be reluctant to admit it, this course seems to have been modeled after PACOM's APCSS, which the Chinese military attended from late 1999 until mid-2002, when, according to Chinese military scholar Senior Colonel Wang Baofu, a new foreign policy strategy was adopted to "refuse to treat Taiwan in isolation from other aspects of the relationship."[44]

Official Chinese talking points blame the presence of Taiwan officers in attendance at other APCSS venues, as well as the continued U.S. arms sales to Taiwan, as the reason for boycotting APCSS. This argument is supported somewhat by Ministry of National Defense Foreign Affairs Office (MND-FAO) interlocutors continuing to research ways to make the PRC seem a more valuable invitee than Taiwan, but weakened by the PLA's willingness to send participants to both West Point and the U.S. Air Force Academy during International Cadet Exchange Weeks. Taiwan attendance at the Academies is well-known by the PLA but apparently overlooked. While the PLA continues to boycott the Center, Chinese nonmilitary organizations without access to the ISC, including the Border Control Forces, have attended APCSS since mid-2008. Apparently, the appreciation and value other PRC government organizations seem to have for interacting with regional neighbors outweighs the PLA's arguments and undermines Wang's claim of a new foreign policy strategy.

While the presence of Taiwan fellows may have caused the PLA to end its participation earlier than planned, another factor seems to have played a part in the decision, the APCSS message itself, and the danger to the political purity of any officer sent to attend. This author, who attended the fifth ISC class in 2003, believes the Chinese reluctance to attend APCSS seminars has more to do with liking the model well enough to emulate it, while being concerned that their message was not competitive in the Hawaii venue, even to their own officers.[45]

Humanitarian Operations.

The PLA was an early supporter of including how PACOM conducted Humanitarian Operations in the military engagement program. Having been the recipient of several PACOM-run operations in support of Chinese natural disasters and embarrassingly dependent on the U.S. Navy to deliver Chinese relief supplies to Indonesian Tsunami victims, the PLA embarked on a period of study and building. In one study, authors from the PLA's Military Transportation Academy termed the U.S. support to China's Wenchuan Earthquake relief effort as "inspiring," and noted the lessons learned would help improve the PLA's intelligence mechanisms, quick-reaction and long-range strategic mobility capabilities, all-weather day-night operations, safety equipment, and integration of their emergency management systems.[46] The lack of heavy lift fixed and rotary wing aircraft was quickly learned in the immediate response period following the earthquake. China has attempted to resolve that problem since 2005 with purchase requests to Russia for both Il-76MD strategic transport jets and more heavy lift Mi-17V7 Search and Rescue helicopters, but to date continues to face problems in negotiating with the Russians. They have also lobbied the United States to sell repair parts for the S-70C helicopters sold them in the 1980s, while allegedly seeking the same parts through espionage and illegal trading.[47] Nirav Patel points out that the "winning hearts and minds" lesson was learned from observing PACOM's Tsunami relief operations in 2004, and included a version of this well-known American strategy in the 2006 *Defense White Paper*. [48]

Since the mid-90s restart of military engagements, the PLA has exchanged disaster relief exercise observers with U.S. Army Forces, Pacific (USARPAC) and the Hawaii National Guard, with more scheduled but cancelled in response to U.S. Taiwan arms sales announcements. The PLAN has also constructed two hospital ships. After briefing Chief of Naval Operations Admiral Gary Roughead on these new ships in 2009, the PLA accepted an invitation to send doctors to join the U.S. Navy's next humanitarian cruise. This cruise happened to be in the Caribbean, so no direct connection can be made to PACOM forces, but doctrinally, the lessons learned would be the same. The *Zhoushan*, a 10,000 ton Chinese hospital ship, recently sailed on its inaugural friendship tour to the Gulf of Aden, ready to dispense their own brand of humanitarian aid in a very familiar manner. The ship's complement of 428, including medical staff, stopped in the African and Asian nations of Djibouti, Kenya, Tanzania, the Seychelles, and Bangladesh during its 87-day voyage.[49]

Civil-Military Coordination.

The PRC has long recognized the need to coordinate defense missions with those of other security strategies and civil defense organizations. The Chinese Ministry of Civil Affairs notes in its information paper posted to the International Civil Defence Organisation

(ICDO) website that while the regional governments should manage disaster response, it also stresses the "commando" roles performed by the members of the PLA, the Armed Police, the Public Security Forces, and Militia Reserves.[50]

The establishment of a "Coast Guard," expanding roles, and consolidating various organizations into a Maritime Security Force is just one example that the Chinese have studied the United States for lessons learned, though it is doubtful they will pursue to the degree the United States has. If the recent interest in securing energy routes and joint fishery patrol agreements with neighboring countries (including the United States) proves anything, it is that the PRC recognizes that trade tops all[51] and that military interests must remain subordinated to security of trade relations and positions.[52] More likely are the recent indications that the five civilian patrol agencies may all be taking on a paramilitary support role. While troubling, the trend matches the history of the U.S. Coast Guard.

Joint Exercises.

PACOM engagement strategies are designed in part to gain regional participation, with the desire of fostering greater regional cooperation. At times, however, PACOM forces conduct unilateral exercises, providing opportunities for internal training, but often timed for their deterrent effect. A long-held theory of engagement by PACOM has included the impact of deterrence to maintaining peace and stability in the region. This has been an especially important part of the command's engagement strategy vis-à-vis China and the potential for another cross-Strait crisis and includes elements of strength (barge tours in Pearl

Harbor), surprise (unannounced deployments of B-52s to Guam), and a little American craziness (officially called ambiguity).[53] As early as 1998, however, a Chinese officer attending a Harvard University program for PLA Officers noted that the deployment of two carrier battle groups into the waters off Taiwan, ostensibly to deter a continuation of the March 1996 Missile-firing exercises into the Taiwan Strait, not only did not deter further launches, but was received in Beijing as confirmation that their message had been received. "Had the U.S. sent fewer than two carrier groups," he said, "China would have been disappointed.[54]"Perhaps the most important lesson learned to date by the PLA about PACOM also came from this event. The deployment of two aircraft carriers into the waters near Taiwan, described by David Shambaugh as "the greatest show of strength directed at China since the Sino-American rapprochement of 1971," signaled in the most unambiguous way that the United States—and PACOM—is prepared to intervene should China attempt to reunify Taiwan by force.[55]

Additionally, this event showed the Chinese the importance of submarines. According to an article in the Taiwan-based "Defense International" ("全球防卫杂志") in February 1997, the "disappearance at sea" of the PLAN nuclear submarines forced the U.S. battle groups to remain 300 nautical miles off-shore. The article credits the 1996 decision to stay outside China's claimed territorial waters to a 1994 encounter between the USS *Kitty Hawk* and a *Han* class submarine west of Japan's Kyushu Island that showed China's seriousness in defending its 200 nautical miles (nm) Exclusive Economic Zone (EEZ).[56] The idea that small, quiet submarines can exploit a vulnerability in Navy fleet defenses was reinforced by Liu Jiangping in a thorough analysis of RIMPAC 2010, during which Japanese and Republic of Korea (ROK) submarines were able to penetrate the anti-submarine shields and directly engage the aircraft carrier. The Rim of the Pacific Exercise (RIMPAC) is a multinational naval exercise hosted by PACOM that China has never been invited to, according to Liu.[57]

A related lesson derived from a more recent U.S exercise is illustrative of another problem of intentional messages being misconstrued; that many deterrence-focused activities only serve to inspire. In a 2007 reference to a U.S. exercise "Dragon Roar" ("龙啸"), the main lesson the author opined should be learned was that the PLA needed to have the capability to fight a regional threat. This exercise was described by the author as a rehearsal of the "mass bombing" of China's coastal cities from [airfields in] Guam and Okinawa. The author concluded that "we can't wait foolishly for a surprise enemy attack on our cities."[58] This perceived threat could be one motivation for studying U.S. dependence on remote communications lines, from seabed to space-based. Over-dependence on long logistic lines was first noted as a disadvantage of the U.S. forces deployed in Korea by Mao Zedong.[59] In a conclusion with a more direct and modern application to PACOM, NDU Institute for National Strategic Studies (INSS) research indicates western scholars believe a primary motivation for China's development of an anti-satellite capability was the ability "to exploit potential U.S. vulnerabilities . . . and reduce the American ability to operate in the Western Pacific."[60]

The PLA has learned lessons from watching PACOM exercises, engagements, and operations. Some of these lessons have been encouraged (high availability disaster recovery [HADR], education reform, NCO Corps, Gulf of Aden anti-piracy patrols); some were unintentional. The outside observer has to also expect that some lessons have been independently derived (such as the need for regional supply bases for long range deployments of naval ships), but it is hard to believe in too many coincidental developments that just happen to be near copies of PACOM capabilities. Some lessons would most certainly not have been intended to be taught by PACOM or any other U.S. military organization.

So I return to my original question, why would the PLA want to take lessons from an organization they seemingly have no desire to emulate? In his 1998 monograph, *The Revolution in Strategic Affairs*, Lawrence Freedman opined that the significance of new technologies developed by the United States in the 1990s was not to create the ability of the United States to dominate all of its adversaries, but that its adversaries would find new ways of fighting. "It was therefore likely that those in conflict with the Americans would use other methods short of challenging them to an unwinnable regular war."[61] Beijing was shocked at the effectiveness of other military campaigns discussed in this volume. Combined with the knowledge that U.S. forces in the Pacific are combat-ready and available for any contingency, Beijing has to conclude that for all of its emphasis on deterrence and stability operations, PACOM forces will be sent into combat by Washington if needed. Beijing has to study them, therefore, in order to develop an asymmetric counter against PACOM interference in Chinese goals and objectives. This represents the single most important lesson the PLA seems to have learned from its interaction with PACOM; the importance of finding another, asymmetric, way of dealing with them.[62] Whether they learned the right lessons will, it is hoped, never be known.

Implications for U.S. Policy.

The Sino-U.S. military-to-military relationship has shifted from the engagement strategy of regional actors centered (for the U.S. side) on Hawaii to a more strategic, globally-focused engagement directly between the capitals. The PLA seems to seek engagement with PACOM only when its strategic position in a particular issue is weak, when their studies assess PACOM can offer them lessons of value, and when engaging does not undermine another, seemingly unrelated but no less important issue (like Taiwan or strategic communications).

Beijing's lowering of the PACOM Commander's counterpart level, significant reduction of approved high-level PACOM-PLA exchanges, and increasingly vocal criticism of PACOM's military operations in the western Pacific all indicate the loss to Washington of a key component of DoD's global engagement strategy in dealing with China. Where PACOM used to be a source for cooperation, it is now seen more as the potential enemy whose mission is surrounding and containing China's peaceful development and against which to base contingency planning. Where proponents of PLA modernization and transformation used to seek best practices and lessons from the U.S. military through PACOM, they are increasingly turning to other sources for the same information, not willing to pay the political price for dealing directly with the United States. And where Washington used to have the ability to dial up or down the rhetoric in bilateral communications, the loss of PACOM as an accepted component in the relationship has forced an unhealthy formality in what should be normal messaging between two militaries. Washington can no longer depend on PACOM to send objective messages to the PLA, because Beijing is too busy studying how to counter their capabilities to listen to their entreaties.

ENDNOTES - CHAPTER 6

1. The well-known quote from Sunzi, "know yourself and know your enemy . . ." is applied in every facet of life by the Chinese. A recent case of its application is the July 2010 Asia Regional Forum (ARF) meeting in Hanoi, Vietnam, where, after repeated attacks from U.S. and Association of Southeastern Asian Nations (ASEAN) delegates on China's South China Seas policies, Foreign Minister Yang Jiechi seemed to threaten Singapore by reminding their Head of Delegation that China was a "big country," and they were not. When this type of relativity is used with U.S. delegations, the comparison is that China is a "developing country" and the United States is not.

2. Peng Guanqian and You Youzhi, eds., *The Science of Military Strategy*, Beijing, China: Military Science Publishing House, 2005, p. 469. See also Colleen K. Holmes, "What the Chinese Learned from Sun-Tzu," unpublished monograph for the Army War College, Carlisle, PA, April 10, 2000, p. 9. Holmes uses the term "calculative strategy" to indicate Beijing's awareness of their current geo-political position and intent to improve on it.

3. While the Chinese do not enter alliances in the western sense, they do depend on short-term alliances of interests to build voting blocs. See Han Xudong (韩旭东), "中国军队要学会打 ' 全球战争'" ("China should learn to fight a 'global war'"), *Global Times* online, June 12, 2010, available from *opinion.huanqiu.com/roll/2010-06/853891.html*. The usage of *shi* as "strategic position/advantage" is derived from Holmes, p. 1. For a more in-depth study of *shi*, see David Lai, *Learning From the Stones: A Go Approach to Mastering China's Strategic Concept, Shi*, Carlisle PA: Strategic Studies Institute, U.S. Army War College, May 2004.

4. The author is using the western concept of Diplomacy, Informational, Military, and Economy (DIME) to address Chinese relations with the world, recognizing that the Chinese would use their domestically-derived Comprehensive National Power (CNP) calculations. With eleven major categories, the CNP is seen by the Chinese as a more precise means of determining relationships between nations.

5. See, for example, the direct translation of an Industrial College of the Armed Forces guidebook for the Joint Staff. Liu Weiguo, Ruan Yongjun, and Wang Jianhua, (刘卫国，阮拥军，王建华), 美军联合参谋军官指南 (*The Joint Staff Officers Guide*), Beijing, China: PLA Press, 2001.

6. For examples of lessons attributed to the U.S. military but clearly meaning U.S. Pacific Command (PACOM) see Sun Jian and Wan Licheng (孙健 and 万里程), "美军欲进驻马六甲海峡的意图及影响" ("An Analysis of U.S. Military Intentions Toward the Malacca Strait"), 东南亚纵横 (*Southeast Asia Affairs*), January 2007; and Zhang Xin, Li Mengyan, Zhou Dongyang, Wu Yang, and Chen Yuxun (张昕, 李孟研，周东阳，吴洋, and 陈玉勋), "透视 '5·12' 美军非战争军事行动及对我军的启示" ("Inspiration of the U.S. Army's Non-war Military Operation in the 'May 12' Earthquake to Its Chinese Equivalent"), 国防交通工程与技术 (*Journal of Traffic Engineering and Technology for National Defense*), May 2009, available from *CNKI.net*, November 11, 2010.

7. With apologies to Peter Senge, B. Garratt, and Arlie de Geus, primary developers of the "Learning Organization" model.

8. Readers will be familiar with the required bonfires of any formalized Chinese military modernization concept, which has grown over the years to now being based on the guidance of Mao Zedong's military thinking, Deng Xiaoping's thinking on building the army in the new period, Jiang Zemin's thinking on strengthening the national defense and the army, and on the important guidelines of Comrade Hu Jintao on national defense and the army under the new circumstances.

9. For an easy-to-read summary of Senge's theory, see Mark K. Smith, "Peter Senge and the Learning Organization," available

from *http://www.infed.org/thinkers/senge.htm*. For the original, see also Peter M. Senge, *The Fifth Discipline. The Art and Practice of the Learning Organization*, London: Random House (1990).

10. Kenneth W. Allen and Eric A McVadon, "China's Foreign Military Relations," Stimson Center Report #32, Washington, DC, October 1999, p. 21.

11. Kuan Cha-chia, "Military Commission Instructs National Defense University to Undertake New Mission of Training New High-Ranking Military Officers of 21st Century," 广角镜 (*Wide Angle*) *Magazine*, Hong Kong, trans. by *Foreign Broadcast Information System* (FBIS). Author's copy is not dated.

12. Briefing to author while touring the Lanzhou Military Region's Army Academy, Xi'an. The briefing included a description of the education network that extended to all remote outposts in the Lanzhou MR, allowing the officers and noncommissioned officers (NCOs) to take courses and exams online. Author's notes, September 2005.

13. Statement made in author's presence by Major General Qian Lihua, Director General of the Ministry of National Defense Foreign Affairs Office, during U.S.-PRC Defense Policy Consultative Talks, held in Beijing, China, February 2009.

14. See Edward C. O'Dowd, "Chinese Military Strategy in the Third Indochina War: The Last Maoist War," for a comprehensive description of the People's Liberation Army's (PLA) inadequacies for modern, professional warfare.

15. Implies a Directive Manager in Senge's concept established in the PLA. Western engagement sees General Xiong Guangkai in this role as primary promoter of China's Revolution in Military Affairs (RMA), but does he represent others?

16. Peng, p. 503.

17. Lieutenant Colonel Jer Donald Get, *What's With the Relationship Between America's Army and China's PLA? An Examination of the Terms of the U.S. Army Strategic Peacetime Engagement with the PLA of the PRC*, Carlisle Barracks, PA: U.S. Army War College Fellowship Research Project, March 25, 1996, p. 3.

18. For more detailed discussion of U.S. Army interactions with the PLA during this period, see Colonel Jer Donald Get, *What's with the Relationship Between America's Army and China's PLA?*

19. See David Finkelstein, "China's New Security Concept: Reading between the Lines," *Washington Journal of Modern China,* Spring 1999/Vol. 5, No 1. Author used Center for Naval Analysis (CNA) Project Asia Issue Paper publication of the same title, dated April 1999.

20. In a 2004 meeting with a visiting U.S. Professional Military Education delegation, Major General Yao Youzhi of AMS noted that since 1990, the PLA was studying the U.S. style of joint services to replace what he described as "coordinated branch/service operations." Author's notes, Beijing, China, June 18, 2004.

21. Personal notes. At the time, author was the J-5 China Desk Officer for U.S. Pacific Command.

22. "China's National Defense in 2008," Information Office of the State Council of the People's Republic of China, January 2009, p. 8.

23. The Pentagon's need to meet requirements under the 1979 Taiwan Relations Act (Public Law 96-8), and the National Defense Authorization Act 2000 (Public Law 106-65, Sec 1201) are often perceived as restrictive to the U.S.-PRC Military relationship. Nothing in either of these laws, nor the pertinent implementing policies, prevents outright any interaction with the PLA, calling instead only for due consideration in each case.

24. At least one western observer has noted the structure of the PLA's new Self-Propelled Gun (SPG) battalion seems to be a copy of the U.S. Army's Paladin SPG battalion. See Martin Andrew, "GI Zhou Newsletter," July 22, 2006, available from *www.oldwardogs.us/2006/07/tongzhimen_shub.html.* For an assessment of the critical components needed to employ an aircraft carrier and how the PLA currently compares to the United States and other military capabilities, see Liu Peng and Ma Xiaojing (刘鹏 and 马晓婧), "浅析航空母舰与中国海军装备能力建设" ("Superficial

Analysis of Aircraft Carriers in the Building of Chinese Navy's Equipment Strength"), 法制与社会 (*Journal of Legal System and Society*), July 2010, pp. 179-183, available from *www.cnki.net*. Author is indebted to David Lai for pointing out this article.

25. For an excellent account of this conflict, see Edward C. O'Dowd, *Chinese Military Strategy in the Third Indochina War: The Last Maoist War*, London, UK: Routledge, 2007.

26. "Naval Expert Yin Zhuo: Chinese Navy Can Explore Establishment of Long-Term Shore Supply Bases," *Beijing National Radio*, December 26, 2009. In Chinese, trans. by Open Source Center, CPP20091230702007.

27. The article states, "Warships on the high seas have complete immunity from any State other than the flag State." See "Chinese Navy Fights Pirates," available from *eng.mod.gov.cn/SpecialReports/2009hjdjhd/2008-12/22/content_4008196.htm*. The author could not find the equivalent posting on the Chinese language site.

28. See *www.paknavy.gov.pk/AMAN/Intro.htm* for information and photos on the series of AMAN (Peace) exercises hosted by the Pakistan navy. According to the site, China sent ships in 2007 and ships and Special Operations Force (SOF) teams in 2009. The 2011 exercise is currently scheduled for March 2011. Photos of Chinese SOF and the "Guangzhou" in AMAN 09 are available from *news.xinhuanet.com/english/2009-03/08/content_10969930_1.htm*.

29. For the most recent compilation of Chinese involvement in United Nations Peacekeeping (UN PK) operations, see Bates Gill and Chin-Hao Huang, *China's Expanding Role in Peacekeeping: Prospects and Policy Implications*, SIPRI Paper No. 25, November 2009.

30. Frank Miller, "Benefits and Challenges to the U.S.-China Military to Military Relationship," Speech to the Security Forum, 2007 George Bush China-U.S. Relations Conference, Washington, DC, October 23-24, 2007.

31. See, for example, Zhang Jinou (张金欧), "美国军官学校的军事思想教育" ("The Education of Military Thoughts in the U.S.

Service Academies"), 比较教育研究 (*Comparative Education Review*), May 2009, available through CNKI:SUN:BJJY.0.2009-05-016.

32. As Army Attaché to Beijing 2003-06, the author was the senior Army representative in country and therefore the sponsor for all exchanges with West Point leadership and cadets during that time. This passage is from author's notes and memory.

33. Kenneth W. Allen, Dean B. Cheng, David M. Finkelstein, and Maryanne Kivlehan, "Institutional Reforms of the Chinese People's Liberation Army: Overview and Changes," CNA Project Asia Report, May 2002, pp. 32-34.

34. This visit and briefing were last in a multi-service tour of China for Admiral Joseph Prueher that, from author's notes, seemed designed to play up the strengths of the PLA. The author is indebted to Larry Wortzel for reminding me of this visit and the theme that in both word and deed pointed to the PLA's emulation of the Geographical Combatant Commander (GCC) concept. Whether the intent was to include the flexibility and freedom of action included in the "combatant" aspect of the U.S. GCC model in the scope of the PLA MR Commander is debatable. Guangzhou, PRC, December 16, 1997.

35. At the time, the counterpart pairings were Secretary-Minister, Chief of the Joint Chiefs of Staff (CJCS)-Chief of General Staff (COGS), and Commander in Chief, Pacific Command (CINCPAC)-Deputy Chief of General Staff (DCOGS).

36. See, for example, Cao Linlin and Wang Yunxiang (曹琳琳，王运祥), "美国加强关岛军士基地建设的战略解读" ("Interpreting the Strategic Connotation of the U.S. Improving its Military base in Guam"), 广东外语外贸大学学报 (*Journal of Guangdong University of Foreign Studies*), January 2010, available from CNKI:SUNGDWY.0.2010-01-015; also Sun Jian and Wan Licheng (孙健 and 万里程), "美军欲进驻马六甲海峡的意图及影响" ("An Analysis of U.S. Military Intentions Toward the Malacca Strait"), 东南亚纵横 (*Southeast Asia Affairs*), January 2007, available from CNKI:ISSN:1672-3953.0.2006-04-004.

37. Li Yu (李雨), ed., 大学军事学教程 (University Course in Military Studies), Shanghai: Shanghai University Press, 2006, p.

27. The editor, a PLA colonel and graduate of PLA National Defense University (NDU), cited PLA NDU's 普通高等学校军事课教程 (Course Lectures for General College Level Military Studies) and relevant General Staff Department directives and specifically acknowledged the assistance of AMS Deputy Commandant Lieutenant General Qian Haihao (钱海皓中将) for his institute's help with the book.

38. Wu Jing, Deng Kun, and Liu Shikao (吴静，邓堃，柳世考), "美军精确制导武器及其对抗技术的分析" ("Analyzing U.S. Military Precision Guided Weapon and Its Countermeasures Technique"), 兵工自动化 (*Journal of Ordnance Industry Automation*), April 2007, available from CNKI:ISSN:1006-1576.0.2007-04-035; Xiong Liang, and Zhu Li (熊良, 祝利), "美军舰载光电对抗系统现状与发展分所" ("Current Situation and Development Analysis of the Ship borne Optical-electronic Countermeasure System in U.S. Military Force"), 舰船电子对抗 (*Journal of Shipboard Electronic Countermeasure*), April 2006, available from CNKI:SCN:32-1413.0.2006-04-006. These are representative examples of intensive studies of every component of PACOM's force structure.

39. Get, Appendix B, p. 24.

40. For a quick explanation of the uses of military diplomacy, see Nan Li, "From Revolutionary Internationalism to Conservative Nationalism; The Chinese Military's Discourse on National Security and Identity in the Post-Mao Era," *Peaceworks*, No. 39, Washington, DC: United States Institute of Peace, May 2001, p. 30-31. It is also interesting to note that the Chinese language version of the Chinese Ministry of Defense website does not have a separate sub-page for Military Diplomacy like its English language counterpart has. Compare *mod.gov.cn* with *eng.mod.gov.cn*.

41. Author's notes.

42. Author's conversations with PLA attendees to Pacific Area Special Operations Conference (PASOC), 2004-06.

43. Author's notes from the Fifth ISC, September-November 2003.

44. Author's notes. Wang was speaking to the Seventh RAND-China Reform Forum Conference, Beijing PRC, August 2004.

45. Author's notes, September 2003.

46. Zhang Xin, Li Mengyan , Zhou Dongyang, Wu Yang, and Chen Yuxun.

47. See "China spy sought Blackhawk helicopter parts, F-16 engines," *World Tribune.Com*, April 25, 2008, available from *www.worldtribune.com/worldtribune/WTARC/2008/ea_china0088_04_25.asp*.

48. Nirav Patel, "Chinese Disaster Relief Operations: Identifying Critical capability Gaps," *Joint Forces Quarterly*, Issue 52, 1st Qtr 2009, p. 113. The 2006 *Defense White Paper* can be found at *eng.mod.gov.cn/Database/WhitePapers/2006.htm*.

49. See Bi Mingxin, ed., "Chinese navy hospital ship sets sail on first overseas medical mission," *Xinhua* online, available from *www.gov.cn/english/2010-08/31/content_1692806.htm*.

50. While I do not know the purpose for using the term "commando" to describe the armed forces' role, the importance of civil-military cooperation is clear. See *www.icdo.org/Directory%20ORIGINAL/Directory-english/China.maj.2006.ang.pdf*.

51. The linkage between a nation's military and its economy is discussed in He Xin and He Zhengbin (何鑫 and 何正斌), "从美国经济看其军事战略走向" ("Viewing the Trend of the U.S. Military Strategy from Its Economy"), 国际问题研究 (*Journal of International Studies*), April 2005.

52. See as an example of their study of the Coast Guard, the translation of "The Pentagon's Fifth Side: The Coast Guard Transfers to the Department of Defense," 五角大楼的第五边：海岸警卫队转隶国防部, *Ordnance Knowledge* Vol. 11B, November 15, 2008, AMS Researcher Major Wang Baocun (王保存少校), trans. The subordination of the Chinese armed forces to the national economy is clearly stated in the 2008 *Defense White Paper*, available from *eng.mod.gov.cn/Database/WhitePapers/2008.htm*. I am indebted to Dennis Blasko for pointing this out.

53. See for example, Federal News Service transcript of "The Heritage Foundation Lecture with Admiral Timothy Keating, U.S. Navy, Commander, United States Pacific Command," July 16, 2008, in which Admiral Keating, responding to a question, stated, "We hope to be a very powerful deterrent. And every day [that] goes by that missiles aren't flying across the strait, I believe our deterrence is effective." This position is not unique to Admiral Keating, however. It is a standard set of metrics by which PACOM has measured success under every commander before and since.

54. Author's interviews with participants of the two seminars. Harvard's Kennedy School ran two Executive Seminars for Senior Chinese Military Officers in 1998. The nonattributable comment cited reportedly was made in the second seminar, March 7-21, 1998.

55. David Shambaugh, "Modernizing China's Military: Progress, Problems, and Prospects," Berkeley, CA: University of California Press, p. 3.

56. The encounter was listed as a 70-hour event on October 27, 1994, without making it clear if that date was the start or end of the encounter. See "PLA Navy-Transforming From a Brown Water to a Blue Water Navy," *Defence International*, Taipei, Taiwan, February 1997, pp. 36-46.

57. Liu Jiangping, "Joint Military Exercise Messes Up Asia-Pacific Situation," *Modern Navy Magazine*, September 2010, Open Source Center trans.

58. Dai Xi (戴旭), "中国需要什么样的新型军队" ("What Kind of New Military Does China Need?"), *Global Times*, No. 1426, May 31, 2007, p. 11. The author, a PLAAF colonel, is described as Senior Strategy Commentator, presumably for *Global Times*.

59. Peng, p. 473.

60. Phillip C. Saunders and Charles D. Lutes, "China's ASAT Test: Motivations and Implications," INSS Special Report, Washington, DC: Institute for National Defense Studies, National Defense University, June 2007, p.g 2.

61. Monograph was published IISS, as cited in Lawrence Freedman, "On War and Choice," *The National Interest*, No. 107, May/June 2010, pp. 10-11.

62. Christopher P. Twomey, "Chinese Doctrines as Strategic Culture: Assessing their Effects," *Strategic Insights*, Vol. IV, Issue 10, October 2005, Naval Postgraduate School, Monterey CA.

CHAPTER 7

THE INFLUENCE OF U.S. COUNTERINSURGENCY OPERATIONS IN AFGHANISTAN ON THE PEOPLE'S LIBERATION ARMY

Martin Andrew

EXECUTIVE SUMMARY

This chapter looks at the influence of U.S. counter-insurgency (COIN) operations in Afghanistan on the People's Liberation Army (PLA).

MAIN ARGUMENT

The PLA has learned many lessons from U.S. COIN operations in Afghanistan, but the primary areas involve battlefield fire support, interdiction, the importance of low collateral damage, helicopters, unmanned air vehicles (UAVs), and fixed-wing close air support in the conduct of conventional operations. These lessons have been applied to the overall development and modernization programs of the PLA, and not exclusively to the development of a Chinese-style COIN capability and doctrine.

POLICY IMPLICATIONS

China has transferred the COIN mission from the PLA to the People's Armed Police Force (PAP). It implies that the China sees this mission in an exclusively domestic context. The PLA itself is not preparing to conduct external COIN operations on the scale of

U.S. operations in Afghanistan. It is unclear how the PLA would respond if it were called upon to perform COIN-like roles in an overseas context.

The PLA has nonetheless used the lessons learned by the U.S. military to inform the developing "jointness" of its own operations. Combined arms operations, with realistic training, have been emphasized to increase the capability of the PLA.

The PLA Air Force (PLAAF) does not have close air support and low collateral damage weapons comparable to those of the United States but fully appreciates U.S. advances in these areas and is trying to replicate them where it can. The PLA also has grasped the importance of helicopter assault, attack, and lift roles as well as the importance of battlefield fire support, especially from fixed-wing close air support assets. Moreover, the PLA sees unmanned systems as having ever-greater importance on the modern battlefield.

INTRODUCTION

The PLA entered the 21st century in the midst of a transformation from essentially an infantry based force into one designed around combined arms mechanized operations. A decade into the new century, the PLA is redesigning its forces into battle groups, using modular force structures and logistics to support operations in high altitude and complex terrains, conduct out of area operations, and develop the core for its vision of a hardened and network-centric army.

In the same period, the U.S. military and other agencies have been involved in an extended COIN campaign in Afghanistan. Operating in a high altitude complex terrain, U.S. forces have employed network centric methods and equipment in wide-ranging operations that feature joint fire control; intelligence, surveillance, and reconnaissance (ISR); and decapitation operations with heavy involvement of UAVs to establish information dominance and to enable targeted strikes of a widely distributed adversary.

The PLA has followed the campaign closely, not least because China shares a short border with Afghanistan, but also because the study of U.S. operations in Afghanistan provides an opportunity to inform the ongoing modernization and development of the PLA. The coincidence of ongoing reforms in the PLA and U.S. combat operations in Afghanistan has allowed for an opportunity for the latter to inform the ongoing transformation in the PLA, ranging in form from inferential lessons learned to a direct application of U.S. operations. This chapter finds that the chief lessons learned for the PLA from U.S. operations in Afghanistan relate more broadly to the development and refinement of PLA conventional operations rather than to a more narrow application to Chinese-style COIN. In part, this is because the PLA sees traditional COIN missions as having only a domestic application, and the mission responsibility for domestic COIN has been delegated to the paramilitary PAP.[1]

This chapter examines how the PLA is "piggy backing" on the lessons learned by U.S. forces in their own COIN operations in Afghanistan to accelerate the modernization of the PLA's own force structure, strategy, and tactics. Chief lessons learned from U.S. operations in Afghanistan include the importance of helicopter assault, lift, and attack roles; fixed-wing close air support; and transformed battlefield fire support and organizational models.

BACKGROUND

The PLA's well-known 1990s pursuit of *xinxihua zhan* (信息化战) "informationalized warfare" has added the supporting concepts of *peishu* or modularization (配属), and *zhichi* or support (支持).[2]

In the early years of this century, the Beijing and Shenyang Military Area Regions main force mechanized infantry divisions conducted exercises utilizing the concepts of *peishu* and *zhichi* to develop the PLA's new brigade/battle group structures in urban and other operational scenarios, with Xinjiang-based units tasked to apply these in high altitude operations.[3] These and subsequent trials developed new doctrine and structures for complex operations in high altitude or plateau regions, and in urban warfare.[4]

These trials coincided with the start of U.S. operations in Afghanistan (Operation ENDURING FREEDOM [OEF]) in late 2001, operations that demonstrated that the combination of precision guided munitions, rapid aerial maneuver, and information dominance could quickly change the dynamics of ground combat. Consequently, the timing and effectiveness of U.S. operations in Afghanistan have had a profound effect on the PLA's own doctrinal concepts and equipment developments, but the impact has been on its broader conventional forces doctrine, tactics and equipment, rather than more narrowly on COIN operations alone.

The key observations that the PLA has drawn from U.S. COIN in Afghanistan about the nature and conduct of war include:

- Maneuver from the air is still a powerful means of power projection.
- Unmanned aerial systems (UAS) are now viable for both ISR and precision attack. New roles will continue to be found and utilized.

- Information and joint operations allowing for precision strikes are the keys to modern warfare. This enables a small-sized force, employing information operations and precision fire power, to achieve disproportionate effects on an adversary.
- Space control now has a direct influence on the modern battlefield, down to the lowest tactical levels, in such areas as global positioning system (GPS) and satellite communications.

This chapter will examine each of these elements in turn.

AVIATION OPERATIONS

One of the biggest weaknesses of the PLA, which has plagued it since the Korean War, has been the movement and sustainment of forces on China's periphery. This shortcoming was painfully exposed during the 1979 Sino-Vietnamese War[5] and has continued to bedevil the PLA until the present day, including notable aerial support failures in the PLA's response to the 2008 Wenchuan earthquake.[6] Two of the biggest issues currently facing the PLA are the ability to move forces quickly by air and high altitude helicopter support.[7] Consequently, force sustainment has become a priority under PLA's modernization in the first decade of the 21st century. *Zhichi* and the creation of a corps-level logistics able to supply and support forces deep inside an enemy's rear area are two ways in which this priority manifests itself.[8]

From the very beginning of the U.S. forces deploying to Afghanistan, the PLA has taken notice of the impact both of strategic transport and the employment of large helicopters both for tactical mobility as well as long-range operations.[9] The PLA, as with other professional military observers, doubtless paid attention to the 640 kilometer (km) air assault operation by U.S. Marines to secure the opium distribution center and runway in the Registan Desert on November 23, 2001, which showed the PLA the combat value of large, air-refueling capable helicopters. Once secured, the airfield was very quickly made operational, and long range C-17 and C-130 transport aircraft rapidly provided support to build up the base. The base itself was totally supplied by air during its operation.

Transport Helicopters. The Chinese aircraft company AVIC has developed the AC313 medium lift helicopter, an advanced development of the old Z-8, itself a copy of the old *Aerospatiale Super Frelon* helicopter.[10] With composite materials comprising 50 percent of the helicopters to reduce its empty weight, and with three Pratt and Whitney Canada PT6B-67A turboshaft engines delivering 20 percent more power, the AC313 can fly up to 6,000 miles (m) and operate in temperatures from -400 Celsius (C) to +500C, enabling it to operate on the Tibetan Plateau with ease.

The U.S. Central Intelligence Agency's (CIA) use of Mi-8/17 transport helicopters would also been of interest as the PLA's current high altitude transport and utility helicopter is the Russian Mi-17 transport helicopter, the export designation of the Mi-8MTV-2 helicopter. The PLA version incorporates a chin-mounted radar enabling bad weather operations, has a limited self-defense capability, and extra engine capacity. Despite the extra power, the Mi-8MT/Mi-17MT can only carry six to eight combat-laden soldiers (each carrying 35 to 40 kilograms (kg) of equipment in addition to his weapon and uniform) below 3,000 meters, and this decreases to only four or five at 3,000 to 4,000 meters altitude.[11] By comparison, the CH-47D *Chinook* transport helicopters deployed in Afghanistan can carry 30 passengers and five tons of cargo at the same altitudes.[12]

Armed Helicopters. As the U.S. military were deploying assets for operations in Afghanistan, the PLA deployed its first army airborne regiment to Xinjiang ostensibly to combat Uyghur separatists.[13] The unit was initially equipped with approximately 30 Chinese-built Z-9G helicopters. The PLA would have taken particular interest in the U.S. operations at high altitudes in Afghanistan, as this new unit's mission was to develop tactics and doctrine for heliborne operations, including night time combat search and rescue, as well as conducting counter terrorist and insurgency missions.[14] Its organization and mission profile was similar to a hybrid mix of a U.S. Army Ranger battalion in combination with the 160th Special Operations Aviation Regiment (Airborne).

The use of attack helicopters in Afghanistan was of particular interest, as the PLA were developing armed WZ-9G helicopters and were deciding on a purposely designed attack helicopter. The WZ-10 attack helicopter similar in size to AH-1W and will be the linchpin of the PLA Aviation's modernization plans. Besides anti-armor, its missions will include escort, armed reconnaissance, and force protection, the latter against enemy attack and reconnaissance helicopters and UAVs.[15]

The PLA continues to have a shortage of long range heavy transports and air-to-air refueling tankers which will continue to plague the PLAAF for many years to come. In 2005, the PLAAF ordered 34 new *Ilyushin Il-76MD* transports and 4 Il-78 tankers; however, the production line in Uzbekistan has closed down, and it remains uncertain as to whether the order will be filled. (See Appendix A for a detailed discussion of the capabilities and characteristics of various helicopter and fixed wing assets.)

Observable Change or Development.

In January 2006, PLA aviation assets were ordered to develop into a rapidly mobile force adapted to integrated joint operations and to transition from a supporting to a combat arm with both attack and maneuver roles by the year's end.[16] The PLA had already started to practice long-range aerial maneuver and massed helicopter raids behind enemy lines, as an October 2005 exercise report from a Jinan mechanized infantry division indicated. The ability to both launch and then defeat a helicopter landing were practiced at that time. A large-scale helicopter-borne insertion was successfully undertaken; however, it was detected by an unmanned aerial system being used in a reconnaissance role, resulting in a notional long-range fire strike defeating it.[17]

UNMANNED AIR SYSTEMS AND INTELLIGENCE, SURVEILLANCE, AND RECONNAISSANCE OPERATIONS

Intelligence, surveillance, and reconnaissance were the primary goals for Chinese UAS until the U.S. forces employed them in various roles, even in the early days of U.S. operations in Afghanistan. The PLA has been very interested in any UAS developments, and Chinese defense industries have developed nearly all of the UAS used by the PLA.[18] The notable exception might well be the HARPY attack UAV, sold by

Israel to the PLA in the late 1990s. PLA special forces have operated UAS since the mid-1990s. Photographs in the Chinese press show the Chinese-produced CH-801 hand-launched micro-UAS to be in service.[19] Larger UAS have also been developed, primarily for the ISR role; the W-50, an older design, has already achieved "combat effectiveness."[20] In the 2008 Sichuan earthquake, at least one Chinese-developed small UAV was deployed to survey the damage.[21] The other operational UAS system is the Z-5, which has the appearance of a large remote control model helicopter.

Increased Use of UAS by the PLA.

In late 2005, the PLA experimented with the use of UAS for the targeting as well reconnaissance and surveillance in night operations. UAS were deployed on operations with thermal imaging equipment and a data link to transmit their images back to a joint operations cell to coordinate strikes based on the data received, which was then distributed to various artillery batteries.[22]

Although these trials were deemed successful, they were not declared combat effective, perhaps due to an incomplete supporting infrastructure and the absence of a long-range guided multiple rocket systems that could exploit the capability of an UAS. The success of the U.S. UAS in Afghanistan may well have spurred the Chinese defense industry to develop new designs, as recent Zhuhai (珠海) air shows and symposia have demonstrated.[23]

In recent Chinese natural disasters, small UAS have been used in disaster relief roles in which they can provide a rapid ability to survey large areas rapidly and require little infrastructure to deploy and operate. The PW-1 close range reconnaissance UAS and the larger PW-2 are recent examples of this trend. (See Appendix A for further details on UAS systems.)

Observable Change or Development of UAS Systems.

The most recent observable change or development that the PLA has adopted from U.S. COIN operations in Afghanistan may well be the development of an indigenous armed unmanned combat system (UCAS).[24] The first Chinese UCAS shown in public was the CH-3, designed by the China Aerospace Science and Technology Corporation and unveiled in November 2008.[25]

BATTLEFIELD FIRE SUPPORT AND COMBINED ARMS TASK ORGANIZATION

Joint Fire Strike.

As part of its informationalization initiative, the PLA has introduced the concepts of joint firepower strike (联合火力打击) and precision strike (精确打击).[26] The former describes the idea of all arms striking, with precision strike referring to the use of advanced targeting equipment and/or precision-guided munitions. These concepts provide insight into the priority the PLA has given to modernizing its doctrine, organization, and equipment in order to reduce the time taken for targets to be identified and destroyed. In particular, the new armored battle groups can bring improved target acquisition and fire control; the U.S. experience in Afghanistan has no doubt provided some insights.

For many years, it appeared that the PLA used a development of the Russian concept of Reconnaissance-

Combat Operations (RBD) in high altitude COIN operations. This involves the extensive use of signals intelligence, special forces, and helicopters supported by ready reaction forces and artillery to provide blocking forces and prosecute attacks.[27] Recent material suggests that they have been more influenced by the ability of U.S. forces in Afghanistan to provide rapid and highly accurate on-call firepower, especially via close air support (CAS) and tube artillery. If they started out using RBD, the PLA appears now to have transitioned to a joint fire support model that looks more like a U.S. approach and may be based on the observations of U.S. operations in Afghanistan.[28]

Moreover, the PLA has internalized how GPS and high technology communications give the United States a huge situational awareness advantage as well as the ability to provide almost immediate accurate PGM strikes on an identified target. In 2004, PLA special forces reconnaissance teams were tasked with providing intelligence information for larger forces and fire coordination for long range fire support, developing their tactics on China's western periphery.[29] The PLA now employs GPS in its armored vehicles for both navigation and to assist in targeting precision guided munitions. Any maneuver platoon can call in fire support on a seamless fire support command and control net.

The PLA has taken on board the use of their equivalent of Joint Terminal Attack Controllers (JTACs) and their attendant equipment, which were first seen in Afghanistan.[30] The PLA employs battalion level scouts to enable rapid destruction of battlefield targets, with close air support now available through the battalion level scouts and artillery fire controllers with their attendant targeting equipment who can be employed at the platoon level when required or operate ahead of the battalion. The PLA changed the structure of their mechanized infantry battalion for the first time since its introduction in the 1960s to allow for this change, going away from the triangular Soviet model to a Western four-vehicle platoon.

The PLA has also been particularly impressed by the U.S. forces' ability to hit small targets in both urban and rural areas quickly and with minimal collateral damage, whether through close air support or artillery.[31] Multiplatform mini-air-to-ground missiles like the Israeli Spike and U.S. Viper Strike are of considerable interest and have been commented upon and written about.[32] The PLA have noticed that the use of too much fire power in urban and high altitude terrain reduces the avenues of approach and provides better defensive positions to an enemy.[33] Destroying mountain passes, which are a good spot for an ambush, denies their use, and rubble in cities from destroyed buildings restricts maneuver while providing excellent concealment for ambushes and improvised explosive devices (IEDs).

The concept of the informationalization of the battlefield saw the PLA change from kinetic warfare to warfare in which nodes and systems are attacked to break down an enemy's ability to resist by destroying their command and control centers. Noncontact combat—using sensors to identify a target deep behind the battlefield and then using long-range precision munitions to destroy them—became a valid concept.[34]

However, a recent article in the *PLA Daily* indicates that the PLA is adapting the joint fire strike concept as used by the U.S. military to its own ends. Specifically, the PLA appears to treating the concept as a tool of operational level, rather than tactical, warfare.[35] This may be due to a shortage of the battlefield command and control equipment and munitions required to conduct a joint fire strike, requiring the PLA to husband its resources to get the most effective use out of these assets. This does not preclude the use of joint fire strike in tactical operations, but such tactical operations must have an operational level effect, such as destroying a headquarters or communications node and thereby creating massive disruption in the adversary's command and control net.

Influence of U.S. developments in Afghanistan: New Organization of the Mechanized Infantry Brigade.

As noted earlier, the PLA thorough informationalization envisions combat formations being flatter, networked, smaller, and more versatile. The ability of small U.S. forces to call in all the available firepower or just a single aircraft no doubt has provided a model for how the new PLA structure might operate, not least because informationalization trials inside the PLA were being developed concurrently with U.S. operations in Afghanistan. Informationalization and the incorporation of U.S. concepts of operation necessarily require better command and control in the PLA. The Type 89 (equivalent to the U.S. M577-series) armored command vehicle attached to every infantry company and above, as well as to mortar and air defense platoons, helps address the demands of better command and control capability. Importantly as well, a fourth infantry fighting vehicle (IFV) has been added to the mechanized infantry platoon for the platoon headquarters.

The PLA conducted an exercise combining informationalization concepts with the *peishu* and *zhi-*

chi concepts and formed a reconnaissance/cavalry battle group for the August 2007-Exercise Peace Mission-2007. The first of its type in the PLA, this reconnaissance/cavalry battle group could have been used to test the aviation brigade and reconnaissance brigades, which are to be part of the new corps. While its exercise mission was asserted to be a counter-terrorism role, the scale of the exercise meant it also involved COIN and out of area entry operations. The battle group was composed of:

- A light (wheeled) mechanized infantry battalion comprising 40 Type 92 wheeled infantry fighting vehicles. (For system details, see Appendix.)
- Two companies of 18 PTL02 assault guns.
- One battalion of 16 Z-9W attack helicopters, some with an under-nose turret mounting a laser range-finder/designator and thermal imager.
- One battalion of 16 Mi-17 transport helicopters, each capable of carrying up to six 57 millimeter (mm) rocket pods containing 32 rockets each or around 16 troops.
- One company of 12 ZBD05 airborne combat vehicles mounting a 30 x 165mm automatic cannon and a co-axial 5.8 x 42mm machine gun and capable of carrying four soldiers in the rear.

The Type 92s could transport a mechanized infantry battalion of three companies with the support provided by two companies of the PTL-02 assault guns, which was an unusually large amount of firepower (火力) for a mechanized infantry battalion. A company of the PTL-02 assault guns could have been used in the traditional cavalry roles of reconnaissance and flank protection, with the Type 92As providing the vehicles for the battalion headquarters and company support weapons. Infantry support weapons deployed included the QBZ87 35mm automatic grenade launcher, PF98 anti-tank rocket launcher, and Type 74 backpack flame throwers. The Mi-17s could lift two infantry companies with their support elements, providing the brigade commander with six company level maneuver elements. The Z-9W attack helicopters provided aerial reconnaissance, fire support and liaison.

Besides being the PLA's new heavy corps reconnaissance and screening force — providing flank protection and serving as the aviation assault brigade — the group is ideally suited for the cavalry's traditional mission of COIN.

Future Developments — Close Air Support.

The PLA is finally achieving the capability for on-call close air support, which previously its personnel in combat have never had. By incorporating the same battlefield command, control, and communications (C3) technology as used for precision strike, the PLA will shortly be able to exercise real time aerial fire support.

Fixed wing close air support is just starting to become reality in the PLA. The Q-5, developed from the Russian MiG-19, has been equipped with the hardware and software to enable the use of the LT-2 laser-guided 500kg bombs. The more advanced LT-3, which is a 500kg bomb mated to a laser seeker in the nose with a GPS guided bomb kit mounted on the rear, is also available and analogous to the U.S. EGBU-24.[36] Presently the PLA uses UAS for ISR and targeting with long range GPS rockets used for prosecution of the target.[37]

COIN Strategy.

Reducing Collateral Damage and Non-Combatant Casualties. As noted in the sections above, U.S. COIN operations in Afghanistan have appeared to influence the PLA in several ways, but mostly in the modernization and development of general PLA efforts to become a better joint operating force. However, there have been some likely impacts on Chinese efforts at COIN. Most notably, these are in the importance of minimizing collateral damage in both people (both combatants and innocents) and materiel. In 2005, in the wake of the media coverage of U.S. operations in Afghanistan and elsewhere, the PLA was reaffirmed in its judgment about the power of the media to rapidly shape events. In an article on modern combat, the authors noted that that "killing too many of the enemy on the battlefield may be strongly condemned by international public opinion."[38]

The PLA has undoubtedly observed that U.S. forces employ a range of means to minimize civilian casualties, including using weapons that are accurate and have warheads designed for minimal damage to other than the intended target. More importantly, U.S. forces receive additional training in the requirements to use force proportionately in COIN operations, so as not to overreact to fire directed at them by calling in a disproportionate response, whether using their own weapons, artillery, or airpower. The Central Military Commission (CMC) has definitely taken measures in COIN operations to reduce noncombatant casualties by employing a wider range of less than lethal munitions and by expanding the role of the PAP. By law, the PLA cannot undertake nondisturbance operations

without the express permission of the CMC, and pro-
tocols are enshrined in law to ensure the PAP is called
out only for recognized anti-disturbance operations.
No longer can the PAP be called on by a local official
to provide muscle for a property developer who cannot get rid of people who will not move.[39]
Are there observable adjustments that the PLA has
made in response to the lessons learned?

> The war in Afghanistan has seen the U.S. military's
> joint operation capabilities reach a new level. When
> people clearly see from the television screen U.S. spe-
> cial forces and Marines using a satellite phone, calling
> the air echelon up against newly discovered targets,
> they feel the real power of joint action.[40]

Joint operations through the PLA's development
of "informationalization" in the entire military is seen
as the keystone to the PLA's way of fighting in the future. The notion permeates all levels of the four services and reflects the PLA goal of a military that can conduct network-centric warfare. U.S. joint operational
capabilities are deeply respected by PLA commanders
and planners and consequently have had an impact
on the development of PLA warfighting doctrine.
As the PLA was already undertaking trials on informationalization and the future structure of its combat units, U.S. COIN operations in Afghanistan have
shown the PLA the value of maneuver from the air
and the power of informationalization in the fields of
fire support, ISR, and command and control of joint
operations.[41] The U.S. ability to provide on-call precision guided munitions strikes and CAS is often cited
as an example of the value of informationalization.
Although in peacetime doctrinal change often takes a
long time to investigate and implement, the combina-

tion of the fortuitous timing of ongoing exercises and the lessons learned from observing U.S. operations sped up this process.

In 2005, in response to CMC Chairman Hu Jintao's call for an increased emphasis on training, the PLA changed the focus of its training to one that examined and built on a realistic appreciation of the modern battlefield.[42] As joint operations were the focus for PLA training in 2006, lessons learned from U.S. combat operations in Afghanistan were being incorporated into PLA training regimes. Along with a continued emphasis on realistic training "with regards to the modern battlefield," the priority of these exercises was to be on joint operations, combat capability, modularization (*peishu*), and sensor fusion to try and create a nascent battle management network-centric capability.[43] In addition, in 2006 the PLA introduced a new mechanized infantry structure as well as a change in the mission and roles of the PLA aviation from a support to a combat arm.[44] These developments resulted in significant changes to the combat structure of the PLA, especially in its use of battle groups within the mechanized infantry brigade, which has become the linchpin of PLA combat power.[45]

UAS were being developed prior to U.S. involvement in Afghanistan, but it was not until the United States started using them in both an ISR and an armed reconnaissance role that the PLA deployed them beyond trials.[46] The PLA continues to develop new UAS vehicles, including an armed model, and may well see an armed UAS (UCAS) in service in a close air support role before a manned CAS system comes on line.

WHAT OTHER UNIQUE LESSONS, PERHAPS IN OTHER FIELDS, DID THE PLA LEARN FROM STUDYING THIS CONFLICT?

Exploiting the Achilles Heel — Anti-Ballistic Missile and Satellite Systems.

The then Secretary of the U.S. Air Force James J Roche, in a speech at the 2002 Massachusetts Institute of Technology Doolittle Award, noted that a bandwidth of 40 gigabytes was required just for the early days of U.S. operations in Afghanistan. He warned that the increasing use of satellites could lead to issues if they became unavailable. The Chinese had already focused on this key vulnerability, the Achilles heel of information operations, and started developing their nascent national missile defense (NMD) system in 1990.[47] The anti-satellite test of January 11, 2009, was a cover for the third of a series of anti-ballistic missile tests, the first two having been conducted on July 7, 2005, and February 6, 2006. It showed that the PLA was also capable of knocking out satellites and an intermediate range ballistic missile, the former showing they could interfere with U.S. information dominance. Of course, the United States is capable of doing the same with its NMD systems.

Infantry Weapons.

By studying the new infantry weapons systems in use by U.S. forces in Afghanistan, the firepower of the PLA infantry soldier has benefited.[48] Selected units now have weapons mounting laser markers, night sights, and other add-on systems via a rail interface system. This is particularly prominent in counterterrorist and special forces units involved in close quarter battle operations and training.

Rail Interface System and Accessories. The U.S. Special Forces that went into Afghanistan had accessories attached to their M4 assault rifle such as reflex and optic sights, visible laser pointers, and night aiming devices/illuminators attached by a rail interface system. These accessories enable more rapid acquisition of targets and greater accuracy in both close quarter battle and at extended ranges in low light conditions. Referring to these, the Chinese weapons designers started work on accessories suitable for close quarter combat work by counterterrorist units. This tied in with an increase in funding for personnel and equipment for anti-disturbance duties.[49] Chinese special forces (机动部队) counterterrorist (反恐) personnel have add-on kits for their Type 81 and 95 assault rifles similar to the U.S. Special Operations Peculiar Modification (SOPMOD) system, utilizing a rail attachment system akin to the Knight's Armament Company rail interface system (RIS).[50]

CONCLUSION

The start of U.S. COIN operations in Afghanistan coincided with the PLA undertaking trials for the restructure of their mechanized infantry and operations in complex terrain, specifically urban warfare and at high altitudes. The PLA was able to piggy back extensively on the lessons learned from the United States in high altitude operations and to improve and accelerate modernization and development of the PLA, especially its informationalization emphasis. This is reflected in the company and platoon structures of the PLA. Others areas that benefited were strategic transport, army rotary wing aviation, battlefield fire support, and, above all, UAS. It may also be the case that the amount of satellites required to provide sufficient bandwidth for even the early days of U.S. operations in Afghanistan informed PLA efforts to focus China's anti-ballistic missile program to provide a near term anti-satellite capability.

Conversely, the direct impact on PLA COIN appears to be much less significant. In part, this may be the case because the PLA understands COIN to be solely a domestic issue for China. The Chinese entity responsible for the domestic COIN mission is the PAP, thereby further diminishing the connection to U.S. conventional forces. The two areas that appear to have been informed by U.S. operations include the importance of decapitation operations and the requirement to reduce unnecessary casualties during COIN operations to avoid international criticism, both of which can be applied in a domestic context. The fallout from the 1989 Tiananmen Square Incident would appear to have been forgotten or not discussed.

ENDNOTES - CHAPTER 7

1. On August 27, 2009, the 11th National People's Congress passed a law codifying the roles and responsibilities of the PAP, which is part of China's armed forces under the dual command of the Central Military Commission (CMC) and the State Council. (See *www.china-defense-mashup.com/china-tightens-restrictions-to-prevent-abuse-using-of-armed-police-force.html*.) The law designated the People's Armed Police Force (PAP) as solely responsible for internal anti-disturbance or *fang bao* (防暴) to deal with the three "isms" of terrorism, extremism (religious), and separatism. As the PAP is solely responsible for internal counterinsurgency (COIN) security and is part of the Chinese armed forces under the command of the CMC, the PAP is the component responsible for conducting COIN.

2. *Peishu* translates to "attaching troops to a subordinate unit," meaning the creation of independent battle groups within the division using modular force groups, as well as augmenting a division or larger structure seamlessly with heavier forces. *Zhichi* translates as "to support," which has seen the creation of a battlefield logistics organization able to supply and support forces deep inside an enemy's rear area.

3. "中国增强机械化步兵师攻击能力" ("China's Strengthened Mechanized Infantry Division's Assault Capability"), 坦克 装甲装甲 (*Tank and Armoured Vehicle*), Issue 11, 2006, No. 249, pp. 12 -13.

4. *Ibid.*, p. 12.

5. Deng Xiaoping, "Streamline the Army and Raise Its Combat Effectiveness," March 12, 1980)," cited in "Deng on Raising Army's Combat Effectiveness," *Foreign Military Broadcasting Service Daily Report: China*, July 26, 1983, pp. K2-K7.

6. "军用运输机: 翱翔蓝天的 '鲲鹏' " ("Military Transport Aircraft: Flying the Blue Sky of the 'Roc'"), 解放军报 (*PLA Daily*), March 11, 2010, available from *chn.chinamil.com.cn/xwpdxw/wqzbxw/2010-11/15/content_4334392.htm.*

7. Li Haijun (李海军), "切实提高我军战略投送能力" ("Effectively Improve the Delivery Capacity of Our Military Strategy"), 解放军报 (*PLA Daily*), March 11, 2010, available from *chn.chinamil.com.cn/xwpdxw/gdylxw/2010-03/11/content_4151489.htm.*

8. "Logistics in the PLA," *Army Sustainment*, March-April 2010, pp. 46-50.

9. "陆军是否需要战略投送力量" ("Does an army need strong strategic airlift?"), 兵器 知识 (*Ordnance Knowledge*), December 2007, No. 242, pp. 16-19; "重型直升机三种枸型的对比" ("Comparing three types of heavy helicopters"), 兵器知识 (*Ordnance Knowledge*), Issue 10A/2009, No. 278, pp. 16-19.

10. "开往蓝天的直升机___由 AC313首飞想到的"" ("Watching a Helicopter Heading for the Heavens___Thinking Flying and by AC313"), 兵器知识 (*Ordnance Knowledge*), Issue 5A/2010, No. 292, pp. 35-37.

11. L. W. Grau, *The Bear Went over the Mountain: Soviet Combat Tactics in Afghanistan*, Fort Leavenworth, KS: Foreign Military Studies office, 2005, p. 101.

12. Patrick Walters, "Hard-working Chinooks: The pack horse of the frontline," in "Special Report on Defence," *Weekend Australian*, November 29-30, 2008, p. 3.

13. Licensed produced Eurocopter AS 565 *Panther 2* helicopters. See "China Dispatched 30 Z-9G helicopters to the Sino-Afghan Border to Prevent Terrorists from Entering China and to Annihilate Terrorists Associated with Eastern Turkestan," *World Journal*, October 23, 2001, p. A7.

14. "Xinjiang Military District Holds Anti-Terrorist Drill," 中国国防报在线 (*China National Defense Dailyon-line*), December 12, 2004; Wei Chuan and Liang Yongli, "Xinjiang MD Army Air Regiment Conducts Nighttime Search-and-Rescue Training," 中国国防报在线 (*China National Defense Daily on-line*), May 4, 2005.

15. "国外媒体热评 中国 武直-10 直升机" ("Foreign Media Heatedly Evaluate Chinese WZ-10 Helicopter"), 坦克装甲装甲 (*Tank and Armored Vehicle*), Issue 1/2008, No. 263, pp. 29-31.

16. "PLA Army Aviation Units seek New Development," 解放军报 (*PLA Daily*), January 8, 2006.

17. "Jinan MR Mechanized Infantry Division Improves Reconnaissance," 前卫报 (*Vanguard Daily*), September 28, 2005.

18. Du Wenlong (杜文龙), "无人机时代真的到来了吗 " ("Are We Genuinely Approaching the Age of the Unmanned Vehicle?") 兵器知识 (*Ordnance Knowledge*), Issue 5A/2010, No. 292, pp. 64-65.

19. "Chinese Army takes on New Look," *People's Daily on-line*, June 19, 2002, available from *english.peopledaily.com.cn/200206/19/eng20020619_98094.shtml*; "CH-801 Micro UAV System," *China Aerospace Science and Technology Corporation*, 2008 brochure.

20. "PLA's UAVs achieve "combat effectiveness," 中国国防报 (*China Military Online*) and 中国日报 (*China Daily*), June 11, 2010, available from *eng.chinamil.com.cn/news-channels/china-military-news/2010- 06/11/content_4237629.htm*.

21. "华鹰翱翔抗震救灾" ("Chinese Eagle soaring providing support to earthquake victim"), 兵器知识 (*Ordnance Knowledge*), July 2008, No. 249, pp. 20-21.

22. "Jinan MR Mechanized Infantry Division Improves Reconnaissance," 前卫报 (*Vanguard Daily*), September 28, 2005.

23. "New type China made unmanned plane debuts at exhibition," China Military Online (Source: *Xinhua*), June 10, 2010, available from *eng.chinamil.com.cn/news-channels/photo-reports/2010-06/10/content_4236847.htm.*

24. "百花齐放 ___ 异军突起军团中国的UAV军团" ("Let a Hundred Flowers Bloom___ a Different Army Suddenly Appears: the Chinese UAV Army Group"), 坦克装甲装 (*Tank and Armored Vehicle*), Issue 4B1/2011, No. 330, pp. 31-35.

25. "China's pilotless aircraft CH3," *People's Daily Online*, November 3, 2008, available from *chn.chinamil.com.cn/90002/95730/index.html*; "CH-3 Medium Altitude Reconnaissance /Strike UAV System," *China Aerospace Science and Technology Corporation*, 2008 brochure.

26. "解放军大 规模演练夜间炮兵火力精确打击" ("People's Liberation Army Artillery Fire Massive Drill Precision Strikes at Night"), 解放军报 (*PLA Daily*), June 30, 2010, available from *chn.chinamil.com.cn /xwpdxw/2010-06/30/content_4249695.htm.*

27. For an explanation and Chinese development of the concept, see Valeriy Kiselev, "Acquired–Destroyed," *Armeyskiy Sbornik* (*Army Digest*), No. 8, 2001, pp. 35-39; "Learn how to fight battles in exercise—Analysis of PLA's training reform from military exercises in 2009 (III)," *China Military Online*, December, 15 2009, available from *eng.chinamil.com.cn/news-channels/china-military-news/ 2009-2/15/content_4095956.htm*; "'Eagle Owls' Over Chechnya," *Nezavisimoye Voyennoye Obozreniye* (*Independent Military Review*), No. 20, June 21-27, 2002, p. 2.

28. Han Jun (韩军), Chong Guang (重光), Chun Xiao (春晓), and Lan Bai (蓝白), "如何实施近距空中支援" ("How to execute close air support"), 兵器知识 (*Ordnance Knowledge*), Issue 9A/2008, No. 252, pp. 16-19; "目标瞄准命中摧毁的区别" ("Distinguishing, Tracking, Aiming at Targets within Range and Destroy-

ing"), 兵器知识 (*Ordnance Knowledge*), Issue 7A/2009, No. 272, pp. 16-19; "如何攻击小目标 " ("How to Assault a Small Target"), 兵器知识 (*Ordnance Knowledge*), Issue 3/2008 No. 245, pp. 16-19.

29. "Airborne Unit Begins Winter Drill to Retrain Troop," 北京空军报 (*Beijing Air Force Daily*), December 11, 2004.

30. "Scouts in target reconnaissance," *China Military Online*, April 30, 2010, available from *eng.chinamil.com.cn/news-channels/photo-reports/2010-04/30/content_4212152.htm.*

31. Han Jun (韩军), Chong Guang (重光), Chun Xiao (春晓), and Lan Bai (蓝白), "如何实施近距空中支援" ("How to execute close air support"), 兵器知识 (*Ordnance Knowledge*), Issue 3/2008, No. 245, pp. 16-19.

32. "迷你长钉: 世界最小的 '射后不管' 导弹" ("Mini-Spike: The World's Smallest 'Fire and Forget' Guided Missile"), 兵器知识 (*Ordnance Knowledge*), Issue 7A/2009, No. 272, pp. 50-52; "城市作战的难点" ("Difficult Points of Urban Combat"), 兵器知识, (*Ordnance Knowledge*), Issue 8A/2010, No. 298, pp. 16-19.

33. "Difficult Points of Urban Combat."

34. "New Characteristics of Annihilation Warfare on Future Informatized Battlefields," 人民前线, (*People's Frontline*), September 30, 2005.

35. Zhou Xuejun (周学军), "联合火力战斗—战术层次的战略影响" ("Joint Fire Fighting—The Strategic Impact of Tactical Level"), 解放军报 (*PLA Daily*), September 2, 2010, available from *chn.chinamil.com.cn/xwpdxw/gdylxw/2010-09/02/content_4290006.htm.*

36. Carlo Kopp, "PLA Guided Bombs," *Air Power Australia*, Technical Report APA-TR-2009-0808, available from *ausairpower.net/APA-PLA-GBU.html.*

37. "济南军区某部开展远程火力打击力量体系作战演练" ("Jinan Military Region to Carry out Long Range Firepower to Combat the Power System Operations Training"), 解放军报 (*PLA Daily*), June 14, 2010, available from *chn.chinamil.com.cn/xwpdxw/2010-06/14/content_4239188.*

38. Zhang Zhiyu, "New Characteristics of Annihilation Warfare on Future Informatized Battlefields," 人民前线 (*People's Frontline*), September 30, 2005.

39. "Reinforce armed police with legal backing," *Global Times online*, August 27, 2009, available from *opinion.globaltimes.cn/editorial/2009-08/461560.html*.

40. Zhang Xu, (张旭), "美军 '联合训练能力' 解析" ("Analysis of U.S. Military 'Joint Training Capability'"), 中国军事网站 (*China Military Online*), April 8, 2010, available from *chn.chinamil.com.cn/xwpdxw/gdylxw/2010-04/08/content_4173915.htm*.

41. *Ibid.*

42. "GSD Military Training Chief on Characteristics of PLA Military Training," 解放军画报 (*PLA Magazine*), January 2006.

43. Cheng Sixun, "Exploration and Practice of Integrated Training of Military Units, Part III," 战旗报 (*National Defense Daily*), February 14, 2006.

44. "PLA Army Aviation Units Seek New Development," 解放军报 (*PLA Daily*), January 8 , 2006.

45. H. Wang, "China's Strengthened Mechanized Infantry Division's Assault Capability ZTZ-98," 主战坦克 装甲 (*ZTZ-98 Main Battle Tank and Armor*), Hailar, Mongolia: Inner Mongolia Cultural Publishing Company, 2002, pp. 73, b 74.

46. "PLA's UAVs Achieve 'Combat Effectiveness'," 中国国防报 (*China Military Online*) and 中国日报 (*China Daily*), June 11, 2010, available from *eng.chinamil.com.cn/news-channels/china-military-news/2010-06/11/content_4237629.htm*.

47. "'CNMD' 亮相了! ___ 解读 我国初次反导挡截试验" ("'CNMD' Revealed! ___ Deciphering Our Country's First Anti-Missile Interceptor Experiments"), 坦克 装甲装甲 (*Tank and Armored Vehicle*), Issue 3/2010, No. 303, pp. 50-53.

48. "系列高技术装备提升保障能力" ("Series of High-tech Equipment to Enhance Security Capabilities"), 解放军报 (*PLA Daily*), May 31, 2010, available from *chn.chinamil.com.cn /xwp-dxw/2010-05/31/content_4228434.htm.* Numerous articles in 轻兵器 (*Small Arms*) show new Chinese developed weapons and their counterparts in the west, often near copies or adaptations of U.S. equipment.

49. "China sets up riot police units," *BBC Asia-Pacific News Online*, August 18, 2005.

50. "中国95式自动步枪展新颜" ("Chinese Type 95 Automatic Rifle Displays New Appearance"), 轻兵器 (*Small Arms*), Issue 12 2008, No. 285, p. 2; "Chinese Type 81-1 7.62mm automatic rifle new appearance," p. 3.

CHAPTER 7 - APPENDIX

SYSTEM CHARACTERISTICS

AVIATION SYSTEMS

MI-17.

The PLA's current high altitude transport and utility helicopter is the Russian Mi-17 transport helicopter, the export designation of the Mi-8MTV-2 helicopter. The PLA version incorporates a chin-mounted radar enabling bad weather operations, and can carry up to six 57mm UB-32 rocket pods containing a total of 192 57mm rockets providing transport helicopters a limited ability to suppress enemy air defenses.[1] The Mi-17 in PLA and PLAAF service has two 1,900 horsepower (hp) turbine engines compared to the Mi-8's engines rated at 1,700hp. The Mi-17 helicopter also carries an auxiliary power plant, which feeds the air starters to the engines, ensuring reliable starting of the main engines up to 4,000 meters (m) depending on the engine type. (During the ill-fated Soviet occupation of Afghanistan in the 1980s, the Mi-8 was severely underpowered at high altitudes. Due to the problems of flying in mountains at high altitudes, helicopters could only fly between 5 and 10 hours in a day, the Mi-8's maximum cargo never exceeded 400 kilograms (kg) and was often dropped at an altitude of between 5 and 30m at a speed ranging between 20 and 70 kilometers per hour (km/hr.)[2] Despite the extra power, the Mi-8MT/Mi-17MT can only carry six to eight combat-laden soldiers (each carrying 35 to 40kg of equipment in addition to his weapon and uniform) below 3,000m which decreases to only four or five at 3,000 to 4,000m altitude.[3] By comparison, the U.S. CH-47D *Chinook* transport helicopters deployed in Afghanistan can carry 30 passengers and five tons of cargo at the same altitudes.[4]

The Z-10 attack helicopter is similar in size to AH-1W and will be the linchpin of the PLA Army Aviation's modernization plans. Besides anti-armor, its missions will include escort, armed reconnaissance, and force protection, the latter against enemy attack and reconnaissance helicopters and UAVs.[5] The Z-10 is in the size and weight range of the Italian A129 *Mangusta*, with many design features directly copied from it including the cockpit. It is awaiting a new engine, because the current 1,531hp Pratt and Whitney Canada PT6C-6TC engine used with the prototype is not available for military use under the post-Tiananmen Square embargo. High horsepower rating is important, because of the negative effect that heat and high altitudes have on helicopter performance.[6] The poor performance of helicopters at high altitudes is why the CH-47D and later versions has become the primary helicopter for delivery of cargo and personnel by air in Afghanistan.

Transport Helicopters.

The Chinese aircraft company AVIC has developed the AC313 medium lift helicopter, an advanced development of the old Z-8, itself a copy of the old *Aerospatiale Super Frelon* helicopter.[7] With composite materials comprising 50 percent of the helicopter to reduce its empty weight, and with three Pratt and Whitney Canada PT6B-67A turbo-shaft engines delivering 20 percent more power, the AC313 can fly up to 6,000m and operate in temperatures from -40° Celsius (°C) to +50°C, enabling it to operate on the Tibetan Plateau with ease.

With a maximum takeoff weight of 13.8 tons, the AC313 can carry four tons in its 1.83m high, 23.5 cubic meter cabin or five tons slung externally below the helicopter. The maximum passenger capacity is 27, with two crew members and 15 stretchers with attendant crew sitting in chairs. It is not supposed to be used in a military role as the engines are embargoed for military missions. If it were, it could carry a crew of four, including a starboard door gunner, and around 14 or 15 fully equipped combat troops entering and exiting by the rear ramp.

Interestingly, no helicopters in the PLA Army Aviation Force have been seen mounting any type of door gun to provide suppressive fire when the helicopters come into land during an assault. Placing a machine gun with mount, ammunition, and dedicated gunner to provide suppressive fire at high altitudes would severely restrict the amount of personnel or cargo that a Z-9 or Mi-17 helicopter could carry.

UNMANNED AERIAL SYSTEMS

CH-801.

A hand-launched micro-UAS is already in service. The wingspan is 900 milimeters (mm) it has an overall length of 800mm, a gross weight of 1.75kg, and a 200 grams (g) payload. It looks like a plastic F-22 with oversized tail fins. Of a pusher configuration, its electric motor gives the CH-801 a maximum air speed of 80km/hr and maximum endurance of 60 minutes. Its cruise altitude is between 50 and 1,000m, with a maximum ceiling of 3,500m. Its L-band control/data link has a maximum line of sight of 10km, with the images viewed on a lap top screen with the UAS control system mounted in a separate back pack.

W-50.

Developed by the Nanjing Research Institute on Simulation Technique, the W-50 has the ability to remain aloft for up to 6 hours and has an operational radius of 100 kilometers, depending on the payload. Nanjing has also developed the Z-3 helicopter unmanned aerial vehicle (UAV) which weighs 130kg with a 30kg payload, and incorporates GPS navigation for pre-planned reconnaissance missions.[8] Of pusher configuration with twin booms connecting a 'V' shaped rear fin 2.1m long, the W-50 has a wingspan of 2.6m and weighs 20kg. It can travel at 110km/hr, reach an altitude of 3,500m and has GPS assisted guidance.

Z-5.

The Z-5 has an all up weight of 450kg including a 100kg mission payload.[9] It has a cruising speed of 160 km/hr, an endurance of between 4 to 6 hrs, and a maximum hover height of 2,500m. It uses automatic controls as well as being command guided.

PW Series.

The PW-1 is similar in shape and size to the Israeli *Aerosky* lightweight UAV.[10] Of twin-boom pusher configuration, it missions include surveillance, reconnaissance, fire control, and target positioning. With a wingspan of 4.4m and 3.8m long, its 16.4Kw piston engine gives the UAV a maximum speed of 170km/hr and an endurance of between 4-6 hrs. The gross take off weight is 130kg with a 20kg payload, and its cruising altitude is 1-3km with a maximum ceiling of

4,600m. The L-band control/data-link has a maximum line of sight range of 100km with its launch being by a small rocket booster that falls away after launch. Landing is by parachute as it only has skids.

The PW-2 is essentially an enlarged PW-1.[11] With a wingspan of 6m and an overall length of 4.1m, its 36.7 kilowatt (Kw) piston engine gives it a maximum speed of 180 km/hr and an endurance of between 6-8 hrs. It has a maximum ceiling of 5,000m with its cruising altitude being between 1,000 and 3,000m. Its gross takeoff weight is 220kg with a 30kg payload. Its S-band control/data-link has a line of sight range of 200km.

PV-2.

The Israeli *Aerostar* UAV, the PV-2, lacks both range and payload.[12] With a wingspan of 6.5m and a length of 4.5m, the *Aerostar* weighs 10kg less, yet carries a 50kg payload with endurance over 12 hrs. It also takes off and lands conventionally, unlike the PW-2 which uses rocket assisted take off and a parachute recovery like the smaller PW-1.

CH-3.

Of tailless canard design, with the flaps mounted on the tips of rear double delta wings. The wingspan is 8m, and it has an overall length of 5.5m. Its 85Kw engine, mounted in the rear of fuselage, has a triple blade propeller giving the CH-3 a maximum air speed of 256km/hr. Missions envisaged include surveillance, reconnaissance, fire control, target positioning, and precision strike. Their possible future use in operations is examined in the next section under battlefield fire support. The projected cruising altitude is between 3-5km, and the device has a maximum ceiling of 6km. It has an 8m wingspan, is 5.5m long, and its 85Kw engine gives it a reported maximum endurance of 12hr. The maximum gross take-off weight is 630kg with a 60kg payload. The CH-3 utilizes a blended fuselage and incorporates a stabilized targeting turret under the forward fuselage that contains a laser ranger/target designator coupled with a charge-coupled device (CCD) or thermal imaging camera. The S band control/data-link has a maximum line of sight range of 200km.

There is a large pylon under each rear wing, which on the mockup mounts an AR-1 air-to-surface missile purposely designed for UAVs. Compared to the U.S. MQ-1C *Warrior*, it appears similar in size although it incorporates a chisel nose instead of the bulbous nose, which contains a Synthetic Aperture Radar/Ground Moving Target Indicator (SAR-GMTI) system, and an AN/AAS-52 Multi-spectral Targeting System (MTS) under the nose. It takes off and lands on grass conventionally with a fixed tricycle undercarriage.

The biggest issue facing the PLA in its use of UAS systems is the Chinese industry's lack of lightweight fuel-efficient engines, composites, and avionics.

BATTLEFIELD FIRE SUPPORT

Close Air Support.

The Q-5, developed from the Russian MiG-19, has been equipped with the hardware and software to enable the use of the LT-2 laser-guided 500kg bombs. The more advanced LT-3 is also available, which is a 500kg bomb mated to a laser seeker in the nose with a GPS guided bomb kit mounted on the rear, and is analogous to the U.S. EGBU-24.[13] The Q-5 is similar to the 1970s *Harrier* GR-3 in capability except that it uses conventional take off and landing. The use of an external pod with a thermal imager and the LT-3 would bring the aircraft up to the early 1990s in capability but the airframe is still old and in need of replacement.

MANEUVER

Armored Group Task Organization.

- Type 92 wheeled infantry fighting vehicles each with a one-man turret with an overhead 25 x 137mm automatic cannon and co-axial Type 80 7.62 x 54Rmm machine gun; and 15 Type 92A wheeled armored personnel carriers, each mounting a semi-enclosed turret with a 12.7 x 108mm Type 54 heavy machine gun.
- PTL02 assault guns, each mounting a turret with a Type 86 100mm smoothbore high-velocity cannon, co-axial Type 80 7.62 x 54mm machine gun, and a cupola-mounted 12.7 x 108mm QJC88 heavy machine gun.
- Z-9W attack helicopters, some with an undernose turret mounting a laser range-finder/ designator and thermal imager. Depending on electronics fit, a Z-9W can carry either eight Hong Jia-8 anti-tank guided missiles; eight TY-90 lightweight air-to-air missiles; or two 57mm rocket; or two cannon pods.
- Mi-17 transport helicopters, each capable of carrying up to six 57mm rocket pods containing 32 rockets each or around 16 troops.
- ZBD05 airborne combat vehicles mounting a 30

x 165mm automatic cannon and a co-axial 5.8 x 42mm machine gun and can carry four soldiers in the rear.

INFANTRY WEAPONS

Rail Interface System and Accessories.

Chinese special forces (*jidong budui*) counterterrorist (*fan kong*) personnel have add-on kits for their Type 81 and 95 assault rifles similar to the U.S. Special Operations Peculiar Modification (SOPMOD) system, utilizing a rail attachment system akin to the Knight's Armament Company rail interface system (RIS).[14] The Type 81 squad automatic weapon has a forward rail interface system to which is attached a forward folding bipod with telescopic legs and a night aiming device on the left hand side towards the end of the RIS. A reflex sight, similar to the U.S. advanced combat optical gunsight (ACOG) reflex sight is also fitted. The Type 95 assault rifle has the same type of reflex sight fitted to the top of the carrying handle giving a poor cheek weld and appears to be used for instinctive instead of aimed fire. The Type 84 sub-machine gun has a RIS with the same bipod and night aiming device (NAD) as on the Type 81 squad automatic weapon. Both have forward handgrips. The bipod is just extra weight on the Type 81 assault rifle, but the system is similar to the close quarter battle kit above. The Type 81 RIS mount fitted to the left side of the weapon incorporates an under barrel RIS. Besides mounting a torch and bipod, the mount above the receiver can fit an ELCAN Wildcat sight.

Type 95 Under Barrel 18.4 x 70mm Shotgun.[15]

This weapon is still a prototype but is expected to go into production. Very much like the XM26, it uses a straight pull bolt and connects under the barrel of the Type 95 5.8mm assault rifle. There is no muzzle brake or flash suppressor fitted and it is fed from a box magazine that appears to hold three cartridges.

XL-Z01 4x4 and XL-Z02 6x6 Prototype Protected Mobility Vehicles-Light.[16]

The Chinese defense industries in Wuhan has developed two new protected mobility vehicles-light (PMV-L), the XL-Z01 4 x 4 and XL-Z02 6 x 6. The latter is an extended version of the former and has the four rear wheels grouped together. They are similar in concept to the Australian Bushmaster PMV-L, rather than the much larger MRAP-L, as the hull is of monocoque construction with the underneath having a 'V' shape to deflect mine blast. The hull is a very clean design, with arrow shaped angled sides which do not allow Molotov cocktails to pool or offer a place for satchel charges to hang onto the vehicle. Other than a turret, the only external protrusions are the heavily reinforced hinges and extended driver's side mounted rear view mirrors. Both vehicles are amphibious with two small shrouded propellers behind the rear wheels. Both are armored against penetration by standard 5.45 x 39mm, 5.56 x 45mm North Atlantic Treaty Organization (NATO) and 5.8 x 42 DBP87 projectiles and two German DM41 grenades exploding simultaneously against the hull. Both are equipped with an anti-lock braking system (ABS) and can climb a 300 slope. The engine on both is mid-mounted on the right side, and doors are provided on either side and at the rear of the hull. Both driver and front passenger have roof-mounted hatches. The XL-Z01 weighs 5 tons and can carry a crew of five. Powered by an 188Kw V8 diesel engine, it has a maximum road speed of 140 km/hr and can be fitted with a small one-man turret that can be fitted with weapons up to and including a QJG02 14.5 x 114mm machine gun. Other weapons can include a 35mm automatic grenade launcher or sniping rifle. The turret includes six Type 85-2 76mm smoke grenade dischargers and a small external rack around the rear of the turret. The XL-Z02 weighs 9t and can carry a maximum of 12 personnel. The vehicle has the same turret ring as the WZ501/Type 86 infantry fighting vehicle (IFV) enabling it to field any weapons the Type 86 can. Its 6.4 liter (L) 240Kw V8 diesel engine gives it a maximum road speed of 130 km/hr.

ENDNOTES - CHAPTER 7 - APPENDIX

1. S. Dolgov, "On a Wing and a Prayer," in S. Roshchin, S. Reznichenko, and S. Saoylyuk, "War Doesn't Sleep," *Armeyskiy Sbornik*, (*Army Digest*), October 2000, p. 59.

2. L. W. Grau and Michael A. Gress eds., *The Soviet-Afghan War: How a Superpower Fought and Lost: The Russian General Staff*, Lawrence, KS: University of Kansas Press, 2002, p. 287.

3. L. W. Grau, *The Bear Went over the Mountain: Soviet Combat Tactics in Afghanistan*, Fort Leavenworth, KS: Foreign Military Studies office, 2005, p. 101.

4. Patrick Walters, "Hard-working Chinooks: The pack horse of the frontline," in "Special Report on Defence," *Weekend Australian*, November 29-30, 2008, p. 3.

5. "国外媒体热评 中国 武直-10 直升机" ("Foreign Media Heatedly Evaluate Chinese WZ-10 Helicopter"), 坦克装甲装甲 (*Tank and Armored Vehicle*), Issue 1/ 2008, No. 263, pp. 29-31.

6. After the paper was presented, the Z-10 program was replaced by the Sino-Russian Z-19 which uses the transmission, tail assembly, and possibly other components from the Z-9W.

7. "开往蓝天的直升机___由 AC313首飞想到的" ("Watching a Helicopter Heading for the Heavens___Thinking Flying and by AC313"), 兵器知识 (*Ordnance Knowledge*), Issue 5A/2010, No. 292, pp. 35-37.

8. "'W-50 Unmanned Air Vehicle', Nanjing Research Institute on Simulation Technique," available from *www.nrist.com/english/e-wurenji-w-50.asp*; Wu Xiaochun, "NRIST Keeps Forging Ahead-Part II," *Military Training & Simulation News*, Vol. 5, Issue 6, November 2003, pp. 54-55.

9. "第五届中国国际警用装备博览会新品收视" ("The Fifth Annual China International Police Use of Equipment Exhibition Viewing New Products"), 轻兵器 (*Small Arms*), Issue 5, 2010, No. 319, p. 21.

10. "PW-1 Close Range Reconnaissance UAV System," *China Aerospace Science and Technology Corporation*, 2008 brochure; "Aerosky," *Israeli Weapons*, available from *www.israeli-weapons.com/aircraft/uavs/aerosky/Aerosky.hml*.

11. "PW-2 Close Range Reconnaissance UAV System," *China Aerospace Science and Technology Corporation*, 2008 brochure.

12. "Aerosky."

13. Carlo Kopp, "PLA Guided Bombs," *Air Power Australia*, Technical Report APA-TR-2009-0808, available from *ausairpower.net/APA-PLA-GBU.html*.

14. "中国95式自动步枪展新颜"("Chinese Type 95 Automatic Rifle Displays New Appearance"), 轻兵器 (*Small Arms*), Issue 12, 2008, No. 285, p. 2.

15. "95式自动步枪首次下挂18.4mm霰弹枪"("Type 95 Automatic Rifle with Suspended 18.4mm Shotgun"), 轻兵器 (*Small Arms*), Issue 5, 2010, No. 319, p. 2.

16. "无惧坎坷路__武汉 '枭龙' 越野车旌演示试验参观记" ("No Fear Rough Road__'Brave Dragon' Cross Country Vehicle Observe and Record Demonstrate Test Vehicles"), 兵器 (*Weapon*), Issue 7/2010, No. 134, pp. 34-38; "特种 甲车显峥嵘 2010年 中国国际警用装备上的装甲车" ("2010 Chinese International Police Use Equipment Vehicles Exhibition Special Type Event Top Equipped Vehicles Display"), 坦克装甲装甲 (*Tank and Armored Vehicle*), Issue 6/2010, No. 309, pp. 43-45.

CHAPTER 8

LEARNING FROM THE NEIGHBORS: THE PEOPLE'S LIBERATION ARMY EXAMINES THE SMALL WARS AND COUNTERINSURGENCIES WAGED BY RUSSIA

Yu Bin

EXECUTIVE SUMMARY

This chapter examines the People's Liberation Army's (PLA) assessment of the Russian counterinsurgency (COIN) operations from the 1990s and beyond.

MAIN FINDINGS

In the absence of large-scale insurgencies in the People's Republic of China (PRC) over the past 40 years, and the distant experience of China's own COIN operations in the 1950s-60s, the PLA pays close attention to the COIN operations of the Russian military, particularly the two Chechen wars (1994-96 and 1999-2009). The PLA analysts seem to have reached a consensus regarding the socio-politico-economic origins of the post-Soviet insurgency and terror issues in Russia. That is, terrorism and insurgencies are forms of "political violence" caused by deeper social ills. They have debated, however, about the effectiveness of the tactics, use of firepower, intelligence gathering, and processing of the Russian COIN operations. While the PLA academia display more favorable views of the Russian operations in the second Chechen War, the PLA intelligence, including their counterparts in the

People's Armed Police (PAP), are more critical about Russia's approaches, particularly about the weakness of the Russian intelligence in COIN operations, as well as in dealing with terror groups in the broader socio-political milieu.

POLICY IMPLICATIONS

- PLA analysts clearly favor broader and more comprehensive treatment of the terror and insurgency issues.
- They attach great importance to intelligence gathering, sharing, processing, and disseminating in anti-terror and COIN operations.
- The PLA discourse over the Russian experience, particularly the structural deficiency of the Russian intelligence community, is perhaps a detour for some analysts, such as in the PAP, to argue for more effective and independent intelligence gathering and processing ability and infrastructure.
- Some, particularly the Intelligence Department of the PLA General Staff, favor the American approach of high-tech reconnaissance and information analysis, something that the Russians seem incapable of doing. It is unclear how this is operationalized.
- The focus on the tactical aspects of the Russian COIN operations by some analysts remains relevant for the PLA in the event that such militarized COIN operations become necessary.
- Recent discussion of anti-terror and COIN shows that PLA is getting interested in cross-border operations.

INTRODUCTION

Perhaps more than anything else, Russia represents a special case for the PLA regarding small wars
and COIN operations for at least four reasons. First,
Russia as a large land power on the Eurasian conti-
nent happens to share long borders with China. On
many occasions in the past, what happened in Russia has tended to have an impact on its relationship
with China. The stability, or instability, of the border
regions has always been a security issue for China.
Second, Russia has undergone major socio-politico-
economic transformations since the end of the Cold
War, with wide-spread social inequality, instability,
and even political and ethnic violence. Third, Russia
(including those former Soviet republics) happens to
border China's Xinjiang Autonomous Region where
ethnic tensions have been on the rise since September 11, 2001 (9/11) and even culminated in 2009 with
large-scale urban riots. Last, if not least, China and
Russia are multi-ethnic nation-states where ethnic
identity has been on the rise in the brave new post-
9/11 world of globalized terrorism, insurgency, and
cross-border criminal activities; and Russia has waged
COIN operations against long-term and large-scale
ethnic violence (Chechnya, etc.).

How does Russia wrestle with its internal tension
and conflicts? To what extent do the Russian military
and security apparatus cope with the increasingly
asymmetrical and deadly violence perpetrated against
innocent people? What is the relationship between
those operations and the broader socio-economic environment in Russia? Will these developments in Russia have a spillover effect in China? How relevant is
Russia's experience for the Chinese situation?

These questions, among others, will be addressed in four specific steps. This chapter begins with a brief survey of China's own experience with COIN operations in both traditional and modern periods. The focus is on the PRC's experience after 1949. This will lead to the examination of how the PLA defines the concept of COIN in both Chinese and non-Chinese terms, and in both traditional and contemporary periods. This paves the way for systematic survey of how the Chinese military and civilian intelligence organizations perceive and assess COIN operations in Russia. In conclusion, some policy relevant issues will be addressed.

THE DYNAMICS OF INSURGENCY AND COIN IN CHINA

The phenomenon of COIN is no stranger to the Chinese. Indeed, insurgency and COIN were enduring features in traditional Chinese politics as almost all of the dynasties were overthrown by rebellions (造反) and/or insurgencies (叛乱). In most cases, insurgent leaders installed themselves as the next dynasties until their dynasties were toppled by another wave of protest-turn-to-insurgency/rebellion. In the minds of the ordinary Chinese, this cycle of dynasty-rebellions was even "normal," because it was legitimate to rebel against the emperor if he was deemed to have lost the mandate of heaven. These types of violent rebellions ended the despotic rule of the first *Qin* Dynasty (221-206 BC), and fatally weakened the last *Qing* Dynasty.[1] Throughout China's dynastic history, it was not uncommon to see the drastic role-switching between rebels and rulers, and vice versa. Insurgency, therefore, was but a symptom of much larger and deeper social illness.

To a large extent, the political history of 20th century China was one of a central government fighting localized forces ranging from heavily armed warlords, disorganized bandits, to organized insurgencies such as Communist guerrillas. From the very beginning, the Republic of China on the Mainland (1911-49) was plagued by its own internal division in the form of Warlordism (1916-26). Many provincially based generals became *de facto* independent from the central government, and fought constantly against one another for territory and influence. It was not until 1927 that Chiang Kai-shek was able to pacify most of these that warlords. After Chiang took Shanghai in 1927, he turned against Communists in the major cities. Those who survived Chiang's "white terror" fled to the countryside where they gradually set up Communist base areas. For Chiang's government, the Communists were simply "bandits" (共匪). From 1930 to 1934, Chiang launched five "extermination," or COIN, campaigns against Communist base areas in Jiang Xi Province. The Fifth Campaign crushed the Communists. Their main forces were forced to embark upon the "Long March" to the northern Chinese Shaanxi Province where they consolidated, expanded, and emerged from the 8 years of war with Japan to confront the Nationalist government. In less than 4 years, eight million Nationalist troops were wiped out, surrendered, or fled to Taiwan. Then, the victorious Communist government started to use the terms "bandits" (Chiang's bandits, [蒋匪]; or KMT bandits, [国民党匪徒]) to describe the Nationalist troops and government in Taiwan.

Militarily, however, the new PRC government would have to engage in its own large-scale "bandit extermination" campaigns (剿匪) to mop up remnants of the Nationalist troops and local bandits whose forces had grown considerably, because of the weak central government in the 1930s-40s. Recently disclosed archives in China indicate that the Nationalists, in anticipating Communist victory on the Mainland, started to train more than 3,000 guerrilla warfare experts in June 1949 and Chiang Kai-shek activated a comprehensive plan for covert and insurgency activities shortly before he left for Taiwan. As a result, there was a deluge of insurgent activities throughout China between late 1949 and early 1950. In a matter of 8 days, February 6-13, 1950, more than 20 counties, prefectures, and provincial governments were attacked by the insurgents, leading to the deaths of tens of thousands of PLA and local government personnel. These numbers, however, do not include large casualties of local masses who supported the new Communist government. Mao, who just returned from a 3-month visit to Moscow, was reportedly stunned by the scale and intensity of the insurgency. Between 1950 and 1952, the PLA launched two nationwide campaigns and "annihilated" (歼灭) some 2.4 million insurgents and Nationalist agents.[2]

The PRC's 3-year COIN operations paralleled much of the Korean War (1950-53), which was a heavy commitment for the young republic with a seriously damaged economy after decades of wars. The PLA would have to engage in both foreign and domestic operations to consolidate much of the ungovernable parts of China, particularly in the border areas. Despite these constraints, major COIN operations were essentially over in late 1952 in most Chinese territories except in three border regions. In the northwestern parts of China (Qinghai, Xinjiang, Gansu, and Sichuan provinces), COIN operations dragged on until late 1953.[3] In Tibet, resistance to the Chinese rule was on and off, and culminated in the 1959 open rebellion. Much of these insurgencies were financed and facilitated by the U.S. Central Intelligence Agency (CIA), whose covert operations did not come to an end until the early 1970s.[4] Along the Sino-Burmese borders, the small wars against the Nationalist troops located in Burma continued until 1966.[5]

At the turn of the century, Xinjiang and Tibet became restless again. Several riots occurred in the late 1980s in Tibet and harsher policies were imposed following the crackdown. In the 1990s, Xinjiang witnessed more incidents ranging from bus bombings to violent demonstrations and crackdowns, several of which took place in Xinjiang's capital city of Urumqi. An armed insurgency reportedly broke out in Xinjiang in April 1990, and in 1996-97, more riots were reported.[6] In the new millennium, ethnic tension in Tibet and Xinjiang began to escalate in both scale and intensity, which peaked prior to the 2008 Beijing Olympics, for example: the March 14 riot in the Tibet capital of Lhasa, the largest since 1988-89; an aborted bombing of Flight CZ6901 of China Southern Airline enroute from Urumqi to Beijing on March 7;[7] and the terrorist attacks 4 days before the opening of the Beijing Olympics, which killed 16 and wounded 16 PAP.[8]

Two sets of factors—internal and external—apparently contributed to the recent trend of terrorism in China. In the first place, the reform decades, while considerably improving the living standards of Chinese people, including that of the minorities, have meant different things for the minorities in Tibet and Xinjiang. In the 1980s, General Secretary Hu Yaobang encouraged more autonomous rule by the minorities. Following several high-profile riots in the mid-

1980s, however, the central government switched to harsher policies. Economic reforms and development also brought in large numbers of Han businessmen and workers, leading to a sense of relative deprivation among the locals, hence the growing ethnic tensions.

Externally, the rise of Islamic separatism in the adjacent Central Asia after the Soviet collapse has also enhanced Uyghurs' cultural identity and ethnic tension in Xinjiang. According to PLA General Xiong Guangkai (熊光楷), pro-Eastern Turkistan separatists launched more than 260 terror attacks inside China in 1990-2003, killing 170 and wounding 400.[9] The year 1996 witnessed two separate developments in this regard. In April, the heads of state of Kazakhstan, China, Kyrgyzstan, Russia, and Tajikistan created the Shanghai-Five by signing "The Treaty on Deepening Military Trust in Border Regions." In September, the Taliban came to power and increasingly turned Afghanistan into a hotbed of religious extremism and even terrorism, thus threatening the stability and security of its neighbors, including China. External influence on China's domestic ethnic tension is not new. Of the more than 20 large-scale insurgencies in Xinjiang during the last Qing Dynasty (1616-1911), most of them had external connections. In the 20th century, according to Chinese analysts, Xinjiang's disturbances and separatism were also connected with "the forces that dominated Central Asia," meaning the former Soviet Union.[10]

Given these historical experiences and recent developments, the Shanghai Five adjusted their mission from force reduction and military confidence building along the border regions to a multidimensional one, including combating the "three forces": terrorism, national separatism, and religious extremism.

In their third summit in July 1998, the Shanghai Five declared in a joint communiqué to strike against the "three forces" and against arms and drug smuggling activities in the region. In the fourth Shanghai Five summit in Kyrgyzstan in August 1999, the organization made it explicit that members of the organization would not allow the actions from their own countries to jeopardize the sovereignty, security, and social order of any other member state.[11] This item was particularly important for China because there are large Uyghur communities in the Central Asian countries, particularly in Kazakhstan, Kyrgyzstan, and Uzbekistan.[12] By the time the Shanghai Five evolved itself into the Shanghai Cooperation Organization (SCO) in June 2001, which was fully 3 months before 9/11, fighting the "three forces" had become an integral part of the SCO's policy. Ten days prior to 9/11, the China Institutes of Contemporary International Relations (CICIR) in Beijing officially put into operation its Center for Counter-Terrorism Studies (CCTS) with the publication of its first study of international terrorism, *Global Terrorism and Counter-Terrorist Campaign*.[13]

The Chinese, as well as their counterparts in the SCO, had a heightened sense of international terrorism, while the new Bush administration was preoccupied with the "vestigial Cold War concerns," such as the Anti-Ballistic Missile (ABM) Treaty, and downgrading U.S. counterterrorist institutions and ignoring the emerging threat against America.[14]

In retrospect, the issues of insurgency and COIN for China have always been part of a broader order-disorder context and they have represented recurring challenges for generations of politicians, officials, and ordinary Chinese. What separates the past and current insurgencies is perhaps the result of heightened ethnic identity, on a globalized scale, and the fluidity of the situation as a result of the revolution of world-wide transportation and communication technologies. In other words, the speed at which information/dis-information is disseminated and the "virtual" space that insurgency forces can operate in make it much harder for established authorities to maintain security and order. All of this, plus the growing trend to target innocent people, has been occurring while China has been steadily growing as a world power over the past few decades. The inexperience and deficiencies of China's anti-terror and COIN operations were clearly revealed during the 2008 Tibet and 2009 Xinjiang riots, particularly in regard to their intelligence, knowledge, preparation, and coordination of and between political and military authorities and between various military and paramilitary units.[15]

It is within this context of the fear of chaos, the long history of insurgency and COIN, the efficiency and power of the modern means of communication, the heightened sense of cultural and religious identity in the post-9/11 world, and the lack of first-hand experience in dealing with contemporary large-scale and sudden riots/insurgencies that the PLA perceives other "peoples' wars" and defines the scope and substance of their own concept of insurgency and COIN. Among China's neighbors, Russia draws particular attention of China's defense and security community for both practical and vigilant purposes.

CONCEPTUALIZATION AND DEFINITIONS

There is a significant gap between the way that China and the U.S./West define terrorism, insurgency, and COIN at three separate but related levels. At the global level where most of the existing definitions of terrorism and insurgency are constructed by the West, PLA analysts believe that they are highly normative and Western-centered.[16] Like their civilian counterparts, PLA analysts also reject the West's "double standard" in defining certain violent actions against the West as acts of terror while ignoring or dismissing those against other peoples and governments.[17] At the regional level such as the SCO, Beijing clearly specifies the target of its anti-terror operation in the "Shanghai Agreement for Combating Terrorism, Separatism, and Extremism" in 2001 (打击恐怖主义、分裂主义和极端主义的上海公约).[18] In domestic debates, most Chinese analysts focus on terrorism, while virtually bypassing or dismissing the concept of insurgency and COIN.[19] One of the reasons for this is perhaps the near absence for several decades of any large-scale insurgency inside China. An implicit reason may well be a historical fact of life that the PLA actually evolved from the insurgent-style of guerrilla forces that conducted asymmetrical warfare against much stronger enemies, be they the Nationalists or the Japanese. Some in the PLA, therefore, do not want to call guerrilla warfare terrorism.

PLA analysts do recognize the similarities between terrorism and guerrilla tactics in revolutionary wars, that is, both terrorism and guerrilla tactics involve asymmetrical tactics against much stronger foes. There are, however, two crucial differences between terrorism and guerrilla warfare. One is that the former targets innocent civilians, while the latter avoids such tactics. The second difference is the goals of the fighting: guerrilla warfare strives to achieve military victory; terrorism aims at expanding political impact through terror because military victory against the much more powerful enemy is impossible. In a way, the difference between guerrilla tactics and terrorism is a matter of degree: the former is a weapon for the weak; the latter is a weapon for the weakest. Despite these differences, the line between the two may become blurred if guerrilla forces use terror tactics by attacking innocent civilians.[20]

Despite the above-mentioned disparities with the West, Chinese analysts do recognize terrorism as a form of political violence. In 2002, three PAP analysts separately used the Clausewitzian treatise to describe terrorist actions as extension of politics by other means.[21] This was a year before Robert Pape's provocative writing regarding the strategic and political goals of contemporary terrorism[22] and is in sharp contrast to popular beliefs in the West that terrorism is driven by, and pursues, religious extremism. "[T]errorism is a kind of asymmetric violent practice with political logics," according to Zhang Jiadong, a prominent scholar on terrorism in Fudan University, Shanghai.[23] Since such an act is targeted against innocent people, it is a crime against humanity. This is similar to many Western definitions.[24]

Beyond this, however, Chinese security experts have deliberated on both the substance and boundaries of politically motivated terrorism. The trend seems to embed various forms of terrorism into the broad paradigm of nontraditional threats. A cursory look at published Chinese works show that Chinese security experts and institutions began to pay attention to the issue in the early 21st century when Lu Zhongwei—who was director of the influential CICIR (1999-2009)—in 2003 published *On Nontraditional Security*.[25] By the end of the decade, the topic attracted more attention from both academic and military circles in China.[26] In 2009, Beijing's Shi Shi Publishing House (时事出版社), which is directly administrated by CICIR, published *Armed Forces and Nontraditional Security Issues*, a co-authored volume by two apparent PLA experts on security issues. Not only does it define the nontraditional security issues for the PLA, but for the first time it also provides a comprehensive survey of how armies of various major powers, including Russia, deal with nontraditional threats including terrorism.[27] It is clear that the PLA realizes that an effective approach to dealing with nontraditional threats including terrorism and its sources cannot be fully developed without gaining insights into the experiences of other militaries, particularly that of Russia.

ASSESSING RUSSIA

The PLA pays close attention to the Russian military's counter-terror and COIN operations primarily regarding the Chechen wars (1994-96 and 1999-2009), and Chechnya related high-profile terrorist incidents that have occurred throughout Russia, which embodied various types of nontraditional threats including terrorism, insurgency, guerrilla warfare, urban terrorism, separatism, etc., almost all of which can be found in China, though to a lower degree. PLA analysts have expressed particular interest in the origins, types, and consequences regarding the Chechen wars and the lessons drawn from them.

Origin and Evolution.

Many PLA analysts noted the long and complicated history that gave rise to the Chechen issue. They identified several root causes of the Chechen terrorism: Czarist expansion into the Caucasus region in the 19th century; the 2-day forced relocation of half a million Chechens and Ingushens to Central Asia and Siberia in 1944 as a way to "punish" their collaboration with the Nazis, which resulted in the deaths of nearly half of those deported within the first 18 months of their relocation; the mismanagement of Russia's relations with Chechnya following the Soviet collapse in 1991, etc. [28]

Russia's mismanagement started immediately after the dissolution of the Soviet Union on December 26, 1991. As the Soviet power structure was melting away, Boris Yeltsin continued to champion democratization and local autonomy, further weakening Russia's already flimsy control of the localities including Chechnya. On November 1, 1991, Chechen independence was officially declared by the radical separatist leader Dzhokhar Dudayev, who was a former Soviet Air Force general, even though Russia's Supreme Soviet dismissed the Chechen "presidential election" a few days before as illegal. At the time, Yeltsin paid little attention to the events in Chechnya because of his preoccupation with political infighting in Russia. This was tantamount to acquiescing Dudayev's *de facto* control of Chechnya.[29] Indeed, a *de facto* independent Chechen state was allowed to exist for two 3-year periods in the 1990s (1992-94 and 1996-99), and this was perhaps one of Russia's biggest mistakes. It encouraged and enabled the Chechen separatist movement to grow, expand, and consolidate during this period to the point of open confrontation with the central authorities, threatening to "Balkanize" not only the Caucasus, but also the entire Russian Federation.[30]

Perhaps the biggest mistake Yeltsin made, according to Yu, was that Russia signed and implemented an agreement with Chechnya to withdraw all troops from Chechnya and to divide the remaining Soviet armament in Chechnya. According to the agreement, the Dudayev government would receive 50 percent of the Russian weapons that were deployed in Chechnya. By the time of the official ending of the Soviet Union in late December 1991, Dudayev issued a "presidential order" that the Chechens have the right to bear arms. In February 1992, there was widespread looting of the Russian military posts and armories in Chechnya. According to Russian sources, the Chechen military was well armed on the eve of the first Chechen War in August 1994, with more than 100 T-62 and T-72 main battle tanks, 260 war planes, 100 antiaircraft machine guns, 18 sets of BM-21 rocket launchers (40 tube - 122mm rockets), and more than 60,000 rifles. Dudayev was quoted as saying that: "The ammunition left by the Russians will be enough for a 20-year war with Russia." It was not a surprise that Russia's first Chechen War ended with huge casualties and a ceasefire on August 31, 1996.[31]

Assessment of "External" Connections.

Like many foreign-assisted ethnic insurgencies in China, PLA analysts find strong foreign affiliations in the Chechen case. During Gorbachev's time, some Chechen Muslims traveled to Saudi Arabia where they were indoctrinated by Wahhabbism. They returned to Chechnya and started to preach this Islamic extremism to the Chechens, Dagestans, and Ingushens. As a result, in the early 1990s, Chechnya became a sanctuary and training ground for Islamic extremists. For example, in 1995, Afghan terrorist leaders set up a "Caucasus Institute" in Chechnya with 40 Afghan

and Arabic teachers. In 2 months, the school gradu-
ated 160 students well trained in Wahhabbism. Many
of them later conducted terrorist operations in both
the Caucasus and Russia. Foreign Islam extremists
also joined Chechen separatists. According to an intelligence estimate by the Russian Defense Ministry
at the end of 2004, some 150-200 foreign mercenaries
from 52 countries were still operating in Chechnya.

A major external connection was foreign financing
of the Chechen separatist and terrorist insurgencies,
and a greatly deregulated Russian financial system,
which collectively created plenty of opportunities for
such transactions. In 2000 alone, the London-based
International Muslim Brotherhood provided the
Chechen separatists $2.5 million. Bin Laden himself
donated $15 million in 2000-01. The Russian govern-
ment claimed that as many as 60 Islamic extremist
groups from more than 30 nations financially supported Chechen terrorism. Many of these groups operated
from Saudi Arabia, Pakistan, Afghanistan, Turkey,
Jordan, Georgia, Azerbaijan, Uzbekistan, Tajikistan,
Kuwait, Qatar, etc. [32]

Both Yang and Yu cited Russia's deep concern
about the "Western factor" behind the Chechen separatist and terrorist operations. The West, particularly
the United States, tolerates, harbors, and even supports
some separatist and terrorist groups for geopolitical
and energy-political reasons, that is, to weaken and
even end Russia's influence in the Caucasus region.
For this goal, the United States has historically supported many terrorist groups including the Taliban,
the Kosovo Liberation Army, and the Macedonian
National Liberation Army. Many Chechen extremists
reside inside America's allies such as Saudi Arabia,
Pakistan, Turkey, Jordan, etc. Yang cited Russian De-

fense Minister Sergei Ivanov's 1999 statement that the United States made sure "to incite controllable conflict in order to weaken Russia's hold of the Northern Caucasus and to strengthen the U.S. posture in the region."[33] The U.S. State Department spokesman insisted that the United States maintain contact with some Chechen political figures after the 2004 Beslan terrorist siege, which led to the death of 350 school children and teachers. Yu went as far as to conclude that the Chechen terrorist and separatist movement could not sustain itself without the financial, human, and spiritual support from the West.[34]

Terror Tactics and Russia's Dilemma.

Terrorism in Russia is known for its cruelty, violent nature, destructiveness, and disrespect of life, which are largely derived from the rugged character of the Chechen mountaineers and the ferociousness of Islamic extremism. Russian chauvinism and the tradition of political extremism are also said to contribute to the extreme violent character of Chechen terrorism. Moreover, Chechen terrorists are well armed and skillful in choosing their time and targets for maximum impact in order to force Russian authorities to change their minds and to grant independence for Chechnya. PLA analysts also noticed that Chechen militants often have good intelligence about the Russians and are able to obtain inside information from all levels of the Russian governmental agencies and local security forces. As a result, they would be able to obtain in advance Russia's operation plans and to get prepared to respond to those plans. In actual combat, the Chechens seldom confront the Russians head-on, but divide themselves into smaller units with specific assignments such as reconnaissance, early warning, firepower preparation, etc. Some units are dispatched to attack Russian supply lines or to cut off Russian units from the rear. These small Chechen units are well coordinated with one another and are very flexible in their maneuvering. Chechen asymmetrical warfare is also assisted by the local population, and many terrorists are ordinary Chechens during the day and engage in combat at night. In contrast, the Russian intelligence community has often failed, particularly in 1994-2004, to gather, analyze, and disseminate information regarding the terrorist groups and their pending operations. One of the reasons for these intelligence failures was the tightly knitted terror groups, which were hard to infiltrate. Inability, or even unwillingness, to coordinate between different security apparatus also led to poor intelligence gathering.[35]

These characteristics of the Chechen terrorists, plus the complexities of the socio-political environment that give rise to the Chechnya issue, made Russia's COIN operations extremely difficult. Even today, Chechen terrorists continue to engage in terrorist actions all over Russia. In his analysis, Yang cited figures from the Russian Interior Ministry showing a significant increase of terror attacks in Russia: 326 in 2001, 561 in 2003, culminating on September 1, 2004, with the Beslan school siege of 1,100 people (including 777 children and their parents and teachers). One day before the Beslan siege (August 31), a female suicide bomber killed nine in addition to herself and wounded 51 others outside a subway station in Moscow.[36] For the rest of the first decade of the 21st century, Chechen terrorists continued to hunt and kill Russians. On March 29, 2010, explosions—set off by two female Chechen suicide bombers in two landmark subway stations in

Moscow—killed 39 people and wounded more than 70.[37] The terror threat in Russia, in the eyes of PLA analysts, remains serious even though the Russians prevailed in the second Chechen War.

Russian COIN Operations.

The PLA's assessments seem to fall into two categories when evaluating Russia's COIN operations: the evolution of Russia's COIN operation and the lessons learned; and the more tactical operations such as the use of fire power, urban warfare, etc. Within the first category, there are optimists and pessimists. Wang Shaomin, an analyst in the PLA's Academy of Military Sciences in Beijing, divides Russia's COIN, or counter-guerrilla operations into three separate but interrelated phases: the Afghan war (the early phase, 萌芽期); the first Chechen War (developing phase, 发展期); and the second Chechen War (mature phase, 成熟期). In the early stage of the Afghan War, the Red Army suffered heavy losses because it employed heavily armed motorized divisions against the more agile Afghan guerrillas. The Soviets were then forced to adapt to the Afghan situation by dispatching small units of special forces and paratroopers supported by attack helicopters and fixed-wing fighter-bombers. The Soviet 103rd Airborne Division, for example, was divided into battalion-size units that operated independently. The main Soviet forces were used only in large-scale "combing" operations. These new tactics helped the Soviets to win a series of battles such as those in the Panjshir Valley where the Afghan guerrillas suffered some 10,000 casualties.

During the first Chechen War (1994-96), the Russians repeated the mistakes that they made in the early stages of the Afghan War. That is, they quickly occupied the Chechen capital of Grozny, while leaving many Chechen guerrillas in the mountains where they were able to regroup and to launch surprise attacks at the times and places of their choosing. Even in the occupied cities, Russian troops were not familiar with the urban environment. Nor did they prepare themselves for street fighting. The Russian military units reportedly did not even have detailed city maps. Once in the city, the Russian units were harassed and attacked from all sides and suffered heavy losses. The 131st Motorized Brigade alone lost more than half of its men in addition to the destruction of 20 tanks and 102 armored personnel carriers. Eventually, the Russian forces were forced to withdraw.

Because of the failures of the first Chechen War, the Russian military significantly revamped its tactics. With careful planning, thorough preparation, and accurate intelligence, the attacking Russian troops divided Grozny into 15 "zones of responsibility" controlled by individual Russian elite units. The Russians also used many long-range precision guided weapons to soften and devastate Chechen resistance before employing their infantry, whose mission was essentially to clear the remnants of the Chechen forces. Because of these effective tactics, the Russian forces were able to clear Grozny and drive the Chechen forces to the mountainous areas in the South.[38]

Several questions can be asked about Wang's rather positive assessment of Russian COIN operations. Despite a rather steep and quick learning curve during the war, the Soviet forces eventually lost control of most of the Afghan territories and had to withdraw. How and why did this final outcome relate to how the Soviets adjusted their operational behavior? Wang simply skips the role of outside assistance to the Afghan guerrillas, which eventually deprived the Soviets of their air superiority. Another question regards the first Chechen War, which was a clear defeat. It is not so clear how and why the PLA analyst defines it as a "developing phase" in Russia's COIN operations, particularly when Russia is said to have repeated the mistakes made during the Afghan War. Russian domestic disarray — and the reorientation of the Russian military — in the first half of the 1990s may be explanations for the clumsiness of its first Chechen operation. In both cases — the Afghan War and the first Chechen War — Wang seems to be interested only in the tactical, but not the broader strategic aspects of the Soviet/Russian COIN operations.

In contrast to Wang's somewhat "benign" treatment of the Russian COIN operations, PLA General Yang Hui, Director of the Intelligence (2nd) Department of the PLA's General Staff and Director of the Anti-terrorist Center at the China Institution for International Strategic Studies (中国国际战略学会, CIISS), tends to be more critical of these Soviet/Russian COIN wars. In his discussion of the "lessons," Yang parallels Russian casualties as shown in Figure 8-1.

	Death	Wounded	Total
First Chechen War (1992-1994):	5,200	20,000	25,200
Second Chechen War (1999-2009):	4,100	16,000	24,100

Figure 8-1. Parallels of Russian Casualties between the First and Second Chechen Wars.

The average annual casualty rate of the Russian military during the second Chechen War was considerably less than its predecessor. Yang, however, argues that the lessons learned from both wars were similar and very costly. Indeed, in terms of the Russian and Chechen losses, the second Chechen War was not necessarily more successful than the first one. There are, however, several key differences in terms of the background and outcomes. In terms of the final outcome, the first war was simply "unfinished," argues Yang. It was unfinished largely because Russia's unsettled domestic political situation, politicking among the political elite, and the hesitations of the Russian leadership, which seriously undermined the decisionmaking and execution. Besides, Yeltsin's war was waged for "restoring constitutional order," a term that tends to be in the gray areas of the post-Soviet politics ranging from self-determination, independence, local autonomy, democratization, to elite politicking for selfish interests. There was also a strong anti-war movement and draft resistant tendency. In contrast, Putin's war on terror enjoyed more support because of the fear of terrorism and subsequent terrorist actions that pervades much of the Russian population.[39]

Yang, therefore, argues that both Chechen wars suffered from a series of similar deficiencies as follows:

- *Lack of preparation and the underestimation of enemy strength.* After the secret operation to overthrow Dudayev failed, top Russian leaders decided to send in Russian troops. At the onset of the war, Russian Defense Minister Pavel Grachev boasted that the city of Grozny could be captured with only one paratroop regiment. Yeltsin, meanwhile, went as far as to declare that Grachev was "the best defense minister of the decade."[40] The Russian civilian and military leadership, therefore, were out of touch with the poor condition of the Russian military and the power of the Chechen guerrillas. Although the lessons of the first Chechen War led to Russia's military reform, the different views of the Defense Ministry and General Staff on how to reform the military seriously hampered the reform process. The 1998 Russian financial crisis further delayed the reform. By the time of the second Chechen War in 1999, the combat capability of the Russian military had not notably increased from that of the first Chechen War. Meanwhile, the Russian military once again underestimated the insurgency's resilience. General Valentin Marilov publicly claimed, shortly after the end of Russia's first offensive operation in the second Chechen War, that it was the last winter for Chechen illegal forces. In the next 3 years, Russian military officials repeated this belief several times. Each was followed by an escalation of the terrorist activities. No matter what the Russian military did—

be they a blitzkrieg offensive, occupying cities and transportation lifelines, etc. — the core of the Chechen insurgency survived.[41]

- *Lack of coordination among Russian units and unclear definition of responsibilities.* Yang finds that in both COIN wars, the Russians never fully resolved the issue of command, control, and coordination between various participating units of the different services of the military, or those of the security, interior, and border control. Even though the first Chechen War revealed many problems in the area of coordination, the second war was still plagued by similar problems. Yang argues that these problems have their roots in the structure of the Russian military. For example, in March 1994 the Russian military established a joint corps consisting of the units of the Northern Caucasus Military Region and those of the Interior Ministry, which was expected to take the command of the operation. Once the first shot was fired, however, the Russian military units refused to be led by the Interior Ministry's commanders. The 1998 "Anti-terror Law" attempted to divide the zone of responsibility for the military and the Interior units. As a result, the second Chechen War began with operations by regular military units and the Interior units followed to mop up the remnants of the resistance and to provide security. By January 2001, however, Russia's Federal Security Service (FSB, or ФСБ) took over Chechnya. In 2003, the jurisdiction went to the Interior units. Meanwhile, the FSB sent its own officials to handle the Chechnya operation. For Yang, the constant shift of command among those agencies created unnecessary hurdles and confusion, and was not conducive to the success of the COIN operation.[42]

- *Structural deficiency of the Russian military.* Yang points out that in both of the Chechen wars, the Russian military failed to create a special force for mountain and jungle warfare. Instead, regular infantry, tank, and artillery units were thrown into the asymmetrical war. Their heavy equipment, which required good roads and bridges, was difficult to supply and maintain, and was incapable of dealing with the flexible and agile Chechen forces. The conventional Russian forces became easy targets. Worse, most Russian units still used communication equipment from the 1970s. Their opponents were armed with advanced communication devices from abroad. This was the main reason for the destruction of a company of the 76th Airborne Division in the spring of 2000. For 3 days, the company was surrounded by the Chechen insurgents and was unable to communicate with the outside until almost all of them were killed.

- *Lack of training and discipline.* Yang notices that in both Chechen wars, the Russian military tended to deploy their forces in a conventional and rigid format. The way some officers coordinated between the different services was similar to the manner utilized in World War II. Officers at all levels lacked knowledge and training of COIN operations. When facing the hit-and-run tactics of the small insurgent groups, the Russians failed to adapt themselves to the situation. Besides, the participating units of the Russian military, particularly the Interior and special forces, had serious discipline problems such as looting, rape, smuggling oil, selling weapons and munitions, human trafficking, and even treason. Yang cites a Kremlin official who stated that there were 748 criminal cases against military personnel from August 1999 to December 2000. These discipline problems not only weakened the combat power of the Russian military, but also jeopardized relations with the locals.

Due to these lessons and problems, Yang cites Russian military experts who came to the conclusion that joint operations between Defense, Interior, FSB, and Border units must be optimized and better coordinated; the use of heavy weapon systems must be selective and limited in order to avoid civilian casualties; priority should be given to high-tech weapons; battalion and company levels of operation should be the force level for COIN operations; and finally, mountain units need to be established.

Yang argues that these operational problems of the Russian military were set against a backdrop of Russia's political transition. As a result of the steep decline of Russia's economic power, the Russian military lacked adequate funding for procurement, training, and salaries. Vladimir Putin, for example, would have to go to the front himself in order to solve the salary shortage for the participating Russian units.

At the socio-political level, Yang argues that the Russian COIN experience indicates the limited utility of the military means in anti-terror operations. It is, and should be, a long-term mission with multiple interventions in the political, economic and social arenas. In the case of Chechnya, some military operations may be able to deal inflict a heavy blow on some separatists and terrorists, but it cannot eliminate the complex origins of the problems. The misuse of the military instrument of power may even backfire. Yang, therefore, believes in "comprehensive" treatment of the COIN issues.[44]

Yang's analysis separates itself from the majority of the PLA experts in their assessments of Russia's COIN operations. It is more critical of the Russian approach to the use of military power, and it argues for more nonmilitary means for the long-term eradication of terrorism and insurgency. Part of the reason for Yang's critique is perhaps the time of his research, which was around 2005 when the Russians were in the middle of the second Chechen War (1999-2009) with no victory in sight. This was also shortly after the September 2004 Beslan terror siege in Russia's Northern Ossetia, during which more than 300 hostages died (among some 1,200 hostages). Even the Russian special forces suffered more than 40 casualties. What is not clear in Yang's writing are the sources for most of his analysis. Unless Yang clearly indicates or directly cites Russian sources, it is difficult, if not impossible, to detect if Yang cites a Russian assessment or expresses his own view. With the exception of a few PLA writers, this group of PLA analysis of the Russian COIN operation does not have references at all.

Tactical Aspects of Russian COIN Operations.

In more recent years, the bulk of the PLA's analyses focused on the tactical issues of the Russian COIN operations such as the use of firepower, offense formation and process, urban warfare, etc. In their assessment of the Russian use of firepower, Li Hongfeng and Pan Menghua, both from the Graduate Department of the Chinese Academy of Military Sciences, give high marks to Russia's tactics during the second Chechen War. They notice that the Russians failed to utilize their superior firepower in the first Chechen War largely due to the lack of coordination between different services, units, and weapons systems. The Russians realized that any one of these weapon systems accomplished fairly little in confronting the insurgents and must be comprehensively combined into a coherent format (综合立体). Some of the specific Russian tactics are as follows:

- Li and Pan describe that the Russians unified the command and control mechanism during the second Chechen War. This was also the case for the use of their firepower and they assigned different weapon platforms to different roles. For example, Su-25 ground attack jets, and attack helicopters such as Mi-24s and Ka-50s, would provide close-range support at mid-low altitude, while the Su-24M would provide precision and area bombing at all altitudes and from variable distances. Ground artillery and rocket launchers would provide saturated bombing to soften insurgent positions. Other small weapons such as grenade launchers, flamethrowers, and sniper rifles would be used in mountain fighting.
- The Russian military always maximized the use of aerial and ground artillery bombardment in what the two PLA researchers refer to as "unconventional" (非常规), "over-saturation" (超饱和), or "repeated over-saturated bombing (连续超饱和轰炸). They cite one case in which

304

the Russian infantry called in 24 aerial support requests against certain insurgent positions. In another operation, Russian bombing almost leveled the entire village before the infantry moved in and combed every house and street. This way, the Russians were said to have almost completely annihilated the insurgents in the village. In still another case, a Russian artillery company was instructed "not to save any ammunition" in its round-the-clock firing. Li and Pan also cite statistics that the Russian Air Force actually carried out 70-80 percent of the bombing missions. In order to avoid hitting civilians, 65 percent of the attacks used precision-guided munitions (1,300 sorties out of some 2,000). The overuse of firepower, according to Li and Pan, helped reduce Russian casualties throughout the second Chechen War.[45]

In many ways, this analysis of the Russian use of firepower directly contradicts the findings and arguments in Yang's earlier writing (2006). What Li and Pan promote is exactly what Yang questions. Just a year and a half apart, the same PLA military journal produced radically different assessments over the same issue, i.e., the excessive use of firepower in COIN operations. Again, this dramatically different view of the second Chechen War has no references and its description sounds more like textbook/manual approach, that is, what each weapon system is supposed to do.

Within the same journal in which Li and Pan praise Russia's use of firepower in the second Chechen War, two other PLA analysts, Mao and Wang, who are from the same Graduate Department of the Chinese

Academy of Military Sciences, assess the "strength and weakness" of the Russian military in its offensive operation in the "special military campaigns." Their piece focuses on the tactical side of the second Chechen War and how the Russian military greatly improved its performance from the first Chechen War. Specifically, they notice how the Russian military achieved surprise in their battle of Grozny. Mao and Wang also discuss how the Russians used deception by deliberately leaving open the southern side of the city while tightly sealing the three other sides. As a result, 3,000 Chechen rebels were ambushed while fleeing to the south, most of whom were either killed (about 1,000) or captured (1,500). Like Li and Pan, Mao and Wang also speak highly of the Russian use of firepower to help reduce infantry casualties, and the higher level of coordination during the second Chechen War. Beyond this, Mao and Wang point out how the Russian military "re-used" some of the Soviet-style political work to boost troop morale to promote patriotism, and to win over the local populace. They say that this was very different from the first Chechen War. They do, however, criticize the Russian army for relying too much on firepower, Russia's difficulties in servicing and supplying a high-tech military during COIN operations, and Russia's antiquated communication system, etc.[46]

Urban COIN operation is another key PLA area of interest. In their 2008 analysis, Fan Lili and Hua Yan examine large-scale urban warfare and anti-terror operations during the second Chechen War and detect six improvements from the first Chechen War:

1. Sealing and squeezing (封锁合围, 逐步挤压). Instead of driving directly to the city center and occupying key installations as were the tactics in the

first Chechen War, the Russian military in the second Chechen War would first attack the peripheries of the key cities and gradually squeeze the insurgents into isolated urban areas. The besieged insurgents were therefore under tremendous psychological pressure, and some actually gave up and surrendered. The Russians used this strategy in attacking the Chechen capital, Grozny; the second largest Chechen city, Gudermes; and Shali (south of Grozny).

2. Using precision-guided munitions against urban targets (火力拔点, 精打要害). This strategy aimed to pick up those scattered urban positions, command-control-communication centers, and weapon platforms of the insurgents. It also reduced civilian casualties. In the battle of the Grozny, the Russian air force launched 100 sorties per day and sometimes 150-200 sorties, 80 percent of which employed precision-guided attacks. The Russian military also distributed ground artillery pieces to smaller units for timely and flexible support. Meanwhile, laser-guided artillery shells were widely used in urban fighting.

3. Cutting urban insurgents into smaller and isolated pockets while driving toward city center (向心突击, 边打边割). This would severely limit the coordination between insurgents.

4. Small units responsible for combing assigned areas (小群多路, 分区清剿). The Russian military split into many small "attacking groups" (攻击群), each with its own armor unit, flamethrowers, engineers, and an Interior unit for area combing. Each attacking group was responsible for eliminating insurgents in the assigned city blocs. Many times, the same area(s) would be combed several times.

5. Using deception and ambush (巧用谋略, 设伏歼敌). In the battle of Grozny, the Russian military

307

deliberately left the city's southern flank open while deploying heavily on the north, west, and east sides of the city. 3,000 insurgents were ambushed while fleeing to the south.

6. Using militia and coordinating with them (重用民兵，协同作战). Militia forces were used in the first Chechen War for logistics and security purpose. In the second Chechen War militias were widely used in combination with the Interior forces, because the main attacking units and were responsible for the postwar stabilization. The biggest advantage of using militias was that they knew the territory and they could identify the insurgents.

Implications for the PLA's Own COIN and Anti-Terror Operations.

As discussed above, the PLA analyses indicate some interesting and obviously different schools of thought in assessment of the Russian COIN experience, not just between the critics and supporters, but also between PLA academics (Li, Pan, Mao, Wang, Fan, and Hua) and the military intelligence branch (Yang). One possible explanation of these differences is the fact that many of the PLA weapon systems are of the same Russian/Soviet designs with identical specifications, capabilities, and perhaps problems. Some PLA researchers therefore may be more receptive to Russian experience and lessons. Another reason is the gradual normalization and development of the Sino-Russian military-military (mil-mil) relations. Additionally, Russia and China have to deal with similar threats from the "three forces" (separatism, terrorism, and religious extremism), and a growing number of these threats and actual incidents of terrorism occur in urban areas, where COIN or anti-terror operations are far more difficult to deal with than in remote and rural areas.

In a way, these different assessments of Russia's COIN operations in Chechnya represent a typical bottle half-full/empty debate. While supporters tend to see the differences between the first and second Chechen wars, critics always point to the high cost of Russia's COIN operations, the outdated strategy, and the persistence of the terrorist attacks to date. Last, but not least, the PLA debate may be driven by the evolution and progress of Russia's COIN operations. In the second half of 2007, the Russians seemed to have turned the corner, as China's civilian intelligence experts observed that the Russians had basically controlled domestic terrorism thanks to a series of policies including its sustained economic growth and progress in Chechen reconstruction; more accommodating policies toward Muslims in Russia; and the strengthening of their anti-terror mechanism, etc.[47]

These PLA and China's civilian intelligence community assessments of Russia's COIN operations are far from conclusive. More recent analyses seem to point to a quite different trajectory. In 2008, General Yang Hui, the intelligence "czar" of the PLA, published a comparative study of Russian and American anti-terror operations. His description clearly favors the more high-tech, better funded, better educated and trained, more flexible and agile American forces. Yang goes as far as to claim that the Chechen wars were the "fourth generation" of wars based on the mechanized technology (机械化), while America's war in Afghanistan today belongs to the "sixth generation" of warfare based on information technology (信息化). Nuclear war is what Yang defines as the "fifth generation" of war. Yang does point to certain improvements in Russia's COIN operations, particularly in Russia's conduct of psychological warfare, use of special force units, and the use of high-tech weapons during the second Chechen War. The Russian military, however, is still prioritizing its "attacking" function (以打为主), while the United States depends more on reconnaissance and information analysis (以侦为主). As a professional intelligence officer, Yang clearly favors the latter.[48]

In a different venue, PAP analyst Liu Xiaoyan also echoed Yang's critique of the Russian approach. Liu points to 69 large-scale terrorist attacks in Russia in 1994-2004, leading to the death of some 1,400 people. The high frequency of the attacks indicated the incapability of the Russian intelligence community, according to Liu, a professor of military intelligence in the PAP academy. In most cases, Russian intelligence had no prior knowledge of many of the terror groups, their network, means of violence, intended targets, finance, etc. But even when some information was obtained, various anti-terror organizations usually did not communicate nor coordinate well. There were multiple reasons for Russia's intelligence failure, including the highly secret and tightly organized terror groups, distrust of government among the local population, and structural deficiencies of Russia's intelligence system.[49]

Does this indicate the PLA's future trajectory toward developing its own COIN capabilities along the American path? To certain degree, the recent questioning of Russian COIN operations does not necessarily mean that the PLA pays less attention to Russia. Russia was considered part of the broader war on terror even before 9/11 in 2001. This was the case of

CICIR's publication, *Global Terrorism and Counter-Terrorist Campaign*, published 10 days before 9/11, and the official debut of its CCTS.[50] In more recent PLA publications on the non-traditional threat, Russia is prominently featured.[51]

The history of Russia's COIN efforts, however, must be considered in the Chinese context. At China's domestic level, the PLA's more critical evaluation of Russia's experience may also be intended for a domestic audience. Liu's strong critique of Russia's intelligence failure may well be an effort to bargain for more independent intelligence gathering capabilities for the PAP, which has until recently depended on other governmental institutions—such as military intelligence (Second Department of the General Staff, [总参二部], Ministry of State Security [安全部], and public security [公安部门])—for intelligence and information regarding terrorism.[52] Even with the creation of the PAP Intelligence Bureau (武警情报局) within the PAP headquarters (武警总部), it is unclear how various military and civilian intelligence gathering organizations will coordinate their effort for COIN and anti-terror purposes. Meanwhile, the issue of command, control, and coordination between the various branches of the PLA in complex anti-terror operations remains an open space for inter-service maneuvering.

Beyond intelligence, various branches of the PLA seem to have developed a certain division of work in relation to their respective Russian counterparts. For example, regular PLA units formed the bulk of the participating forces in multilateral exercises such as SCO's "Peace-Mission" in 2005, 2007, 2009, and 2010;[53] while the PAP units, particularly its special forces such as the Snow Leopard commando unit (雪豹突击队), participated in bilateral training exercises with their foreign counterparts such as units from Russia's Interior.[54] These exercises do not necessarily imply what the "final solution" for the type of forces that should be used for large-scale COIN operations or smaller, yet high profile, counterterrorist operations will look like. A PAP analyst, for example, argues that China's anti-terror operations should be the work of public security institutions and PAP units; regular PLA units should not be overloaded with anti-terror assignments, which may divert their attention from bigger responsibilities such as safeguarding China's territorial integrity, i.e. Taiwan. An "obsession" with the anti-terror issue may cause China to fall into the trap like that of the United States.[55]

In closing, the Russian COIN experience has been both valuable and limited for the PLA. It is valuable because both Moscow and Beijing confront the complexities and difficulties of the growing terrorist threat in the post-9/11 world. China's own experiences in COIN operations in traditional, modern, and contemporary times are simply not adequate in this new world of identity sensitivity, clash of civilizations, weapons of mass destruction, and preemption. It is limited because of the two totally different domestic settings. Terrorist and insurgency activities in China, which have been considerably lower than those in Russia in terms of severity and frequency, have been essentially countered with public security and PAP forces. This was the case even for the recent large-scale urban unrests (in Tibet in 2008) and riots (in Xinjiang in 2009).

This, however, may change in the future if transborder terrorist activities escalate with increasing destabilizing effects on China's domestic situation, and if Chinese nationals abroad increasingly become the targets of terrorist activities. Already, the PLA's ground and air units have been dispatched to join various anti-terror exercises in SCO member states and beyond. More recently, the PAP is paying increasing attention to the experience of its foreign counterparts, including that of Russia, in conducting anti-terror operations outside their respective national boundaries.[56] It remains to be seen how the PLA and PAP will coordinate their operations outside China should there be such a necessity.

ENDNOTES - CHAPTER 8

1. This includes the Taiping Rebellion (太平军起义, 1851-1864), the White Lotus Rebellion (白莲教起义, 1774-1804), the Nian Rebellion (捻军起义, 1853-68), and the two Muslim rebellions (1855-73 and 1862-78). These rebellions led to the death of perhaps as many as 100 million people, and the Qing never recovered from the destruction. See Kenneth Lieberthal, *Governing China: from Revolution through Reform*, 2nd Ed., New York: W. W. Norton & Company, 2004, pp. 20-21; Keith Schoppa, "From Empire to People's Republic," in William A. Joseph, ed., *Politics in China: an Introduction*, Oxford, UK: Oxford University Press, 2010, pp. 40-41.

2. Qu Deqian (屈德骞), "共和国史册上的大匪患" ("Major Insurgencies in PRC History"), 当代中国研究所 (Institute of Contemporary China), 中华人民共和国国史网 (*History of the People's Republic of China*), October 15, 1995, available from *www.hprc.org.cn/cnki/zdsj/200906/t20090610_9805.html*.

3. 中国人民解放军第一野战军战史 (*History of the First Field Army of the People's Liberation Army*), Beijing, China: PLA Press, 1995, p. 363.

4. Kenneth Conboy and James Morrison, *The CIA's Secret War in Tibet*, Lawrence, KS: University Press of Kansas, 2002; Robert Barnett, "Tibet," in William A. Joseph, ed., pp. 321-23; Li Ye and Wang Zhongchun (李晔, 王仲春), "美国的西藏政策与'西藏问题'的由来" ("The U.S. Tibet Policy and the Origin of the 'Tibet Problem'"), 美国研究 (*America Studies*), No. 2, 1999, available from *www.tibet328.cn/zxss/01/200902/t264002.htm*.

5. Li Jian (李健), 共和国之战, 上卷 (*Wars by the Republic*, Vol. 1), Beijing, China: China Social Press, 1996, pp. 336-82; "打击逃缅国民党军窜扰的作战" ("Combat against the Hit-and-run Operations by Nationalist Troop Fled to Burma"), available from *baike.baidu.com/view/1151353.html*.

6. Guardner Bovingdon, "Xinjiang," in William A. Joseph, ed., p. 348.

7. "警方通报针对南航班机未遂恐怖袭击案" ("Police Report on Aborted Attack of the China Southern Airline"), 新华网 (*Xinhua Net*), March 28, 2008, available from *news.xinhuanet.com/mrdx/2008-03/28/content_7874040.htm*.

8. "新疆喀什市发生一起严重暴力袭警案件 16人死亡" ("A Violent Attack of Policy in Ka Shi City, Xinjiang, 16 Dead"), 新华网 (*Xinhua Net*), August 4, 2008, available from *news.sohu.com/20080804/n258578985.shtml*.

9. Xiong Guangkai (熊光楷), 国际战略与新军事变革 (*International Strategy and Revolution in Military Affairs*), Beijing, China: Qinghua University Press, 2003, p. 20. Xiong is former PLA Deputy Chief of Staff (1996-2005) and former Director of the General Staff Intelligence Department (1988-92).

10. See Zheng Yu (郑羽) ed., 中美俄在中亚：合作与竞争 (*Cooperation and Competition: China, Russia, and the U.S. in Central Asia*), Beijing, China: Social Science Academic Press, 2007, p. 381.

11. "Shanghai Five" ("上海五国"), 百度百科 (*Baidu Encyclopedia*), available from *baike.baidu.com/view/259646.htm*.

12. It is estimated that China is home for some 8.5 million Uyghurs, while Kazakhstan, Kyrgyzstan, and Uzbekistan have some 200,000. See Zheng Yu (郑羽), ed., 中美俄在中亚：合作与竞争 (*Cooperation and Competition: China, Russia and the U.S. in Central Asia*), Beijing, China: Social Science Academic Press, 2007, p. 375.

13. 国际恐怖主义与反恐怖斗争 (*Global Terrorism and Counter-Terrorist Campaign*), Beijing, China: Shi Shi Chubanshe, 2001, available from *www.wl.cn/1265254*.

14. Lewis Clarke, *Against All Enemies*, New York: Free Press, 2004, pp. 234, 230-231.

15. There was a sense of overconfidence among certain experts of Tibetan issues in managing local affairs at the end of 2007. This was the author's impression while attending the conference "China's Geopolitics," sponsored by School of International Affairs and Public Policy, Fudan University, Shanghai, December 15-16, 2007. Regarding Xinjiang, some analysts actually anticipated the increase of religious extremist activities prior to the 2009 Urumqi riots. Actual information sharing and policy coordination, however, were inadequate. See Pan Guang and Zhao Guojun (潘光，赵国军), "9/11以来东突势力的新变化及其动因" ("Eastern Turkistan Terrorist Organizations' Development and Causes After 9/11"), 现代国际关系 (*Contemporary International Relations*), No. 10, 2008, pp. 47-54.

16. Pan Menghua and Wang Fang (潘孟华, 王芳), "恐怖主义与游击战概念辨析" ("On the Definition of Terrorism and Guerrilla Warfare"), 外国军事学术 (*Foreign Military Science*), No. 5, 2008, pp. 74-75.

17. Pan Menghua and Wang Fang, p. 76; Wang Shuyou (王树友), "恐怖主义感念体系研究" ("The Conceptual Frameworks of Terrorism"), 武警学院学报 (*Journal of the Chinese People's Armed Police Force Academy*), Vol. 18, No. 6, December 2002, p. 60; Yu Shujie (于淑杰), "俄罗斯对恐怖主义的界定" ("Russia's Definition of Terrorism"), 外国军事学术 (*Foreign Military Science*), No. 11, 2003, pp. 21-24.

18. One of the most comprehensive definitions of China's version of terrorism is articulated by Wang Shuyou (王树友), associate professor of the People's Army Police (PAP) Academy, in his "恐怖主义感念体系研究" ("The Conceptual Frameworks of Terrorism").

19. A notable exception is made by Zhang Liwei (张立伟) in his analysis of the similarities of anti-terror and counter-guerrilla operations of the Soviet and U.S. militaries. See "现代反恐怖作战反游击战理论初探" ("Initial Theoretical Exploration of Modern Anti-terrorist and Anti-guerrilla Warfare"), 武警学院学报 (*Journal of the Chinese People's Armed Police Force Academy*), Vol. 20, No. 5, June 2004, pp. 87-89.

20. *Ibid*, pp. 74-76.

21. Wang Shuyou (王树友); Xia Mingxing and Xu Daqiang (夏明星，许大强), "当代恐怖主义活动浅析" ("On Contemporary Terror Activities"), in *Ibid.*, pp. 61-62, 68.

22. Robert Pape, "Strategic Logic of Suicide Terrorism," *American Political Science Review*, Vol. 97, No. 3, August 2003, pp. 343-361.

23. Zhang Jiadong (张家栋), 恐怖主义论 (*On Terrorism*) Beijing, China: Shi Shi Chubanshe, 2007, p. 1. Also see, Zheng Shouhua and Ren Jian (郑守华 任剑), "国际恐怖主义活动特点与反恐怖措施" ("The Operational Features of International Terrorism and Counter Measures"), 外国军事学术 (*Foreign Military Science*), No. 11, 2003, pp. 16-20.

24. See Randall Law, "Terrorism: A History," *Polity*, 2009; Robert Pape, "The Strategic Logic of Suicide Terrorism," *American Political Science Review*, Vol. 97, No. 3, August 2003, pp. 343-361.

25. Lu Zhongwei (陆忠伟), 非传统安全论 (*On Nontraditional Security*), Beijing, China: Shi Shi Chubanshe, 2003.

26. See, for example, Yu Xiaofeng, Pan Yihe and Wang Jiangli (余潇枫，潘一禾，王江丽), and 非传统安全概论 (*Nontraditional Security: An Introduction*), Hangzhou, China: Zhejiang Renmin Chubanshe, 2006. In the same year, The Zhejiang University set up the Center for Non-Traditional Security and Peaceful Development Studies, which is China's first think tank on nontraditional security issues (*www.nts-pd.org/center_intro.php*). Also, see Gao Taicun (高太存), "中国非传统安全面临的挑战及思考" ("Challenges to China's Non-traditional Security"), 武警学院学报 (*Journal of the Chinese People's Armed Police Force Academy*), Vol. 23, No. 1, January 2007, pp. 6-8; 国家安全与非传统安全 (*National Security and Nontraditional Security*), Shanghai: Institute of World Economics and Politics, Shanghai Academy of Social Sciences, 2008; Li Luping and Xian Fengli (李陆平, 贤峰礼), 军队与非传统安全 (*Armed Forces and Nontraditional Security Issues*), Beijing, China: Shi Shi Chubanshe, 2009. The journal, *Foreign Military Science*, even published a piece by a Singapore scholar on the use of military against nontraditional threats, see Wang Yuling (王毓麟), "运用军队应对

非传统安全威胁" ("Using Armed Forces in Dealing with Nontraditional Threats"), 外国军事学术 (*Foreign Military Science*), No. 5, 2009, pp. 42-45.

27. Other militaries include the United States, the countries of the European Union, and Japan. See Li Luping and Xian Fengli, *Ibid.*

28. Yang Hui (杨晖), "俄罗斯反恐怖斗争研究" ("Russia's Anti-terror Struggle"), 外国军事学术 (*Foreign Military Science*), No. 5, 2006, p. 1; Yu Nina (于尼娜), "俄车臣恐怖主义产生的主要根源" ("Main Sources of Chechen Terrorism"), 外国军事学术 (*Foreign Military Science*), No. 1, 2005, p. 16. Yu is a member of the Graduate program, Chinese Academy of Military Science.

29. Yu Nina, p. 17.

30. Yang Hui, p. 1.

31. Yang Hui, p. 2; Yu Nina, p. 17.

32. Yang Hui, p. 3; Yu Nina, pp. 18-19.

33. Yang Hui, pp. 3-4.

34. Yu Nina, p. 19.

35. Liu Xiaoyan (刘肖岩), "俄罗斯反恐情报失误研究" ("Russian Anti-terrorism Intelligence Failures"), 武警学院学报 (*Journal of the Chinese People's Armed Police Force Academy*), Vol. 26, No. 5, May 2010, pp. 90-93.

36. Yang Hui, p. 4-5.

37. Clifford Levy, "Moscow Attack a Test for Putin and His Record against Terror," *New York Times*, March 29, 2010, available from *www.nytimes.com/2010/03/30/world/europe/30moscow.html.*

38. Wang Shaomin (王绍民), "俄军反游击战浅析"("Russian Military's Counter-Guerrilla Warfare Operation"), 外国军事学术 (*Foreign Military Science*), No. 10, 2006, pp. 10-11.

39. The Chinese Institute for International Strategic Studies (CIISS) is a "civilian think tank" for the PLA's General Staff, which was established in 1979, available from *gb.cri.cn/27824/200 9/06/24/1965s2544429.htm*.

40. Yang Hui, p. 9.

41. "Pavel Grachev," *Wikipedia*, available from *en.wikipedia. org/wiki/Pavel_Grachev*.

42. Yang Hui, p. 10.

43. *Ibid*.

44. Yang Hui, p. 11.

45. Li Hongfeng and Pan Menghua (李红峰, 潘孟华), "俄军反恐作战中火力运用的特点研究" ("Russia's Use of Firepower in Anti-terror Operations"), 外国军事学术 (*Foreign Military Science*), No. 11, 2007, pp. 45-47.

46. Mao Xiang and Wang Jiliang (毛翔, 王继亮), "俄军特种战役背景下进攻战斗的强弱点" ("Strength and Weakness in Russian Military's Offensive Operations under Special Operation Environment"), 外国军事学术 (*Foreign Military Science*), No. 11, 2007, pp. 48-50.

47. Fan Lili (范莉丽), "俄军大规模城市反恐作战方法探析" ("Tactics of the Russian Military in its Large-scale Urban Anti-terror Operations"), 外国军事学术 (*Foreign Military Science*), No. 3, 2008, pp. 55-58.

48. Zhang Jian (张建), "国际反恐战略研讨会纪要" ("Summary of the International Anti-terror Strategy Conference"), 现代国际关系 (*Contemporary International Relations*), No. 10, 2007, pp. 61-62.

49. Yang Hui (杨晖), "俄美反恐怖军事行动比较研究" ("A Comparative Study of Russian and American Anti-terror Military Operations"), 外国军事学术 (*Foreign Military Science*), No. 4, 2008, pp. 1-7.

50. Liu Xiaoyan (刘肖岩).

318

51. 国际恐怖主义与反恐怖斗争 (*Global Terrorism and Counter-Terrorist Campaign*), Beijing, China: Shi Shi Chubanshe, 2001, available from *www.wl.cn/1265254*.

52. Li Luping and Xian Fengli (李陆平, 贤峰礼), 军队与非传统安全 (*Armed Forces and Nontraditional Security Issues*), Beijing, China: Shi Shi Chubanshe, 2009.

53. For PAP's lack of its own independent intelligence gathering mechanism, see Wang Hongjun (王洪军), "警卫部队应对恐怖主义的对策研究" ("PAP Units' Counter-terror Measures "), 武警学院学报 (*Journal of the Chinese People's Armed Police Force Academy*), Vol. 18, No. 6, December 2002, pp. 66-68; Wang Hongjun (王洪军), "我国反恐怖斗争对策研究" ("China's Anti-terror Measures"), 武警学院学报 (*Journal of the Chinese People's Armed Police Force Academy*), Vol. 20, No. 5, October 2004, pp. 83-86.

54. Peace Mission-2005, which involved 10,000 troops, Russian strategic bombers and China's submarine-launched missiles, and was not a typical anti-terror exercise.

55. See 新华网 (*Xinhua Net*), "中国武警司令: 演习提高中俄内卫部队反恐能" ("PAP Commander: Drill Increases Terror-fighting Capabilities of the Chinese and Russian Interior Forces"), September 6, 2007, available from *mil.news.sina.com.cn/2007-09-06/1803463036.html*.

56. See Wang Hongjun (王洪军), 2004.

57. See Zhang Liwei (张立伟), "境外反恐行动的理论研究和实践探索" ("Theories and Practices Regarding Anti-terror Operations outside National Boundaries"), 武警学院学报 (*Journal of the Chinese People's Armed Police Force Academy*), Vol. 25, No. 9, September 2009, pp. 84-87.

ABOUT THE CONTRIBUTORS

MARTIN ANDREW was a member of the Royal Australian Air Force from February 1977 to February 2005. His Air Force career was primarily in the areas of education and training, and included postings to the Australian Joint Warfare Establishment and the Royal Australian Air Force Staff College. For the period 1991 to 2003, he was in the Northern Territory, a highlight of his service was being an International Military Liaison Officer in Darwin with the Foreign National Support Elements for their deployed forces in East Timor from November 1999 to July 2000. He publishes a monthly *GI Zhou Newsletter* on the Chinese military, and the second edition of his book, *How the PLA Fights: Weapons and Tactics of the People's Liberation Army*, was released in September 2009. He has also conducted research on insurgencies in Southeast Asia, the origins of Communist guerrilla warfare, terrorism, and weapons of mass destruction (WMDs), among other topics. He received a Ph.D. in philosophy in February 2009.

DEAN CHENG is a research fellow on Chinese political and security affairs at The Heritage Foundation. He specializes in China's military and foreign policy, in particular, its relationship with the rest of Asia and with the United States. Cheng has written extensively on China's military doctrine, technological implications of its space program and "dual use" issues associated with the communist nation's industrial and scientific infrastructure. He previously worked for 13 years as a senior analyst, first with Science Applications International Corp. (SAIC), the Fortune 500 specialist for defense and homeland security, and then with the China Studies division of the Center for Naval Analyses – a federally funded research institute. Before entering the private sector, Cheng studied China's defense-industrial complex for a congressional agency, the Office of Technology Assessment, as an analyst in the International Security and Space Program. Cheng has appeared on public affairs shows such as John McLaughlin's "One on One" and programs on National Public Radio, CNN International, BBC World Service, and International Television News (ITN). He has been interviewed by or provided commentary for publications such as *Time Magazine*, *The Washington Post*, *Financial Times*, *Bloomberg News*, *Jane's Defense Weekly*, South Korea's *Chosun Ilbo* and Hong Kong's *South China Morning Post*. Cheng has spoken at the National Space Symposium, the National Defense University (NDU), the Air Force Academy, the Massachusetts Institute of Technology (MIT) and the Eisenhower Center for Space and Defense Studies. Cheng earned a bachelor's degree in politics from Princeton University in 1986 and studied for a doctorate at MIT.

JUNE TEUFEL DREYER is a Professor of Political Science at the University of Miami, Coral Gables, Florida. Dr. Dreyer is a Senior Fellow of the Foreign Policy Research Institute, a member of the Board of Scholars of the U.S.-China Research Institute of the University of Southern California, and a member of the Institute for Strategic Studies. She was appointed Commissioner of the United States-China Economic and Security Review Commission by Speaker of the House Dennis Hastert, and served three terms thereon. She formerly served as Senior Far East Specialist at the Library of Congress and as an Asia advisor to the Chief of Naval

Operations. Her research work centers on ethnic minorities, the Chinese military, Asian-Pacific regional relations, cross-strait relations, and Sino-Japanese relations. Dr. Dreyer is the sole author of *China's Forty Millions: Minority Nationalities and National Integration in the People's Republic of China* and *China's Political System: Modernization and Tradition,* which is being prepared for its eighth edition. Her current project is a book on Sino-Japanese relations. Her articles have appeared in numerous scholarly journals. She is also a co-author and/or editor of numerous other books, including the 2005 *Report to Congress of the United States Economic and Security Commission.* Dr. Dreyer has served on official observation groups for four Taiwan elections. She has also testified at numerous U.S. congressional hearings. She serves on the board of editors of *Orbis* and the *Journal of Contemporary China,* and has received numerous teaching awards. She received a joint Ph.D. in government and East Asian studies from Harvard University.

ROY KAMPHAUSEN is a Senior Associate for Political and Security Affairs (PSA) at The National Bureau of Asian Research (NBR) and an adjunct faculty member at George Washington University and Columbia University's School of International and Public Affairs. He advises and contributes to NBR research programs on political and security issues in Asia. Mr. Kamphausen previously served as Senior Vice President for Political and Security Affairs and Director of NBR's Washington, DC, office. Prior to joining NBR, Mr. Kamphausen served as a U.S. Army officer, a career that culminated in an assignment in the Office of the Secretary of Defense (OSD) as Country Director for China-Taiwan-Mongolia Affairs. Previous assignments include the Joint Staff as an intelligence analyst and later as China Branch Chief in the Directorate for Strategic Plans and Policy (J5). A fluent Chinese (Mandarin) linguist and an Army China Foreign Area Officer (FAO), Mr. Kamphausen served two tours at the Defense Attaché Office of the U.S. Embassy in the People's Republic of China. He is a member of the National Committee on U.S.-China Relations, the International Institute for Strategic Studies (IISS), the Asia Society, and the Council for Security and Cooperation in the Asia-Pacific (CSCAP). His areas of professional expertise include China's People's Liberation Army (PLA), U.S.-China defense relations, U.S. defense and security policy toward Asia, and East Asian security issues. Mr. Kamphausen co-authored the chapter "Military Modernization in Taiwan" in *Strategic Asia 2005–06: Military Modernization in an Era of Uncertainty*, with Michael Swaine; he was the co-author of the chapter "PLA Power Projection: Current Realities and Emerging Trends" in *Assessing the Threat: The Chinese Military and Taiwan's Security* (2007), with Justin Liang; he co-edited the volume *Right-Sizing the People's Liberation Army: Exploring the Contours of China's Military* (2007), with Andrew Scobell; he co-edited the volume *The People in the PLA: Recruitment, Training, and Education in China's Military* (2008), with Andrew Scobell and Travis Tanner; and he co-edited the volumes *Beyond the Strait: PLA Missions Other Than Taiwan* (April 2009), and *The PLA At Home and Abroad: Assessing the Operational Capabilities of China's Military* (July 2010) with David Lai and Andrew Scobell. Mr. Kamphausen holds a B.A. in political science from Wheaton College and an M.A. in international affairs from Columbia University. He studied Chinese at both the Defense Language Institute and Beijing's Capital Normal University.

DAVID LAI is a Research Professor of Asian Security Studies at the Strategic Studies Institute (SSI) of the U.S. Army War College. Before joining the SSI, Dr. Lai was on the faculty of the U.S. Air War College. Having grown up in China, Lai witnessed China's "Cultural Revolution," its economic reform, and the changes in U.S.-China relations. His teaching and research interests are in international relations theory, war and peace studies, comparative foreign and security policy, U.S.-China and U.S.-Asian relations, and Chinese strategic thinking and operational art. Dr. Lai is a co-editor with Mr. Kamphausen and Dr. Scobell of *The PLA at Home and Abroad: Assessing the Operational Capabilities of China's Military* (Carlisle, PA: Strategic Studies Institute, U.S. Army War College, June 2010). Dr. Lai holds a bachelor's degree from China and a master's degree and Ph.D. in political science from the University of Colorado.

FRANK MILLER, is a retired U.S. Army colonel currently serving in the Defense Intelligence Agency as the Defense Intelligence Officer for East Asia. He has over 30 years of active duty in the Infantry, Special Forces, and as a China Foreign Area Officer with 23 years of extensive interaction with all Asian militaries in or focused on Asia at the local, regional, and national levels. Mr. Miller previously served as a military attaché (Vietnam and China), a regional security assistance officer (Pacific Command [PACOM]), and as a political-military analyst (PACOM and Joint Staff). His last assignment was as Director, Northeast Asia Division, Joint Staff Strategic Plans and Policy Directorate (J5).

ANDREW SCOBELL is Senior Political Scientist at RAND's Washington, DC, office. Prior to this he was an Associate Professor of International Affairs at the George H. W. Bush School of Government and Public Service and Director of the China Certificate Program at Texas A&M University located in College Station, TX. From 1999 until 2007, he was an Associate Research Professor at the Strategic Studies Institute, U.S. Army War College and an Adjunct Professor of Political Science at Dickinson College, both located in Carlisle, PA. Dr. Scobell is the author of *China's Use of Military Force: Beyond the Great Wall and the Long March* (Cambridge University Press, 2003), he co-authored *China's Search for Security,* with Andrew J. Nathan, (Columbia University Press, forthcoming, 2012), he has written more than a dozen monographs and reports, as well as several dozen journal articles and book chapters. He has also edited or co-edited 12 volumes on various aspects of security in the Asia-Pacific region. He is a co-editor with Mr. Kamphausen and Dr. Lai of *The PLA at Home and Abroad: Assessing the Operational Capabilities of China's Military* (Carlisle, PA: Strategic Studies Institute, U.S. Army War College, June 2010). Dr. Scobell holds a Ph.D. in political science from Columbia University.

CHRISTOPHER P. TWOMEY is currently an Associate Professor of National Security Affairs at the U.S. Naval Postgraduate School in Monterey, CA. His previous assignments were as an Associate Chair for Research and as Director of the Center for Contemporary Conflict from 2007-09. He works closely with the Office of the Secretary of Defense (Policy) and the State Department on a range of diplomatic engagements across Asia and regularly advises the U.S. Pacific Command (PACOM), the U.S. Strategic Command (STRATCOM), and the Office of Net Assessment. He has previously taught or researched at Harvard, Boston College, RAND, the Chinese Academy of Social Sciences, and Institute on Global Conflict and Cooperation (IGCC), and is currently a Research Fellow at the National Bureau of Asian Research. Dr. Twomey is the author of *The Military Lens: Doctrinal Differences and Deterrence Failure in Sino-American Relations* (Cornell, 2010), which explains how differing military doctrines complicate diplomatic signaling, interpretations of those signals, and assessments of the balance of power. He edited *Perspectives on Sino-American Strategic Nuclear Issues* (2008), and his articles have appeared in journals such as *Asian Survey, Security Studies, Arms Control Today, Contemporary Security Policy, Asia Policy, Current History,* and the *Journal of Contemporary China*. Dr. Twomey holds a Ph.D. in political science from MIT.

YU BIN is a professor of political science and the director of East Asian studies at Wittenberg University in Springfield, Ohio. He is also a Senior Fellow in the Shanghai Association of American Studies. He is the author and coauthor of six books in both Chinese and English, more than 100 articles/chapters in academic and policy journals and books, and numerous op-ed pieces in English and Chinese media outlets. He is also a regular contributor to the Pacific Forum and its online journal *Comparative Connections* (on Russian-China relations), as well as a senior writer for *Asia Times* online. His research interests include international relations, Sino-Russian relations, and East Asian security and politics, among other topics. Yu served in the PLA infantry from 1968-72 and was a research fellow at the Center of International Studies, State Council in Beijing from 1982-85. He received his MA in journalism from the Chinese Academy of Social Sciences in Beijing and his Ph.D. in political science from Stanford University. He is currently working on a book about Western studies of the Soviet Union and Russia to be published by the Eastern China Normal University Press in Shanghai in 2012.

CHRISTOPHER D. YUNG is a Senior Research Fellow at the Institute for National Strategic Studies (INSS), National Defense University. Dr. Yung provides insights and counsel for the Office of Secretary of Defense, the Joint Staff, and the Combatant Commanders concerning Chinese defense and national security decisionmaking; Chinese force structure and doctrinal developments; Chinese military capabilities and current operations; Chinese engagement activities with the United States; and China's political-military relations with other nations in the Asia-Pacific region. Prior to his entering into government service, Dr. Yung was a Senior Research Analyst at the Center for Naval Analyses (CNA). While at CNA, Dr. Yung led projects or was involved in analysis related to China, Northeast Asia security, the Chinese Navy, the Chinese Military, and U.S. inter-operability with the militaries of the Far East. In addition to Dr. Yung's China and Asia-related expertise, he also has direct Military Operations Analysis experience. Between 1998 and 2001 he was a special assistant and operations analyst for the Commander, Amphibious Group Two — the senior U.S. Navy amphibious command in the Atlantic Fleet. This was followed up with an assignment as a special assistant and operations analyst for the Commander, U.S. Marine Corps Forces Atlantic — the highest ranking Marine Corps operational command on the East Coast. Dr. Yung holds a Ph.D. in international relations from the Paul H. Nitze School of Advanced International Studies (SAIS). He also holds a master's degree in East Asian and China studies from the same institution. He received language certificates from Columbia University and the Beijing Foreign Language Teacher's Institute, where he studied Mandarin Chinese.

U.S. ARMY WAR COLLEGE

Major General Gregg F. Martin
Commandant

*****

STRATEGIC STUDIES INSTITUTE

Director
Professor Douglas C. Lovelace, Jr.

Director of Research
Dr. Antulio J. Echevarria II

Editors
Dr. Andrew Scobell
Dr. David Lai
Mr. Roy Kamphausen

Director of Publications
Dr. James G. Pierce

Publications Assistant
Ms. Rita A. Rummel

*****

Composition
Mrs. Jennifer E. Nevil